English in Practice

English in Practice

In pursuit of English studies

PETER BARRY

University of Wales, Aberystwyth

A member of the Hodder Headline Group
LONDON
Distributed in the United States of America by
Oxford University Press Inc., New York

First published in Great Britain in 2003 by
Arnold, a member of the Hodder Headline Group,
338 Euston Road, London NW1 3BH

http://www.arnoldpublishers.com

Distributed in the United States of America by
Oxford University Press Inc.,
198 Madison Avenue, New York NY 10016

The advice and information in this book are believed to be true and
accurate at the date of going to press, but neither the author nor the
publisher can accept any legal responsibility or liability for any errors or
omissions.

British Library Cataloguing in Publication Data
A catalogue record for this book is available from the British Library

Library of Congress Cataloging-in-Publication Data
A catalog record for this book is available from the Library of Congress

ISBN 0 340 80885 3 (hb)
ISBN 0 340 80886 1 (pb)

1 2 3 4 5 6 7 8 9 10

Typeset in 10/13pt Utopia by Phoenix Photosetting, Chatham, Kent
Printed and bound in Great Britain by
MPG Books Ltd, Bodmin, Cornwall

What do you think about this book? Or any other Arnold title?
Please send your comments to feedback.arnold@hodder.co.uk

To Maureen and Gerard

Contents

List of illustrations

Preliminaries

What kind of book is this? That is a natural question to ask whenever we pick up a book in a bookshop or library. Here is the answer: this book is a practical reflective overview of the study of English at degree level. It is selective, of course, as all overviews must be; for instance, it doesn't discuss those areas where English Studies shade into Cultural Studies, and there is little in it about drama other than Shakespeare. Nor does it make any attempt at dispassionate neutrality, so the *over*view offered here is also a point of view, though one which has, I hope, a distinct 'edge' and 'bite' which will compensate for its partiality. It tries to get the 'bite' by always explaining matters through fully developed 'worked examples', rather than just setting out general principles, and it doesn't strive for an even-handed comprehensive coverage of all possible angles.

Who is this book for? This is another vital question, and my answer is: it's for you. I mean by this that you probably wouldn't have picked up a general book of this kind about English Studies, from this section of the bookshop or the library, if you were not involved in the teaching or learning of English, and wanted something more than just author-specific criticism, or an account of some particular school of literary theory. Throughout the writing of the book I have tried to visualize you, and have aimed to talk to you as directly and as intimately as I can. As I did so, I have to confess, you flickered between two identities, like that duck/rabbit drawing which, when you glance at it, is sometimes a duck and sometimes a rabbit, but never a mixture of the two. Mostly, I see you as a student just embarking on an English degree, or perhaps already quite a way in, but wanting to re-establish your bearings and take stock of what you are doing. At other times I see you as a teaching colleague, seeking a brief respite from the endless slings and arrows of initiatives, audits, and briefing papers, and wanting to reshape or rediscover what it was that first brought you into this subject, to which, after all, you are giving pretty much your whole life. Whichever reader you are, I know that our needs and views can never entirely coincide, but I hope that reading the book will help you to define (or redefine) your own requirements and purposes in doing English.

Why was this book written? Well, the simple answer is that I wrote it because Christopher Wheeler of Arnold Publishers invited me to, for which I am very grateful. But, of course, I accepted the invitation (as he foresaw I would) because it's the kind of book I like writing, not least because it gives me an opportunity to talk with a wide audience, right across the whole field of English Studies. Furthermore, anyone writing such a book has to stand back a little from the hurly-burly of teaching and learning and think again about fundamentals – about what there is to be gained from doing English, and why people decide they want to take it on. This kind of broader-scale reflection is an especially urgent need in our discipline today, for there is some evidence that our traditional recruiting strengths have suffered some erosion. Professional pressures cause us to specialize more and more in ever narrower topics, but the intellectual 'closing down' which that requires can narrow our debates and exchanges without offering adequate compensation in terms of profundity of insight. Sir Roy Strong once remarked that the most satisfying kind of writing always makes a bridge between a new audience and an old, and I agree with that absolutely – hence the attraction of my 'duck/rabbit' notion of the reader. The kind of book which is *only* for experts, or *only* for those just starting out, easily degenerates into a routine professional production which can be tiring and dispiriting, both to read and to write.

Producing this one, then, has enabled me to meet that need to stand back and 'recollect', a fine word, which is only partly about remembering the past. To be specific: in this case it's partly about repaying a debt to those who taught me and transmitted to me their enthusiasms (and some of their idiosyncrasies). It's a way of trying to keep that enthusiasm kindled for the next generation. 'Recollecting' is also about reflecting and pondering, sometimes without coming to firm conclusions (or 'learning outcomes', as we now call them), but emerging with a new sense of engagement and purpose. In my distant Catholic schooldays we had a monthly half-day of silent reflection known as *'Recollectio'*, when individuals would seek out remote parts of the grounds and walk the paths at a certain pace which was neither very fast nor very slow. I suspect that some such activity is highly beneficial to mental health and intellectual wellbeing, and I wish it could still be part of my routine today.

When I went to university myself (at King's College in London) I had to learn to walk much faster, slipping into the rapt and rapid human tide that flowed one way along the Strand in the morning and back the other way at night. Of course, like everybody else, I seem to have been rushing along at that pace ever since. Writing this book, during a sabbatical semester (for which I thank the University of Wales, Aberystwyth), gave me that old *'Recollectio'* feeling again. Instead of just *doing* English, I have been able to think about it, and have come back to the doing of it with a sense of re-engagement. I hope it will in some small way perform the same function for you.

* * *

I have kept the structure of the book as simple as possible. The first chapter attempts the task of saying what it is about English which keeps attracting people to it. The next three chapters (2–4) are about the 'hard core' of the discipline, which is reading: we learn to read the lines, and then between the lines, and then beyond the lines. I illustrate the first with poetry, the second with prose fiction, and the third with poetry again. The preponderance of poetry examples is not meant to imply that poetry should take precedence over prose, or that it should form the culmination of our studies: it's simply that I hate working with extracts, and like to use whole texts for illustrative purposes whenever possible. However, the example used in the second half of Chapter 4 is Tennyson's 'The Lady of Shalott', which is a substantial narrative piece rather than a short lyric, and can be seen as 'poetic fiction' (a form much liked by the Victorians), rather than just poetry.

After this initial group of chapters the book broadens out to wider issues, beginning with Chapter 5 on English and History, which is the most overtly polemical chapter in the book and is about the currently contentious issue of context in literary studies. Chapter 6 is about literary theory, and it does two things: firstly, it gives an overview of the arrival and impact of literary theory in English Studies since the 1970s, and, secondly, it gives two detailed examples of how theory can operate in actual reading practice. It does not give a detailed exposition of the various kinds of literary theory, because I have done that in another book (to which I refer you in the bibliography – naturally). Chapter 7 is about the history and development of English Studies, a topic which can help us to be aware that the 'scope of the possible' in the discipline may extend beyond currently approved or prescribed modes. This, I think, is the second most polemical chapter. Chapter 8 looks at how the literary text we study in class and write essays about comes into being as a printed artefact: in other words, it's about the shadowy world of textual editors, those literary midwives who move in their mysterious ways to bring literary texts into the world, often labouring for decades over the (re)birth of a single work. I have included the chapter because I believe that some basic aware-ness of 'the text as text' should be part of degree-level study. Chapter 9, 'Online English', is about 'English and it', that is, IT (Information Technology), as it was called until 'it' became 'ICT' (Information and Communication Technology) a few years ago. Whatever we call it, it is obvious that it will keep on becoming more and more vital to literary study, but *it* will start using *us* unless we have pretty clear ideas about how *we* want to use *it*.

Chapter 10 is the longest, because it looks at a cross-section of the different kinds of language study that can be included on English degrees. This too can be a contentious area, and the friction between literary study and language study has a long history. To some extent, the friction is inevitable – it's like the friction always felt between adjacent cities, and I try to show that the propinquity can be beneficial, provided that outside forces don't try to make the two cities amalgamate into a new disciplinary megalopolis. The brief Chapter 11 registers the recent rapid rise in the popularity of creative writing as an element in English degree courses, a trend which may have profound effects on the culture of English departments, and which may help us to counter the slight dip in the popularity of our 'traditional' and conservatively anarchic subject during the early part of the present century. English in practice, finally, always means having to write essays, so Chapter 12 offers a practical way of conceptualizing what progress in this skill might entail. The bibliography at the end of the book is conceived on very simple principles: it is annotated, and it lists five books relevant to the topic of each of the chapters.

* * *

I am most grateful to Sarah Barrett for her meticulous copy-editing of the final text. Several friends and colleagues (David Grylls, Andrew Hadfield, Paulina Kewes, Sean Matthews, Lyn Pykett, Tom Wharton, and Tim Woods) have read or heard sections of this book, making valuable suggestions, and (which is even more important) giving me much-needed reassurance that I am not (as we say in our department) 'completely barking'. So I am, of course, very grateful for that. But I am just as grateful for being invited down to the New Inn at lunchtimes (with former colleagues, in days gone by), or, these days, to *Brynamlyg* or *Penbryn*, where the Aberystwyth English Department usually lunches *en masse*, to the evident bemusement of staff in other, less favoured, departments.

P.B.
Aberystwyth
April 2002

Acknowledgements

The author and publisher would like to thank copyright holders for permission to quote the following: 'Brief Thoughts on Maps', by Miroslav Holub, from *Notes of a Clay Pigeon*, translated by J. and I. Milner, published by Martin Secker & Warburg, reprinted by permission of The Random House Group Ltd; 'Why Dorothy Wordsworth is Not As Famous as Her Brother', by Lynn Peters (9 lines), from *The Virago Book of Wicked Verse*, ed. Jill Dawson; 'Oread', by HD (Hilda Doolittle), from *Collected Poems, 1912–1944* © 1982 by The Estate of Hilda Doolittle, used by permission of New Directions Publishing Corporation; 'Transit', by Adrienne Rich, from *A Wild Patience Has Taken Me This Far: Poems 1978–1981* by Adrienne Rich © 1981 by Adrienne Rich, used by permission of the author and W.W. Norton & Company, Inc.

1 Introduction: The Appeal of English

SEEKING FIT WORDS

I sat down a few moments ago to begin this book by describing the appeal of English, intending to say why the subject still engrosses me, after many years of learning and teaching it for a living. But this turned out to be one of those tasks which are far more difficult to undertake in practice than to contemplate as a distant prospect, and, after several false starts, I find myself starting again. What has been passing through my mind – or hovering within it, really – in connection with the task of writing this opening are sentences from three literary works I have studied in the past. Yet, strangely, the first two of these are not from twentieth-century literature (my specialist field), but from much earlier periods which I have not studied closely for many years.

The first sentence is from the poet Philip Sidney (1554–86), whose sonnet sequence *Astrophel and Stella* opens with a famous poem about what T. S. Eliot (in the 'East Coker' section of *Four Quartets*) was later to call 'the intolerable wrestle / With words and meanings'. Here is Sidney's poem:

> Loving in truth, and fain in verse my love to show,
> That she, dear she, might take some pleasure of my pain:
> Pleasure might cause her read, reading might make her know,
> Knowledge might pity win, and pity grace obtain,
> I sought fit words to paint the blackest face of woe,
> Studying inventions fine, her wits to entertain:
> Oft turning others' leaves to see if thence would flow
> Some fresh and fruitful showers upon my sun-burn'd brain.
> But words came halting forth, wanting Invention's stay,
> Invention, Nature's child, fled step-dame Study's blows,
> And others' feet still seem'd but strangers in my way.
> Thus great with child to speak, and helpless in my throes,
> Biting my trewand pen, beating myself for spite,
> Fool, said my Muse to me, look in thy heart and write.

Sidney says here that he's in love ('Loving in truth . . .') and that he wants to express his love in poetry ('and fain in verse my love to show . . .'), but he can't get the words to do what he wants them to do, so that they come out sounding lame and uninspired ('But words came halting forth, wanting Invention's stay'). He is in a rage of helpless frustration ('beating my self for spite' – writer-rage, let's call it) until he 'hears' a voice within him (and this is the sentence *I* kept hearing) – 'Fool, said my Muse to me, look in thy heart and write.' This must have solved Philip Sidney's writer's block (as we might call it today) because this is the first poem in a very long sequence of sonnets, so he obviously got himself going again by reminding himself of the need to 'speak from the heart'. Of course, Sidney's sonnets (in spite of what he says in this poem) are anything but artless, and the writer's block may well have existed only when he was 'in role', speaking as the traditional lovelorn sonneteer. But art and heart have to go together in some way, and to speak memorably 'from the heart' in sonnet form you need to have learned the *art* of doing so (which involves compressing thoughts and ideas, using metrical patterns, rhyming, and so on). But the art without the heart would be as unengaging as its opposite (artless, heartfelt outpourings), and that, I think, is what the remembered sentence from the sonnet was telling me about this book. It was reminding me that I must say what I *really* think and feel, rather than (for example) just seeking to impress friends and colleagues. That, indeed, is what I want to do, with all my art and heart. Yet, oddly, the words to express such deep-down resolves and convictions are often already there, somewhere within the basement of the memory, and often they derive from literature we thought we had forgotten, which says it to us much more powerfully than we could say it to ourselves with our own words. This realization of the enormous and abiding power of the vast archives of the 'already said' is one major aspect of the appeal of English.

THE FLIGHT OF A SPARROW

The second sentence which seemed to be hovering in my mind came from an even earlier piece of literature, one which I had encountered in the Anglo-Saxon section of my undergraduate degree. It's a famous passage from Bede's *Ecclesiastical History of the English Nation*, which was in my mind (again) without my really knowing why.[1] At one level, now that I begin

1   The Venerable Bede, as he is known (673–735) spent his life in the monastery at Jarrow in the north-east of England. He is the first English historian, and his *History* was written in Latin. In the ninth century it was translated into English (i.e. Old English, which is also known as Anglo-Saxon) at the instigation of Alfred (871–99), king of the West Saxons.

to think about it, the association between the passage and the study of English is clear, because when I took an undergraduate degree in English (in the late 1960s) the study of Anglo-Saxon literature was a compulsory part of the course, and this anecdote is found in the textbooks familiar to my student generation. The passage tells how, in the seventh century, King Edwin of Northumbria, after a great deal of pondering and soul-searching, was finally converted to Christianity by Bishop Paulinus. But not quite by Paulinus himself, the hot-shot missionary sent by Pope Gregory for that express purpose, who had found the cerebral and conscientious Edwin no pushover, but by an odd combination of the high priest of the old pagan religion of the court (who had concluded that prayer to the old gods was useless) and one of the king's own elders. The elder in question spoke up during the debate at court about whether they should change their religious allegiance, making the point that if this new religion could explain what had happened before life began, and what will happen after death, then it should be embraced. But he didn't say it in that abstract way: he used the hauntingly vivid anecdote of the sparrow which flies briefly through the mead-hall during a feast, passing in through one window and straight out through another, so that for a few moments it is in the warmth and cheer of the hall, before passing out into the winter darkness again. Human life, the elder said, is as fleeting as that brief moment when the sparrow is in the hall, and we are ignorant about what happened in the darkness before life began, and what will follow afterwards in the darkness of death. This is the passage (the inserted numerals will help you to identify the corresponding sentences in the Old English original text which is given in the footnote overleaf):

/1/ Another of the king's chief men, approving of Coifi's words and exhortations, presently added: /2/ 'The present life of man, O king, seems to me, /3/ in comparison of that time which is unknown to us, /4/ like to the swift flight of a sparrow through the room wherein you sit at supper in winter /5/ with your commanders and ministers, and a good fire in the midst, /6/ whilst the storms of rain and snow prevail abroad; /7/ the sparrow, I say, flying in at one door, and immediately out at another, /8/ whilst he is within, is safe from the wintry storm; /9/ but after a short space of fair weather, he immediately vanishes out of your sight, /10/ into the dark winter from which he had emerged. /11/ So this life of man appears for a short space, /12/ but of what went before, /13/ or what is to follow, we are ignorant. /14/ If, therefore, this new doctrine contains something more certain, /15/ it seems justly to deserve to be followed.[2]

The king and his court were at once persuaded, not by the precepts of the missionaries alone, but by those precepts as crystallized in this vivid example, which has a power over the mind beyond that of mere *saying*, for it has the force of an image, which is to say that it is the vivid concrete embodiment of an idea. The kind of mind which finds it difficult to resist the force of ideas embodied in this way (rather than in a series of logical or philosophical propositions, no matter how elegant they might be) is the kind which is attracted to English. That, it seems to me, is the English Studies mindset in miniature – that love of hard specificity of image or illustration. Here, then, is another major element of the appeal of studying English, namely the fact that it is a discipline which privileges the concrete and specific over the general and the abstract. It is always interested in the *embodiment* of ideas in an image, or as represented in character or incident. Ezra Pound defined an image as a kind of vortex into which ideas are continually rushing. Such vortices are the very heart of English.

The other aspect of the anecdote in Bede which makes it expressive, for me, of the whole point of English is the way it draws so much from an apparently trivial incident (the remembered moment when an actual sparrow flew through the hall). On the surface this incident is simplicity itself and quite without meaning, and yet it is 'read' with vivid and imaginative insight, so that it gives access to a hidden realm of conceptuality overflowing with significance. What we *can* see leads us to speculate about what we *can't*, and this

---

2   *Bede's Ecclesiastical History of the English Nation*, Everyman's Library, repr. 1954, book 2, ch. xiii, p. 91. In Old English the passage is as follows (the unfamiliar letters 'þ' (called 'thorn') and 'ð' (called 'eth') represent the two slightly different forms of the sound represented today by 'th': there are no silent letters: rine (rain), for instance, in the fifth line, is pronounced 'reener':

/1/ þaes wordum oþer cyninges wita and ealdormann geþafunge sealde and to þaere spraece feng and þus cwaeð: /2/ 'þyslic me is gesewen, þu cyning, þis andwearde lif manna on eorðan /3/ to wiðmetenesse þaere tide þe us uncuð is: /4/ swylc swa þu aet swaesendum sitte /5/ mid þinum ealdormannum and þegnum on wintertide and sie fyr onaelaed and þin heall gewyrmed /6/ and hit rine and sniwe and styrme ute /7/ cume an spearwa and hraedlice þaet hus þurhfleocume þurh oþer duru in þurh oþer ut gewite. /8/ Hwaet, he on þa tid þe he inne bið ne bið hrinen mid þe storme þaes winters ac þaet bið an eagan bryhtm and /9/ aet laesste faec ac he sona of wintra on þone winter eft cymeð. /11/ Swa þonne þis monna lif to medmiclum faece /12/ aetyweð hwaet þaer foregange /13/ oððe hwaet þaer aefterfylige we ne cunnun. /14/ For ðon gif þeos niwe lar owiht cuðlicre ond gerisenlicre brenge /15/ þaes weorðe is þaet we þaere fylgen.

seems to me ('thus it seems to me ...') like the reading of literature, when a detail we see on the page (a description of a room in a novel, for instance) suggests or connotes things we are not explicitly told at all. For instance, in a Victorian novel, a room might be described as having windows draped in thick and elaborate curtains, which are presented in minute verbal detail, so that we can almost smell the mustiness of the heavy fabrics. This is what we 'see', as everyone in the mead-hall could see the passage of the sparrow. But to 'read' the seen detail takes us into the realm of the *un*said, which is yet somehow implied (perhaps that the family within is over-anxious, in some way which will affect the story, about the wider life beyond the safety of the home). The novelist may not *tell* us this, but we deduce the un-said from the said, the unseen from the seen, as in the anecdote of the sparrow. When I realized (at about the age of 17) that doing English could take us beyond the merely seen and said, I was instantly converted, just like those troubled and pondering Northumbrians in Bede's conversion narrative. Herein, in my view, lies a second major aspect of the appeal of English, this way of giving us a means of access to covert realms of signification which often lie beneath the most mundane remark or detail.

THE TROUBLE WITH MAPS

The third item which has been at the back of my mind as I have been thinking about how to start this book comes from a much more recent piece of writing, not in fact from English literature at all, but from the work of the modern Czech poet Miroslav Holub (1923–98), whose work was made popular in English translation during the 1970s, mainly through the medium of the Penguin Modern Poets series. I was thinking along the lines of how this book should provide an outline map of degree-level English Studies, and was feeling very daunted at the prospect of attempting this. But maps are strange things. None of us has ever seen an accurate map, since that very notion of absolute accuracy actually makes little sense in relation to maps. The only 'accurate' map there could be of a place would be the place itself. Think, for instance, of a road map of a country, which you might buy and use as a tourist or traveller. If that map were a strictly accurate, true-scale representation of the country, then the roads would in reality be about five miles wide. On the other hand, if the roads were shown in accurate scale you wouldn't be able to see them on a map that you could hold comfortably in your hands – so it wouldn't be a 'road map' at all. The purpose of a map, then, is to be helpful, showing you what you need to see in order to achieve your purposes of the moment.

The same is true of the map this book hopes to provide – it offers a way of looking at the terrain, one which I hope will be helpful to you now. Later on, you will see lots of complexities not included in this map, but found, perhaps, in others that strive to meet different needs. As writer and reader in partnership, we don't have to anticipate those needs now, and no such book as this could ever be written, or usefully read, if we did. Certainly, if I thought that I had to anticipate your every need and every possible query, I would stop writing now. But I don't. Indeed, if the map is to work at all, it will do so not because of my input, but because of yours.

As before, all these thoughts were already expressed in the poem by Miroslav Holub which I remembered in outline as I thought about the book, and was prompted by all this to track down. It's a poem about a particular map, a map that saved lives, and it relates an event which actually happened. The title of the poem is 'Brief Thoughts on Maps':

> Albert Szent-Gyorgi, who knew a lot about maps,
> according to which life is on its way somewhere or other,
> told us this story from the war
> due to which history is on its way somewhere or other:
>
> The young lieutenant of a small Hungarian detachment in the Alps
> sent a reconnaissance unit out into the icy wasteland.
> It began to snow
> immediately, snowed for two days and the unit
> did not return. The lieutenant suffered: he had despatched
> his own people to death.
>
> But the third day the unit came back.
> Where had they been? How had they made their way?
> Yes, they said, we considered ourselves
> lost and waited for the end. And then one of us
> found a map in his pocket. That calmed us down.
> We pitched camp, lasted out the snowstorm, and with the map
> we discovered our bearings.
> And here we are.
>
> The lieutenant borrowed this remarkable map,
> and had a good look at it. It was not a map of the Alps
> but of the Pyrenees.
>
> Goodbye now.[3]

3   'Brief Thoughts on Maps', *TLS* (4 Feb. 1977), p. 118, and reprinted in Holub's collection *Notes of a Clay Pigeon*, trans. Jarmila and Ian Milner (Secker & Warburg, 1985).

The purpose of this book is to provide you with a map to keep in your pockets as you set off into the Alps of English Studies. As the blizzards of set texts, theoretical approaches, and essay deadlines set in, it is easy to panic. But perhaps you will remember the map in your pocket, and calm down, and pitch camp till the blizzard clears. Much later, when the crisis has passed, and you take out the map again in a moment of idle curiosity, you may well find that it isn't really a proper map of English Studies at all, just as the map which saved the soldiers lost in the Alps was actually a map of somewhere else entirely. But the important thing is that when it was needed it gave you a feeling of security, a sense of direction, and a sense of knowing what you have to do, not just to survive as an English student but also, I very much hope, to enjoy your studies and move beyond them.

'ENGLISH' ISN'T JUST ENGLISH

Finally, an important word about the usual name given to our discipline. The word 'English' in 'English Studies' is often felt to be unsatisfactory and mis-leading. For one thing, on English degrees we don't just study the literature of England, but usually a sample, at least, from that of Ireland (W. B. Yeats, James Joyce, Seamus Heaney, for instance), of Scotland (Walter Scott, Robert Louis Stevenson, Edwin Morgan), and of Wales (Dylan Thomas, David Jones, R. S. Thomas). So, even when we are thinking just of the British Isles, doing English involves the literature of the whole group of islands sometimes known as the 'British Archipelago'. But, of course, it isn't just that either, for on English degrees we also study world literature *in* English, that is, writing from the United States (Herman Melville, Edith Wharton, Toni Morrison), from the Caribbean (Derek Walcott, V. S. Naipaul, Kamau Brathwaite), from Canada (Margaret Atwood, Alice Munro, Earle Birney), from the Indian subcontinent (Rabindranath Tagore, R. K. Narayan, Anita Desai), from Australia (Patrick White, Peter Carey, Les Murray), from South Africa (Athol Fugard, Nadine Gordimer, Ezekiel Mphahlele) and so on.

But even these wide-ranging national divisions of literature in English are hardly satisfactory or sufficient. In the United States, for instance, the various ethnic communities each has its own body of literature, and many of these have grown dramatically in recent years both in scope and variety, and in terms of national and international prestige. A selective listing would need to include: African American writers (Ishamel Reed, Gloria Naylor, Toni Morrison), Asian American writers (Carlos Bulosan, Amy Tan, Maxine Hong Kingston), Native American writers (N. Scott Momoday, Louise Erdrich,

Sherman Alexie), and Chicano/a writers (Rolando Hinojosa, Rudolfo Anaya, Sandra Cisneros).[4] Furthermore, all four of these 'trans-national' groupings are themselves a yoking together of writers from many different regions, and to approach a true picture of the range of contemporary literary activity in English they would all need to be further sub-divided. For instance, the broad category of Asian American writing includes (but is not confined to) Chinese American, Japanese American, Korean American, Filipino American, and South Asian American literatures, and in each of these fields there is a wide range of available literature, mainly prose fiction, often vividly representing the multicultural history and experience of each of these groups.[5]

But even if we were to extend our listing along these lines, so that a wide range of national and trans-national groupings of writers in English was represented, we would still be offering a very conservative map of 'English Literature' (in the sense of Literature in English), if we were to view it from a different angle. For instance, if our viewpoint were 'generic' (which is to say, concerned with the various forms and genres of writing in English), then it would have to be admitted that nearly all the writers just listed are novelists. So, while the list just given is progressive in one way, it is conservative in another, for it doesn't even cover the conventional generic triad of fiction, drama, and poetry, and it makes no attempt to move out beyond those to forms in which the boundary between literature and other kinds of writing is blurred or called into question.

For instance, we might argue that accounts of extreme experiences, like prison or captivity narratives, constitute an important kind of writing which deserves close study. This might lead us to a collection like *Women's Indian Captivity Narratives* (ed. Kathryn Derounian-Stodola, 1998), representing a form of narrative which is, the editor suggests, 'arguably the first American literary form dominated by the experience of women' (the ten examples in the collection cover the period 1682–1892, and show considerable diversity). Likewise, we might wish to study the narratives, not just of a *period* of captivity, but of *lives* of captivity, as represented in a volume like *The Classic American Slave Narratives* (ed. Henry Louis Gates Jr, 2002). Equally, it might be the increasingly popular and significant genre of travel writing, as found, for instance, in *Colonial American Travel Narratives* (ed. Wendy Martin, 1994), or, on the other hand, voyage accounts (a very different genre, since the main thing to be discovered on a long sea voyage is yourself). We could go on to

---

4   The work of all 12 writers mentioned in this sentence is discussed in detail in *Beginning Ethnic American Literatures*, ed. Helena Grice *et al.* (Manchester University Press, 2001).

5   For suggested reading in each of these areas see Grice *et al.*, pp. 185–7.

include conversion narratives (that is, life narratives which pivot around the moment of religious conversion or transformation), or, more recently, 'coming out' stories (life accounts in which the focal moments are those of recognizing, acting upon, and making known one's true sexual orientation).

But even a list supplemented with all these would remain a fairly conservative sketch of the generic coverage which studying English might, or should, involve – you might be asking where are the cyberpunk prose, the graphic novels, the 'sudden fiction' (also known as 'short-short-fiction'), the performance poetry, and the improvised drama? All these different kinds of writing have valid claims for inclusion on English courses, and one of the great transformations of the past 20 years has been that many of these claims have been met, so that the kind of material cited in the last few paragraphs is increasingly indicative of the exciting scope and scale of English degrees in the twenty-first century. But a book like this one, which works mainly through the discussion of detailed examples, has to take its examples from those areas of the curriculum which are traditional and long-standing, and which tend to be covered at some point on nearly all English courses, almost wherever in the world they are taken. Otherwise, the danger is that the material would be of enormous interest and relevance to readers in certain parts of the world, or even to a substantial minority of readers worldwide, but perhaps almost completely unfamiliar to many others. The examples used here, then, come from the middle range of the syllabus – Philip Sidney, Jane Austen, John Keats, Alfred Tennyson, Joseph Conrad, 'HD' (Hilda Doolittle), Adrienne Rich, for example – that is, mostly from authors you will probably touch upon at some point wherever you take your English degree.

* * *

At its most basic, English is about reading the lines of the text, but then, you could say, so is history or philosophy. What distinguishes English from other textual disciplines, it can be argued, is the intensity of the reading: English is high-intensity reading, or supercharged reading, and it produces its own characteristic mental atmosphere in which the words seem to glow with an aura of high verbal energy, as we scan them rapidly, perhaps driven by an accelerating current of dawning comprehension, or else, as if becalmed, scrutinize them minutely, almost one by one, turning them this way and that, in the light of an idea which is still only half-formed in the mind. Either way, it's the lines themselves we are following, and everything which happens in this discipline has to begin happening there. So the first chapter after this introduction is about that difficult task which looks so easy – reading the lines.

2 Reading the Lines

This chapter is about the interpretation and evaluation of literary texts. Its first two sections mainly concern the former and the second two mainly the latter. Since the next chapter is about prose, this one concentrates on poetry in its detailed examples, but the two media are not, of course, separate universes. Poems tell stories as well as fiction (often in both senses of 'as well') – they just do it differently. The contemporary poet Ian Duhig once defined poems as 'novels without the waffle', and he was, I think, only half joking.[1] Likewise, we may admire Coleridge's famous definition of poetry as 'the best possible words in the best possible order', but this should not lead us to imagine that novelists are content with anything less than this (more or less adequate words in an on the whole acceptable order, for instance). Gaining access to the realm of the *un*said, as discussed in the introduction, is something we can *learn* to do, just as we can learn to play tennis or poker, so I want to offer an indicative list of the kind of operations we perform when we 'tackle textuality' without any particular resort to literary theory. The following section, then, itemizes some of the things we do when we interpret literature, whether it be poetry or prose.

YOUR STARTER FOR TEN

The list sets out ten interpretive processes, and it does not claim to be comprehensive. In practice, the ten processes feed off each other, operating in any order or combination. They are not instinctive; indeed, I think they are representative of the kind of things which those who do English learn to do when reading. So, what do we do when we interpret a work of literature in the usual 'close reading' situation without making any specific use of literary theory? The following is indicative of the repertoire of practices we draw upon.

1 Duhig is the author of *The Mersey Goldfish* (1995) and *Nominies* (1998), both published by Bloodaxe. He made the remark in an edition of the British TV arts programme *The South Bank Show* which was broadcast in 1997 to celebrate the so-called 'New Generation' poets.

(1) *We look for some overall structural pattern – that is, something which provides a structural frame or backbone for a whole work.*
We can call these 'macro-patterns' to distinguish them from the smaller-scale patterning referred to later (in point 8). For example, two characters or two couples in a novel or a play may be paired and contrasted throughout (for example, the two sisters in Jane Austen's *Sense and Sensibility*, or the two women in John Osborne's play *Look Back in Anger*). The contrast may be supported by image-patterns linked to each, by speech styles characteristic of each, by symmetrical or parallel plots lines applying to each, etc. Once the structural pattern has been perceived, a whole line of interpretation can be built.

(2) *We look for similarity beneath apparent dissimilarity, or vice versa.*
The two couples may be presented at first as the opposites of each other, but a close reading might show that what at first seemed true is actually untrue. For instance, one couple may be presented as very materialistic and the other as highly idealistic. But, in the end, events may show the idealists to be unyielding and inflexible, while the materialists are seen to be generous of heart and forgiving of human frailty. So they *are* opposites, but not in the way that first appeared.

(3) *We distinguish between overt and covert content – that is, between apparent content and real content.*
For example, e. e. cummings has a poem about driving a car which is actually about making love – it's not a very good poem.[2] Herman Melville has a novel about hunting a whale which is actually about searching for the meaning of the universe. It's called *Moby Dick*, and it's a very good book.

(4) *We distinguish between meaning and significance.*
'Meaning' is like something *inside* the work, whereas 'significance' is something we *perceive* in the work, something which is necessarily shifting.[3] If a literary work is regarded as being like the sea, then 'meaning' is like the salt – it's one of the 'ingredients' of the water, whereas significance is like its colour, that is, something that changes with the prevailing light conditions. Here is an illustration: in his book *Literary Theory: An Introduction* Terry

---

2 'She being Brand// -new', pp. 15–16 in *e. e. cummings: Selected Poems 1923–1958* (Faber, 1960).
3 The distinction is put forward in *Validity in Interpretation*, by E. D. Hirsch (Yale, 1967).

Eagleton says that we can probably be sure that *King Lear* is not about Manchester United. He should have said that Manchester United is not part of the *meaning* of King Lear but it may well be part of the *significance*. *King Lear* is about somebody who retires, but won't let go. He still wants a hand in team selection: he wants to be able to name his squad of a hundred knights and keep on having a say in running the club (or the kingdom). In other words, the parallel between *King Lear* and the one-time Manchester United manager Sir Matt Busby is actually pretty close. It's a play about devolving power and yet trying to hold on to power. And, after all, the play does mention football: Edmund says to Kent 'Out of my way, you base football player.'[4]

(5) *We think in terms of genre or literary type – that is, we ask how the literary genre affects the content of the work.*
For instance, in a Renaissance stage tragedy an evil character may openly declare his evil intentions, as when Richard III (in Shakespeare's play) announces, 'I am determined to prove a villain.' But we don't conclude that he is a person of unusual self-knowledge and honesty, because this kind of announcement is one of the conventions of the genre; it allows the author to address the audience by proxy through the character, enabling the action to be greatly accelerated (and, in a sense, anticipating forms of direct authorial comment about characters which would develop later with the rise of the novel).

(6) *We frequently read the literal as metaphorical – that is, especially in reading poems.*
For example, a contemporary poem mentions a 'bullet lodged inside before we knew it was growing'.[5] At first this seems to suggest an assassination by some outside figure. But literal bullets can't grow, and this is the clue which shows that it is actually a metaphorical bullet, and it becomes clear that it is a metaphor for a fatal illness which one of the characters is found to be suffering from. This kind of interpretive move (literal details like bullets read metaphorically) is very common in the reading of poetry.

---

4   This response to Eagleton on *Lear* is Ken Newton's; it originally appeared in an article entitled 'Interest, Authority and Ideology in Literary Interpretation', in *British Journal of Aesthetics*, 22 (1982), pp.103–14, and in expanded form in his book *In Defence of Literary Interpretation: Theory and Practice* (Macmillan, 1986).

5   See 'The Forked Tree' in *The Peepshow Girl*, by Marion Lomax (Bloodaxe, 1989).

(7) *In spite of this, we read the surface of the work accurately – in other words, we recognize the importance of the precise literal words of the text and do not take liberties with them.*

For example, a poem discussed in Chapter 6 contains the line 'We were as close as sisters'. It is important for the reader to realize that this means, precisely, two things: (a) that we were *like* sisters, and (b) that we were *not* sisters.

(8) *As readers we look for patterns in literary works. Not overarching structural patterns this time, but 'micro-patterns', such as a series of words with the same tone, register, or flavour.*

Often the significant point is where the perceived pattern is broken, for the item in question must have been chosen either in spite of breaking the pattern or because it breaks the pattern, and is thereby 'foregrounded' in the reader's attention. In the same way, if you look at a hundred rows of flowers in a wallpapered room, the only ones which will catch your attention are the ones which are not properly aligned – all DIY people know this.

(9) *As readers we identify stages and phases within a literary work.*

Some of these are formally marked by divisions into acts, or books, or chapters or verses. These are breaks in the text, but often in literature the transitions are more important than the breaks. Across these breaks, there is a moment when the 'exposition phase' slides into the 'development phase', and another phase begins when the development has put everything in place for the dénouement or the conclusion. The reader needs to be aware of the moment when the introduction of setting and characters pivots into the first significant incident, or choice, or denial. For example, in Shakespeare's Sonnet 73, which I will comment on in Chapter 6, it is important to decide whether the three images of ageing are meant to represent some kind of progression and development, or just three static examples of the same thing.

(10) *Finally, as readers, we read in linguistic period, aware (among other things) of semantic change (that is, changes in the meanings of words).*

For instance, in Shakespeare's *Henry V* Falstaff talks about his womb ('My womb undoes me'). Do we conclude that he is unmanning himself, or claiming some kind of double-gendered universality? Well, it's tempting to some critics, but the explanation is simple. In Elizabethan times the word 'womb' still had its older meaning of 'stomach', and was used of both men and women. Falstaff is simply saying that his large stomach prevents him from being a brave and agile soldier. (For more about such changes of meaning see the section 'Meanings on the move' in Chapter 11.)

* * *

These, then, are some of the main ways in which readers and critics engage with literary texts and begin to put forward accounts of what they mean. So, where does it leave us? The situation is this. We will always need these ten elements of interpretation. Literary criticism can never outgrow them, and they can never be superseded. It's impossible to do English without them. It always was, and it always will be. But, as we will argue in later chapters (especially Chapters 4 and 6), though we can never grow out of them, we will need, as we progress into degree-level study, to supplement them with techniques and attitudes ultimately derived from literary theory. For the moment, though, I want to suggest some very specific reading techniques for the 'close-up' reading of very short texts, these being the kind which tend to be subjected to the most intense forms of scrutiny.

THE END IS NIGH: READING SHORT POEMS

Reading should be a predatory activity

(Thomas Kinsella, contemporary Irish poet)

The practice of 'unseen close reading' is still taught at school and university as the main way to cope with short poems. The practice, though, can seem to invite a *reverence* for poems, building a mystique of invulnerability about the poet (who produces 'the best possible words in the best possible order', and all that), and inviting us merely to *contemplate* the result, which can be very intimidating and disempowering for readers. We seem to be asked to enter the poem, taking off the cycle-clips of day-to-day thinking, and merely standing in awkward reverence, like the speaker in Larkin's 'Church Going'. What we need to do is to *intervene* in the poem in some way. The white space around a poem on the page is quasi-sacramental, like the space between priest and people at a church service: it's a kind of barrier between word and world, as if the poet were a priestly being and the poem a service going on in the distance at the 'holy end' of literature, which we readers have to witness passively. The method recommended here involves *taking* back this white space and *talking* back to the poem. It involves *writing* on the poem, *substituting* words, *dividing* the poem up – *doing* things with it in fact. In this way we try to make connections between ourselves and the poem – to read ourselves back into it, so that it becomes a part of ourselves. All this will perhaps help us to *reappropriate* poetry, refusing it its status as the revered verbal icon in the inner temple of literature. The 'method' described here is a way of 'negotiating' with a poem, and it should provide you with plenty to say in circumstances where you are expected to write analysis or commentary as part of an essay or exam. The four steps are:

1. Read through the poem two or three times, then circle the word or phrase which is for you the strangest or most surprising in the poem. This word or phrase is the focal point of your view of the poem: look across the poem for others that seem related to it: circle them too and link them to your focal word. Try the experiment of changing the focal word to one which you would initially consider less surprising. How is the overall effect now changed? Later you can ask why the focal word stands out: it may have unexpected content, or tone; it may be combined in a surprising way with other words; it may be part of a phrase in which the words are unusually ordered.

2. Poems (no matter how short) have *phases*: there is a part which is introductory, then a development (probably the longest section), then a concluding part (which may double back, or break off from the logic of the development, or transpose what had been merely literal and one-dimensional into something more complex). Mark the phases on the poem (e.g. with cross-page dotted lines). This helps you to look for an overall structure, to see the poem as meanings unfolding, moving, going back, etc, (in contrast to the first stage which focuses on single words). There may be different ways of phasing the poem according to different ways of reading it: it may 'phase' one way if seen as primarily literal and another if seen as primarily figurative, but identifying parts gives us a strong sense of familiarity with the poem, of 'ownership', even.

3. Few poems are easy all the way through. Nearly all poems have a 'crux', or 'nub', or 'node', or 'vortex': this is a section of daunting complexity or baffling simplicity, from which we tend to look away. Find the bit in the poem which has this 'ardent obliquity' (J. H. Prynne's term, meaning, more or less, passionate indirectness): box it in on the page: spend some time with it: write about it in the margin: talk back to it: 'brainstorm' it: free-associate round it. Difficulty in poetry often indicates the presence of thematic

significance: facing up to this part of a poem is a cure for poetry phobia. Don't worry, the other side of this coin is that no poem is difficult all the way through.

4. Poems have *patterns*. Identify some in the poem and find a way of marking them. Having identified a pattern, look for a point where the pattern is broken. Breaks in a pattern are always significant. Patterns can be made out of almost any aspect of a poem: obvious examples are: line length, stanza length, rhyme, rhythm, type of vocabulary, angle of view. Lines or verses which are longer or shorter than the rest: words which are more formal or more colloquial than most others in the poem, an observation which stands out as cruder, or more reverent than most others in the poem – all these will almost certainly indicate significant points in the poem.

Being aware of what we called in the introduction the power of the 'already said' does not mean that we should adopt a superstitious evaluation of the mystique of literature in general or poetry in particular. On the contrary, we must always find ways of becoming *involved* with it, and this is not compatible with passive reverence. The short poem often has a kind of gem-like quality which can make engagement with it quite difficult. As a reader, you may find the stark simplicity of an ultra-short lyric like Robert Frost's 'Stopping by Woods on a Snowy Evening' to be mesmerizing and dazzling. But merely saying so doesn't make any critical point, or contribute to any possible analysis, so it is of very little use for study purposes. To write about the poem you will have to get beyond your sense of awe and set up some kind of dialogue between yourself and the poem. The four stages of 'dialogue' just described try to help you to do this.

* * *

Let's see how this approach could work with a suitable short poem: the piece below is by contemporary poet Johnston Kirkpatrick and originally appeared in *The Times Literary Supplement*.[6] Kirkpatrick says that his main subject matter has mostly been his 'growing up in working-class Belfast', and this poem is about a blind friend from his childhood:

6   *TLS*, 15 Feb. 1980 p. 185: Kirkpatrick's work has also appeared in *Trio Poetry 3* (Blackstaff Press, 1982), as one of three poets in the collection; in *English*, 40, no. 167 (1991); and in the anthology *A Rage for Order: Poetry of the Northern Ireland Troubles*, ed. Frank Ormsby (Blackstaff Press, 1992, repr. 1994).

APOSIOPESIS

Wet days, Sammy Hill's sitting room,
Sammy on holiday from the 'Blind School',
his spectacles thick as bottle bottoms,
reading buff-paged riddled books of Braille,
nervous fingers divining the words.

I held the page to the window.
My dumb touch read nothing in spite
of seeing the bullet-proof page,
groped over the stopped rivets,
the darkness of dot dot dot dot.

Beginning, then, with the single word which seems to be the focal point of the poem, I suspect that the title word itself might well be the one which takes much of your initial attention, for its air of learned technicality is strikingly at odds with the extremely ordinary and simple language of the poem itself. It isn't a word in common usage, and most readers would need to look it up. The dictionary informs us that it is the term which denotes a printed indication that something is missing from a text, the most common of which are such devices as: the apostrophe in a word such as *don't*, which indicates that in this contracted version of the words 'do not' the 'o' of 'not' has been omitted; another example of aposiopesis is the dash which indicates an item of held-back information (as in a Jane Austen novel, when we might be told of a character that he is 'a Colonel in the ——shire Regiment'); a final example is the spaced full stops (. . .) which indicate omitted material within a quotation. The last example is the most relevant to the poem. Aposiopesis, notice, is not the act of leaving something out, but the means of *indicating* that something has been left out. The root meaning of the word is to pass over something in silence (from Greek roots *apo* + *siopesis*, together meaning 'in silence'), but this isn't precisely the same as simply leaving it out – a blank page wouldn't be an example of aposiopesis, unless there is an indication that there should be, or had originally been, something on it.[7] The pages of Braille writing

---

7   In Laurence Sterne's novel *Tristram Shandy* (1760–67) a page is left blank when the author professes himself overcome by grief at the death of his friend Yorick, so that words fail him. The page is printed black, which is an aposiopesic device indicating the omission, and making it clear that the blank page is not just a printer's accident. Valentine Cunningham discusses *Shandy* (though not this example) and aspects of aposiopesis in the section 'Give me an Aposiopesic Break' in his *In the Reading Gaol* (Blackwell, 1994). The novelist B. S. Johnson, too, in *House Mother Normal*, prints whole pages of aposiopesis (dot dot dot dot) within the interior monologues of some of the elderly characters represented in the book, in order to indicate their intermittent senile dementia. The effect is very moving.

held up to the light by the speaker look like an endless aposiopesis, as indeed they are, in the sense that for him the *entire* sense of the words is omitted by the Braille, since he understands nothing of it at all. The 'dot dot dot dot' at the end of the poem tells the speaker that there is something he doesn't understand, and indicates the existence of a gulf between himself and his friend.

On the matter of the 'stages and phases' of the piece, clearly the first stanza of the poem is mainly about Sammy and the second is about the speaker. The first shows Sammy reading, and the second shows the speaker trying to read. Sammy may be awkward and nervous, but he is succeeding, and in this sense he penetrates the darkness which surrounds him: the speaker, by contrast, fails – his touch is 'dumb', and he can merely grope in the darkness. Structurally, then, the second stanza is a kind of mirrored reversal of the first.

On the third stage (concerning the 'node' or 'crux' within the poem), for me this occurs in the last two lines of the first stanza: 'buff-paged' simply describes the nature of the paper – it doesn't look or feel like the pages of an ordinary book because it has to be thick enough to hold the perforations which form the text. So the page is 'riddled' in two senses, firstly in the sense that it is full of holes (as in an expression like 'riddled with bullets'), but secondly it is 'riddled' in the sense that it poses a 'riddle' or problem for the sighted reader because it is written in code (like the Morse Code suggested by the 'dot dot dot dot' at the end). The remaining difficulty, though, is the word 'divined', which oddly suggests that there is something supernatural or uncanny in the decoding which Sammy is learning at the 'Blind School'. Of course, it *looks* that way to the person who has not learned the code, but there is something here of our own tendency to invest this disability with an aura of the supernatural, as if we want to romanticize it by believing that in return for the physical disability some kind of spiritual '*in*sight' is given – hence the recurrent figure in literature and legend of the blind seer ('seer' meaning 'prophet'), such as the Tiresias who features in Sophocles' play *Oedipus Rex* and in T. S. Eliot's poem *The Waste Land,* and the blinded Gloucester in Shakespeare's *King Lear* who, after he has been blinded, tells us 'I stumbled while I saw', meaning 'I was morally blind until I lost my sight'. Does the poem collude with this spiritualization of a physical disability or does it expose it, saying that blind people differ from everybody else only in not being able to see?

On the final point, concerning what patterns the poem contains: the major one is a pattern of reversals between the two stanzas: Sammy's fingers may be nervous, but they *are* reading, whereas the speaker's touch is 'dumb' and can read nothing. He holds the page to the window, but he can see nothing. The indicators of disability are shifted from Sammy to himself as the poem progresses – he is dumb and gropes in darkness. Looking at Sammy in the first stanza, he sees an awkward, ill-at-ease character (the thick glasses, the heavy pages of the book, the nervous fingers), but in the second, as the awkwardness is transferred to himself, he gropes in a darkness which his sight cannot help him to penetrate, and seems to achieve a degree of empathy with Sammy, an achievement to which either seeing or not seeing is irrelevant. 'Aposiopesis', in my view, is an excellent poem, but nobody would argue that it is a complicated one. Paradoxically, its not being complicated makes it easy to enjoy but difficult to write about. The four-stage method just described and exemplified suggests some ways of working out worthwhile things to say about poems, and in doing so exposing the basis on which poetic excellence is built.

But 'excellence' is a very loaded term. If some pieces of writing are indeed 'excellent', then others must be less than excellent, and yet others must be mediocre, or even downright poor. These are evaluative terms which express judgements about degrees of quality. On what kind of criteria can literary judgements of this kind be based? That is the topic of the next section.

LITERARY EVALUATION

Writing about literature is not exclusively concerned with making judgements about literary quality, but attempting to make such judgements is a significant part of it. Notice, though, that evaluation is not the same thing as interpretation (which we have talked about so far in this chapter), even though in practice the two often work in combination. In different ways, *both* were marginalized as a result of the dominance of literary theory within English Studies during recent years (as discussed in Chapter 6): interpretation, firstly, was sidelined because it is primarily to do with the consideration of individual literary works, and the dominant literary theorists were keen to turn our attention to broader issues, such as the nature of literariness itself. Hence, the theorist Roland Barthes made his well-known assertion (in his essay 'The Death of the Author') that, while everything in a text could be *disentangled*, nothing could be *interpreted* (my italics). This approach can be thought of as *dismantling* the text, rather as an alarm clock might be dismantled in order to understand what makes it tick. In those circumstances, the dismantler would have no particular interest in that individual clock, since the whole object (presumably) would be to understand the workings of alarm clocks in general. Evaluation, secondly, was sidelined by theory, for many reasons, but not least because of a strong suspicion of hierarchical distinctions in general, and a consequent desire to avoid the 'privileging' of anything at all (such as 'canonical' authors over less well-known authors, mainstream 'highbrow' novels over popular genres like the detective story, the historical romance, the thriller, and so on). So literary theory, in spite of its name, tended to see 'writing' as its object of enquiry, rather than 'literature'. The latter category, indeed, was viewed with some suspicion, as if it were a kind of hereditary aristocracy which owed its superior status to class-bound judgements passively received by posterity. My own view is that this distrust of interpretation and evaluation was misplaced, and there is considerable evidence that this view is now widespread. Furthermore, as practices, interpretation and evaluation are by no means incompatible with the outlook of literary theory (as is argued in the section 'Seven types of continuity' in Chapter 6).

Literature, then, is inescapably a world in which some works are more equal than others, and identifying the strengths and weaknesses of literary works is one of the skills you might reasonably expect to develop over the course of an English degree. But we must be realistic about the amount of agreement likely to be achieved. When a dozen competent mathematicians take up a calculation they will, I suppose, all come up with the same answer, but if you ask a dozen critics to evaluate a poem or a story the likelihood is that you will end up with a dozen different opinions (perhaps more, as literary critics will even argue with themselves). The problems arise because evaluation is usually highly contested and often very personal. But let's see to what extent it might be possible to agree on some general evaluative principles, even though we realize that the application of these criteria to specific instances will probably not produce universal agreement.

Let's start by emphasizing that poetic excellence means different things in different literary periods. My admiration of Kirkpatrick's poem is heightened by the fact that it dispenses with many of the conventional external features of poetry (such as rhyme and a fixed metre), and appears 'naked' before the reader, and yet without losing a certain poised and compressed precision which is immediately recognizable as the real thing in poetry. But this kind of completely 'unadorned' poetic excellence is not a kind which was available to, say, a Renaissance poet, for the English poetry of earlier centuries, by contrast, kept to laid-down rules of poetic form and diction, and poets had to find a way of being original within the restraints of that kind of framework. In the same way, a chess player has to be daring and original *within the rules of chess.* Placing a pawn on an opponent's head, though original, and probably quite daring, can never be a brilliant move in a chess game. So, in making a judgement about the quality of a piece of writing, we have to consider it within the context of the rules to which the writer has subscribed. It would therefore be difficult to devise criteria of excellence that would apply equally to Kirkpatrick, writing in the 1970s, and, say, Edmund Spenser, writing in the 1590s. All the same, let's see how far we can get in formulating some actual criteria for poetic excellence. An attractive criterion would be to require that every word in a text should earn its keep and have a specific job to do, a definite *semantic* role to play (that is, one concerned with establishing the meaning) – words shouldn't just be decorative. Much of the 'practical criticism' and 'New Criticism' which was prevalent from the 1920s to the 1970s (see Chapter 6) seemed to subscribe to this criterion, but it should soon become apparent that we can't really accept it in these absolute terms, for it is actually very genre-specific. An epic poem, for instance, could be much more effectively evaluated by thinking about the impact of complete episodes, rather than that of single lines or phrases. So, let's refine our original formulation to take this into account: this gives us the final form of our evaluative criterion in the area of language: *the briefer the verbal structure, the more important it is that every word should have a precise semantic function.* This is a *contingent* criterion, rather than an 'absolutist' one, for it is genre-sensitive in a fairly precise way.

SPENSER'S 'SECOND HAND'

In practice, I suspect, the above criterion will turn out to be still not flexible enough, partly because it doesn't make any distinction between the poetic tastes and practices of different historical periods; but, for the moment, let's see how useful it is in evaluating the following sonnet, from Edmund Spenser's *Amoretti* sequence:

> 75
>
> One day I wrote her name upon the strand,
> but came the waves and washéd it away:
> again I wrote it with a second hand,
> but came the tide, and made my pains his prey.
> Vain man, said she, that doest in vain assay,
> a mortal thing so to immortalize.
> for I my self shall like to this decay,
> and eek my name be wiped out likewise.
> Not so, (quod I) let baser things devize,
> to die in dust, but you shall live by fame:
> my verse your virtues rare shall eternize,
> and in the heavens write your glorious name.
> Where when as death shall all the world subdue,
> our love shall live, and later life renew.

The sequence was written the year before Spenser's marriage (at the age of 40) to Elizabeth Boyle, who may be taken as the 'she' addressed in the poems. What the criterion we are testing does, in essence, is to condemn mere decorative padding, insisting that every word and phrase in a short poem should be 'load-bearing', that is, should be necessary in some way to conveying *the sense*, so that 'verbal redundancy' should not occur. Now, this is a test which Spenser's sonnet might have some difficulty in passing, for there seems to be a clear example of verbal redundancy in line 3. The speaker opens the poem by saying how he wrote the name of his beloved in the sand; it was washed away by the tide, so he wrote it again – 'again I wrote it with a second hand', he says. But isn't the entire sense of this line conveyed by the first phrase, 'again I wrote it'? The second phrase, 'with a second hand', *adds* nothing to the sense. So it fails the 'verbal redundancy' test. Is that the end of the matter, though? Is the poet really guilty here of faulty technique?

Well, let me argue against myself, as I said critics are prone to do. If we apply a strictly utilitarian test to the words in the sonnet, then it may be that we would rule out many of the effects which sonnets are most geared to creating. In other words, we need to redefine the notion of *utility* with specific reference to the sonnet, taking into account the fact that in a sonnet the concept of 'utility' (what works and what doesn't, what has a job to do, and so on) is more various than mere semantic precision. The sonnet's primary requirements are for verbal and conceptual ingenuity within the framework of a very tight and inflexible set of rules for rhyme and rhythm. So the sonnet's principle of utility would be anything that is conducive to these ends. One aspect of the verbal ingenuity found in sonnets is the use of (to take a phrase which post-dates Spenser) 'elegant variation', which can involve, for instance, repeating what has already been said but using a different form of words. For example, lines 2 and 4 describe exactly the same thing (the incoming sea washing away what is written in the sand), but they use different verbal formulae ('waves' becomes 'tides' and 'washed it away' becomes 'made my pains its prey'), so that the principle of variation is maintained. In this light, the phrase 'with a second hand' may be said to conform to the sonnet's generic requirement for 'repetition-with-variation', so that it doesn't actually fail the redundancy test at all.

This approach involves seeing the sonnet as a form of compressed verbal entertainment akin (let's say) to text-messaging. Text-messaging too has its own verbal conventions which are imposed by the genre, and within which those who employ the medium strive to be witty and inventive. It wouldn't make sense to accuse the text-messager of not using the proper grammar and spelling of Standard English, or to condemn the medium as an inadequate vehicle for conducting a conversation about the meaning of the universe. Not even Milton would have tried to justify the ways of God to man in a sonnet – he realized it would take an epic, at least, to do that (hence, *Paradise Lost*) – nor would it be sensible to try to use text-messaging to teach open-heart surgery. This amounts to saying, again, that it doesn't make sense to set up open-ended criteria (like the absolute condemnation of verbal redundancy) which don't take into account the *totality* of the aims, customs, and capabilities of a medium of communication (whether we are talking of sonnet-writing or text-messaging). Every medium or genre, then, has its own norms of appropriateness or 'decorum' which determine what can be said, and how, within it. Thus, you might text-message a friend to let her know what time you will all meet this evening, but not (surely) to tell her that her grandmother has died. If you had to do that, you would go round to see her if you could, or phone her if you couldn't. And it wouldn't make sense to judge your way of breaking the news by the criterion of verbal redundancy – on the contrary, the more verbal redundancy you employ, the kinder your manner is likely to seem and the more genuine your concern will be taken to be. If we consider the sonnet, then, as verbal entertainment, or even simply as effective communication, we might conclude that the strict verbal redundancy criterion is not really an appropriate one to apply – indeed, it may well be one which is at odds with the 'decorum' of the sonnet medium.

So, have we convinced ourselves that Spenser's 'second hand' is OK after all? Well, in my case, not entirely. I've made the best case I can for it, but I still have a twinge of doubt. If we think of poems in the way that the American poet/critic Charles Olson (1910–70) did, which is to say as a flow of energy, then the phrase about the second hand does seem to be a moment when the current goes slack and simply marks time for a few beats.[8] It seems to puncture the flow of the sonnet, because it is such an inert repetition, too obviously just needlessly saying the same thing a second time.

---

8   This same 'Olsonian' attitude to the words of poetry is finely expressed in a recent poem by Matt Simpson, entitled 'Making an arrangement', addressed to fellow poet Gael Turnbull. The poem begins: 'Each word as required/ by thrust of will/ by pulse of need' (in Matt Simpson's collection *Getting There*, Liverpool University Press, 2001, p. 44). As the title suggests, the ideal poem (if we accept this aesthetic principle of concision) is above all an economical *arrangement* of words, and the result should be as clean and spare as a piece of Shaker furniture. Johnston Kirkpatrick, writing about his own working methods, describes something very similar: 'As soon as I begin telling, I am aware of complications. That's when the work begins, the toil of packing the right words in the right place, the desire for form, the ear listening for the click of the snib [i.e. the lock]' (in the poetry magazine *Windows*, 10, ed. Janet Ashley, Peter Barry, Robin Haylett, and Marianne Taylor, East Sussex College of Higher Education, 1982).

It will be clear (and this may well have been in your mind while reading the last couple of pages) that, in evaluating the poem in terms of strict linguistic concision, we have inevitably strayed into wider territory; and this will often be the case. Indeed, the defence just mounted essentially involved switching our attention strategically to broader aesthetic issues, and arguing that the pleasure afforded by sonnets often has to do with patterns of repetition combined with variation. In the same way, if we were trying to judge the aesthetic quality of (say) a Georgian town house, it wouldn't be a valid criticism to say that a given window was the same as the ones on either side of it, since the whole concept of Georgian buildings involves elements which are repeated and have an effect *collectively*, that is, as a *row* of windows.

This notion of the 'collective' will serve to take us into a second area, structure, since it raises the question of smaller patterns or structures which are contained within larger ones. In our Spenser example, the point is that this individual sonnet is part of something bigger, just like the individual window in the façade of the Georgian house, and that this is something which needs to be taken into account when evaluating it. The criteria so far used have had the built-in assumption that the piece under consideration is an integral and complete work. But we should bear in mind that a sonnet sequence is a composite work, which is to say that the component parts (the individual sonnets) are at the same time self-sufficient items, *and* part of a sequence. A sonnet sequence, then, is a *composite* work – it is made up of 'stand-alone' parts – whereas a novel is a *cumulative* work – its parts (chapters) are not 'stand-alones'. What the composite and the cumulative work have in common is that their constituent parts interact with each other, either well, or not so well. The crucial difference in critical practice is whether we emphasize the claims of the larger whole or of the constituent part. In the case of the composite work (a sonnet sequence or a sequence of short stories, let's say), the aesthetic *autonomy* of the constituent parts (the individual sonnets and stories) is much greater, and we have a much greater right to expect them to work effectively on their own. For a cumulative work, on the other hand, the aesthetic effect of the whole is of more importance, and should receive proportionately greater evaluative weighting.

Though less so than in the case of the cumulative work, then, factors relating to the overall structure of the sonnet sequence do require some comment. We should remember, too, that between the micro-level of the individual sonnet and the macro-level of the sequence as a whole there will often be structural 'sub-components' – for instance, there may be sub-groups of several sonnets which treat the same idea, emotion, or dilemma, or a gradual shift of mood as the sonnets progress, or else significant juxtapositions between adjacen   'transitions' which are just as important as th   ier, and they constitute the work's 'stages and ph   the beginning of this chapter). My point, then, i   t that a complete evaluative account of an indivi   make some reference to its role and status with   e might, then, formulate a criterion to cover this   ollowing lines: when a work is composite or cumu   istituent part should be effective both as a quasi-i   relation to the whole structure. A period specia   his as an important element in the overall pictu   et sequence. Clearly, a criterion like this will ena   ich broader picture than a mere close verbal scr   tem could allow.

          structure, then, is this individual sonnet part of?   Larsen, editor of the most recent scholarly edition   nposite character of the work lies in the fact that it   artifact', meaning that many of the sonnets in the sequence   n on specific identifiable days in 1594, drawing on the scriptural re ings prescribed for these days in the liturgical calendar of the Church of England. From these daily readings are drawn 'conceits, themes, ideas, imagery, words, and sometimes their rhetorical structure'.[9] Thus, the 46 sonnets between *Amoretti* 22 (with its reference to Ash Wednesday, the first day of Lent) and *Amoretti* 68 (with its reference to Easter Sunday, the end of the penitential season) mark in turn the 46 days of Lent (Larsen, p. 4). Within this sequence, Sonnet 75 corresponds to 'Low Sunday' (the Sunday after Easter), and was originally intended to bring the sequence to an end, and the remaining sonnets (76 to 89) do not have liturgical correspondences. Low Sunday is associated with baptism (in the early Church, those baptized on Easter Sunday wore a white garment until Low Sunday). Hence, Larsen links the references to water and immortality in Sonnet 75 with these aspects of Low Sunday, and also with the conclusion of Ovid's *Metamorphosis,* in which the poet talks of gaining his own immortality through verse. These liturgical elements must be taken into account in any evaluation of the sequence, whether the whole or just certain parts are in question. Indeed, Larsen's publishers make the large re-evaluative claim that 'these scriptural associations also make a rather impenetrable and seemingly uninteresting cycle of poems a highly personal,

9 Kenneth J. Larsen, *Edmund Spenser's Amoretti and Epithalamion: A Critical Edition* (Arizona State University Press, 1997), p. 3.

very funny, and often risqué sequence', which is a very large claim indeed, one which it is not possible to assess here.

My point in raising all this is partly to show how 'close reading' can sometimes be *too* close, ignoring the facts of the movement and dynamic of the sequence as a whole, and fixing somewhat artificially on just one item within it. This can be like trying to follow with the eye an individual item of flotsam being carried along by a river current, rather than looking at the river as a whole as it flows past. All the same, readings like Larsen's do have a cost: the learned liturgical and Ovidian parallels convert the material to a densely wrought textuality, layered with allusions and references. The attractive actuality of a specific incident (the speaker's writing his lover's name in the sand) is downplayed – in his notes, this becomes for Larsen just 'a possible occasion of writing', as if he doubts that any such incident ever really happened, so that it is seen primarily as a typical 'conceit', or elaborated image, which enables this genre to play out variations on the notion of 'mutability', one of its favourite themes. All this, then, confronts us with an ultimate evaluative question: which do we think more valuable, the convincing glimpse of personal actuality (two actual people from centuries ago playing affectionate, silly games on the seashore), or the multi-layered textual puzzle? But why do we have to choose, you may be thinking, why can't we have a reading which combines both elements? Of course, we *should* always strive to make such combinations. But it isn't easy, since these two kinds of reading (the 'lived actuality' reading on the one hand and the 'allusive-generic' reading on the other) do not seem to find it easy to negotiate with each other: I suspect that poetry readers usually prefer the former, and poetry scholars the latter. Only in the Romantic period did the poetry of the 'personal actuality' type finally tip the balance against the poetry of referential textuality. This might be to say that the reader of Spenser who longs for that kind of glimpse of actual lived reality, in the poetry of the 1590s, is reading in a way more appropriate for Romantic poems of the 1790s. Likewise, it might be said, the reader who wants to weigh every word 'by pulse of need' has arrived at an Early Modern poem with expectations more appropriate to the 1970s. Our conclusion must be, to reiterate, that the reading practices we develop should be appropriate in terms of period and genre, which is another way of saying that we need to approach the text with realistic and informed expectations. That is the only way to gain access to the enjoyment which the writing of all periods has to offer.

* * *

In this chapter we have considered in a practical way the two basic literary-critical activities of interpretation and evaluation, taking poetry as our focus.

We have emphasized reading close, and this seems entirely appropriate for smaller-scale poetry, but towards the end we began to think about larger works, and here it makes less sense to focus exclusively on individual lines. In reading prose, even more so, we will need to begin to shift our attention away from the impact of the localized phrase, the individual line, and onto the cumulative movement and unfolding of the whole work. In the next chapter we move from poetry to prose, and I have called it 'Reading Between the Lines' to emphasize the need for that kind of shift. In fact, saying that we have to read between the lines is perhaps a way of reminding ourselves again that sometimes close reading can be *too* close.

THE FACTS OF FICTION

'Every picture tells a story' says the familiar cliché, but what can a picture tell us which shows someone telling a story? The one I have in mind is a famous painting called *The Boyhood of Raleigh* completed in 1870 by the Victorian artist John Everett Millais. It shows the young Walter Raleigh, later explorer and naval hero, listening (along with a companion) to a veteran sailor who is telling them stirring tales of adventure at sea, and, we must suppose, inspiring Raleigh to take up his future career. It's a picture which has greatly interested literary academics: Kate Flint discusses it in her book *The Victorians and the Visual Imagination* (2000), and Jeremy Hawthorn uses it as an emblem of the storytelling process in his edited collection *Narrative: From Malory to Motion Pictures* (1985). This is what Hawthorn says about the picture at the start of his preface:

> In Millais's famous painting *The Boyhood of Raleigh* two young boys stare with rapt attention at the figure of a sailor who is telling them a story. The sailor points out to sea with one arm, but his other arm forms itself into a familiar interpersonal gesture directed towards his auditors. His gaze does not follow the direction of his pointing arm but is fixed upon the two boys who, in return, stare not out to sea but at the person who is addressing them: the narrator. (p. vii)

I am grateful to Hawthorn for the idea of using the picture to discuss the narrative process, but it has to be said that this is not an accurate description of the painting, as I think you can see by looking at the illustration (the original is in the Tate Gallery in London). Is it really true that the two young boys 'stare with rapt attention at the figure of a sailor'? Surely Flint's description is closer to what we see: 'The eyes of one of the small boys are fixed intently on him; those of the other, Raleigh himself, are directed more downwards, suggesting an inward, imaginative visualisation of the sailor's words' (p. 285). This is more accurate, but still not completely so, for even the second boy does not seem to me to have his eyes 'fixed intently' on the sailor, and he too, though with less intensity, seems to be looking at something which is suspended, so to

3.1 *The Boyhood of Raleigh* (1870), Sir John Everett Millais

speak, between the mind's eye and what is physically before the eye. And what do *we* look at as we look at the picture? Our viewpoint is low down, as if we too were auditors of the tale, sitting or reclining like the two boys, and constructed by the perspective as fellow childish listeners to the stirring tale. And though the sailor's finger points out beyond the horizon, our gaze, like that of the children in the picture, doesn't follow it, but fixes, surely, on the pale, inward-seeing face of the young Raleigh.

The narratee

Already we have touched upon a number of the salient points of the narrative process, but let's try to use the picture in a more systematic way to bring out some of the major elements of storytelling. First, though the story points out beyond the frame of the narrative to the 'real' world, as the sailor is doing, the tale actually happens within the 'narratee', which is to say, the hearer, auditor, or reader. It is the narratee (who may indeed mentally 'sub-vocalize' the narrating voice) who produces the tale by a process of sustained imaginative introspection, which is triggered, of course, by what the teller points to, and yet is not limited by that. This imaginative collusion will vary in intensity from reader to reader (as it evidently does for the two boys), but it will always involve the vicarious (that is, 'proxy') living out of the depicted events, as if they were happening to ourselves, as if we were Elizabeth Bennet, in Jane Austen's *Pride and Prejudice,* or Dickens's David Copperfield, or Toni Morrison's Seth in *Beloved.* This vicarious identification does not depend upon our being a woman, or working-class, or black – on the contrary, a reading of *Pride and Prejudice* in which the male reader's vicarious identification is with Mr Darcy rather than Elizabeth is necessarily a misreading. In other words, we put ourselves imaginatively into the frame of the book, just as the young Raleigh is 'living' the sailor's tale as it is told, reacting mentally as if it were happening to him. The reading of fiction, then, requires this kind of collusion, this coming out of yourself, so that you allow the thoughts of another person to 'think' within you.

Yet, at the same time, we are not asked as we read to *lose* ourselves in the story, or to believe that we are really somebody else and that the narrated events are really happening. Rather, what is required is what the poet Samuel Taylor Coleridge finely called a 'willing suspension of *dis*belief' (my italics). In other words, we have to stop *not* believing in the truth of what is said, without quite going so far as to believe that what is happening is real. Hence, a fearsome ghoul on the cinema screen may make you cringe in your seat as if terrified, but it probably won't make you run screaming from the cinema in fright, for you are taking the events on the screen as both real and not real at the same time, suspending, as Coleridge said, your rational disbelief in the reality of what happens on stage, or on screen, or in the inner-projected theatre of the mind which operates as we read a novel. So, Raleigh's eyes in the picture are not closed. Even though they are focused on an image projected from within, he is still in touch in some way with an external reality. He doesn't look in the direction of the sailor's pointing finger because he doesn't need to, since the story isn't taking place out there beyond the horizon, but within his own mind.

The narrator

The narrator, however, strives for a kind of invisibility; we only look directly at the teller when we are sceptical about what is being said, when the spell is broken. If we were to look directly at the pointing finger we would become conscious of the narrative process, at the way we are being manipulated, and when this happened the implicit trust between teller and auditor would have broken down, and the narrative would falter. Of course, many twentieth-century writers were profoundly interested in the narrating process itself, and deliberately cultivated a technique whereby the teller of the tale is recalled from anonymity and rendered visible again, perhaps even receiving the main spot-light of attention, so that as we read we constantly speculate about whether the narrator is 'reliable' or not; authors felt anxious about the rapt, inward gaze of the auditor, and about the comparative vulnerability of this state. They found something disturbing or morally distasteful in the kind of authorial hypnotism which placed readers in this state, and in any case, the spell of realism no longer seemed an artistic challenge – on the contrary, working this spell seemed all too easy, so that a whole body of early twentieth-century writers (Joseph Conrad, James Joyce, Virginia Woolf, and many others) began to experiment with ways of redirecting the reader's 'gaze' away from that projected inner theatre of imagined events, away from the things the teller pointed *at*, and onto the teller, and the act of telling itself. Hence, they would deliberately draw atten-tion to the voice and actions of the teller (that left hand of the sailor, for instance, which seems to manipulate or orchestrate the boys' reactions as a puppeteer determines the actions of the puppet – what is it doing, exactly, and how is this trick achieved?). Indeed, the sailor's is the only gaze in the picture which is unambiguously directed – his attention is unswervingly on the reac-tions of his auditors as he produces his finely calculated effects. Significantly, he does not follow the direction of his own pointing finger. As developing readers of literature, we need to look both at what is pointed at and at the pointing itself (to use a distinction made by Hawthorn), asking such questions as Why now? Why at this? Why not at that as well?

'Site' or 'domain'

In the painting, it is perhaps obvious that we should 'read' and interpret the two boys and the sailor, since they are clearly the collective focus of the picture. But there are plenty of other things in the picture which also need to be read, for we must read the 'site' or 'domain' of the action as well as the action itself. Flint, for instance, reads some of the objects in the 'site' as follows:

> On the left of the picture, a toy sailing ship, placed on the same diagonal as the sailor's outstretched arm, suggests how childhood enthusiasms, mediated through the narratives and inspiration of the sailor, will transform into adult exploration and adventure. The red ensign on this

ship signals its Englishness; the strange feathered cap, and the exotic plumage of a dead bird behind the sailor, represent the cultural and natural trophies awaiting the voyager across the ocean. (p. 285)

Flint reads these objects plausibly in emblematic or symbolic terms, but it is clear that there is a degree of subjectivity here; this cannot be avoided, but we ought to be conscious of it, as we slide from *delineation* (noting that the object in the left foreground is a toy sailing ship, for instance) to *interpretation* (suggesting that its meaning is that 'childhood enthusiasms . . . will transform into adult exploration'). Obviously, such details would lend themselves to different interpretations, for instance, that the ship in the left foreground is a 'proleptic' (that is, anticipatory) emblem of the eventual outcome of Raleigh's brilliant career (that is, his disgrace and beheading), for it is positioned so as to look like a ship wrecked on a rocky shore. In the right foreground are objects representing a different possible outcome – we can see the fluke of an anchor, the anchor (associated with landfall and homecoming) being a traditional symbol of hope and fulfilment, with the parrot suggesting a return from distant parts of the globe. Nobody in the picture is pointing towards these objects, so it takes an effort to pick them out and figure them out; but being aware of this kind of peripheral significant detail is an essential way of adding depth and nuance to our reading. Yet with the interpretation of such details it is notoriously difficult to know when to stop – once we become readers we sometimes become obsessives who are determined to leave nothing at all *un*read. So we might see the enclosing wall of the rampart as the protective horizon of childhood, behind which the boys are still sheltered, pending the time when they will face the open horizon beyond, its dangers perhaps suggested by the cliff just visible on the left. Furthermore, we might speculate about the ship's timbers which the sailor is seated on: are these the detritus of a shipwreck, rotten timbers in which weeds have taken root, or are they wood still being seasoned from which the ships of the future will be built, just as the boys will supply the 'hearts of oak' from which the future navy will be fashioned? Here we have moved away from what seems to be the central focus of the picture, and have started to construct a kind of alternative narrative.

This other narrative is implied by the objects in the picture, which we read as emblems or symbols that construct a series of 'silent statements' constituting (to use a musical metaphor) a kind of *counterpoint* to the main narrative, which is to say, another tune which is interwoven or contrasted with the first one, making the overall musical experience more complex. A slightly different way of putting this (though still keeping to the musical analogy) is to say that the 'silent statements' made by the emblematic devices are a kind of accompaniment which harmonizes with the 'tune' being played by the main narrative line, giving it added depth and subtlety, in the way that the 'chordage' played by the pianist's left hand sets off the basic melody played by the right. But the emblematic dimension of a narrative is easily misread or over-interpreted, and, unless we can reintegrate this narrative 'shadow line' with the basic patterns set up by the central narrative elements (plot, character, direct authorial commentary, and so on), then we ought perhaps to be cautious, and should at least pause to ask ourselves whether we have gone too far.

So far, then, what have we said here about narrative? We have commented on the role of the listeners or readers, and the way they bring the story to life by their inward gaze, which becomes unconscious of the narrating voice, and on the role of the objective world beyond, in which the events take place. We have also commented on the narrator, and on how the manipulation of the reader's response is his or her exclusive concern ('Have eyes only for your reader,' novelist Ford Maddox Ford (1873–1939) said to writers, a phrase which perhaps reminds us of the sailor's intense gaze at the two boys who are 'taking in' his story). Narrators may point outwards to events in the real world, but their real concern is with what happens within. Finally, we commented on a more loosely defined aspect of the story which lies beyond the main events of the plot and the protagonists. This is the realm of significant details of setting, emblem, or symbolism, which add nuance and depth to the overall effect. We have called this aspect of the text the 'site' or 'domain' of the story, and defined it as those parts of the narrative which are *not* explicitly pointed to during the process of narration.

The narrator's fear of the narratee

A while ago, I said that early modernist writers engaged in a sceptical foregrounding of the narrating role, employing a device often known as the 'unreliable narrator'. Many of these features of narrative come to our attention only when the story-line 'pauses' in some way, which authors sometimes deliberately make it do. A famous example occurs in Joseph Conrad's 1899 novella 'Heart of Darkness', when the narrating persona, whose name is Marlow, interrupts his own story with anxious introspection about the inevitable limits of knowing and telling. For Marlow is struck in mid-tale by the sheer impossibility of ever conveying to others the unique flavour of an occurrence, or the precise nature of another human being; it's as if an acrobat, crossing a cataract on a high wire, were to look down suddenly and become aware of the immense vulnerability of his own position. Marlow is trying to convey to his hearers, through his tale, the precise lure of the corrupt Mr Kurtz, but he breaks off with: 'Do you see him? Do you see the story? Do you see anything?'[1] Here, as it were, that other old sailor, the one in Millais's painting, breaks off, and asks those two boys, who are not looking at him as he tells his tale, what exactly (if anything) they see in their mind's eye. And then, of course, the spell is broken, not just because the tale which the boys are projecting within themselves is interrupted, but also because the storyteller has lost faith in a fundamental way in the narrative process itself, and is suddenly just floundering. This is Marlow:

> He was silent for a while.
> '. . . No, it is impossible; it is impossible to convey the life-sensation of any given epoch of one's existence, – that which makes its truth, its meaning – its subtle and penetrating essence. It is impossible. We live, as we dream – alone. . . .'
> He paused again as if reflecting, then added –
> 'Of course in this you fellows see more than I could then. You see me, whom you know. . . .'

What we see here is the narrator's fear of the gaze of the narratee (the 'recipient' of the tale). The former's desire is that the auditors should look anywhere but at him, for if they look at him they will inevitably see more than he himself can, because they will also see his 'bias', which is to say the point of view which determines the limits of his vision. In other words, the telling of a story is always an act of self-exposure, for in the process we inevitably reveal our obsessions and our weak spots, making it embarrassingly obvious precisely what 'makes us tick'. So what makes Marlow able to continue? Crudely, it is the cover of darkness, which restores narratorial invisibility. As they sit on deck, listening to Marlow's tale and waiting for the tide to turn, darkness has descended, so that Marlow loses his solid individuality as a real person – the person his old friends know only too well – and becomes a kind of disembodied voice, an impersonal narrating function, the voice not of the teller but of the tale:

> It had become so pitch dark that we listeners could hardly see one another. For a long time already he, sitting apart, had been no more to us than a voice. There was not a word from anybody. The others might have been asleep, but I was awake. I listened, I listened on the watch for the sentence, for the word, that would give me the clue to the faint uneasiness inspired by this narrative that seemed to shape itself without human lips in the heavy night-air of the river.

1 'Heart of Darkness', new edn, ed. Robert Hampson (Penguin, 2000), p. 50.

This powerful passage again seems in accord with the storytelling in the Millais picture. In Conrad the listeners are isolated from each other, each one projecting a different realization of the tale in his mind, just as the two boys are both isolated in a private world of vicariously lived experience (not, for instance, looking at each other and sharing open-mouthed wonder, as a cruder representation of the narratee might have had it). The unnamed 'principal narratee' in Conrad will later (presumably) write down the tale Marlow told, so that it can be relayed eventually to us, but for the moment the energizing thread is not mere suspense (the desire simply to know what happened next) but the desire to identify the source of the vague feeling of unease which Marlow's tale induces in his listeners. This isn't a desire for mere narrative closure, then, which is to say that it is not a desire to *know*, but a desire to *understand*. Yet, too, the remarks of Marlow already quoted show an awareness of the fact that this is a desire which can never be fully satisfied, so that, in a real sense, *every* story is a never-ending story, or (to say this differently) a story which ends differently every time we read it. In the lines from the tale just quoted, this sense of endemic uncertainty is built into Conrad's very grammar – is it the narrative which 'seemed to shape itself without human lips' or the 'faint uneasiness' which that narrative inspires? In Millais, it is the narrator himself who is least likely to know the ending of the tale he tells (it continues in Raleigh's life, and ends with Raleigh's execution); in Conrad, Marlow supplies a false ending to his tale of Kurtz's life when he confronts the dead man's fiancée and deceives her into believing that 'The last word he pronounced was – your name.' Since we know for certain that Marlow deceived *her*, how can we ever be sure that he isn't also deceiving *us*?[2]

The account of stories given in this section has, as you will have noticed, focused mainly on story*telling*. Its primary emphasis has been not on content, but on the act of representation, that is, on how narrators present matters and how readers respond. Its end-point has been to recommend a certain scepticism about what the storyteller says; this scepticism will necessarily prise the reader away a little from the spell of the story, and set up a space in which readers, in effect, can enter into a kind of dialogue with it. However, this is not to plump for a wholesale dethronement of authors, since, if reading is to be seen (as I believe it usefully can be) as a form of conversation between reader and writer, then it still remains the case that the conversation is initiated, and

---

2 A good answer to this question would be to say 'because he himself reveals to us his deception of the Intended – it isn't something he tries to hide'. All the same, it remains true (even though he himself is the one who says it) that as readers we can always see more than he (or any tale-teller) sees, because we see the tale-teller too.

largely directed, by the author. Likewise, it is not to assume that readers know better than authors what authors mean, and hence are always able to expose authorial ideologies and purposes to which authors themselves are naïvely blind (an illusion common in literary critics). After all, the scepticism about narrative omniscience which came to a head in the high modernist period of the early twentieth century was not instigated by a readers' revolt in which readers refused any longer to believe in authorial omniscience – rather, the writers (James, Conrad, Joyce, Woolf, and many others) were themselves the instigators of that kind of scepticism. Thus, one of the linking factors between the way we discussed poetry in Chapter 2 and the discussion of fiction here has been precisely this emphasis on the reader 'writing back', or talking back, to the text. We could even say that this kind of 'writing back' is supremely what doing an English degree is all about.

* * *

The next chapter takes matters a stage further, going 'beyond the lines', so to speak, in the sense that it begins to take into account some of the external factors which impinge upon the text, starting with those texts which have a prior relationship with the text under discussion, that is, with its sphere of *inter*textuality, and then opening up the question of how it relates to the world beyond, that is, its *con*textuality. Both the examples used in this next chapter are poems, but they are also narratives, thus bringing together some of the concerns of Chapters 2 and 3.

4 Reading Beyond the Lines

INTERTEXTUALITY: WORDSWORTH'S 'BEGGARS'

No literary text exists in a vacuum. Every text is intimately related to a great web of circumstances outside itself (that is, it has *con*textuality) and every text has relations with other texts, some literary, some not (that is, it has *inter*textuality). To strive for a comprehensive investigation of the web of contextuality within which all literary works are entangled is, surely, an impossible ideal, for extricating even a single text from all the strands of its web of contextuality could occupy a literary scholar for a lifetime (though some seem willing to pay this price). To take an instance: among specialists in the 'Early Modern' period (formerly known as the Renaissance), there is a powerful impetus – partly the slipstream of the movement known as New Historicism – towards reconstructing the culture and outlook that produced the cultural institution known as the Early Modern Stage. Hence, there are increasing numbers of books by literary scholars about how it was financed, its cultural affiliations, the make-up of its audience, and the gendered assumptions that governed its stage practices and determined its repertoire of plays.[1] This historical entity 'the Early Modern Stage' is now a prime object of *literary* study, rather than the plays of Marlowe, Webster, Kyd, and Middleton, whose names no longer seem to feature in the titles of books by literary academics. Similar historicizing tendencies are equally evident today in the study of other literary periods, including the medieval, the Romantic, and the nineteenth century. The assumption, then, is that the process of meticulous contextualization is the prime means of achieving literary understanding, so that the study of context seems to have become dominant in literary study (of which, more in the next chapter). My own unease about these tendencies will be evident from

1 Representative books are: Theodore B. Leinwand, *Theatre Finance and Society in Early Modern England* (1999); Anthony B. Dawson and Paul Yachnin, *The Culture of Playgoing in Shakespeare's England: A Collaborative Debate* (2001); Roslyn Lander Knutson, *Playing Companies and Commerce in Shakespeare's Time* (2001); and Bridget Orr, *Empire on the English Stage, 1660–1714* (2001), all from Cambridge University Press.

the tone of the above. I suspect that as literary scholars we have exaggerated the amount of literary understanding which can be derived from the study of context. So we need (sometimes, at least) to entertain the counterview that there is a sense in which we can only understand and appreciate the literature of the past by detaching it from its web of contextual strands and filiations. This is to advocate a combination of historicism (see Chapter 5) and formalism (see Chapter 6), rather than the current disciplinary fashion which requires the rejection of the latter and embrace of the former.

The study of intertextuality is generally less problematic than that of context, because the area of relevance is usually much more limited and specific, and less the selective construction of the individual critic. Many literary works, for instance, have close relationships with other printed texts, from which they derive or to which they respond in some way. For instance, the Victorian poet Gerard Manley Hopkins wrote his epic-scale poem 'The Wreck of the *Deutschland*' in response to an account of this tragic shipwreck in *The Times* newspaper of 11 December 1875; it is possible to compare the two, and by doing so gain an insight into the poet's thinking and methods of composition. Beyond this (as we might call it) *primary* level of intertextuality, there are in the case of this poem other levels of more generalized inter-textuality, such as the poem's relationship with the Victorian sub-genre of ship-wreck poems and ballads, with its set pieces of 'vivid and repeated descriptions of the storm, heroic drama, prayer, a powerless crew . . . and horrific detail', so that 'Hopkins was drawing on literary convention for subject, details, emotion, and vocabulary'.[2] Hence it was natural then, as it would not be now, that, when Hopkins discussed the newspaper account of the event with his religious superior, the latter should make the comment that somebody ought to write a poem about it. And there are further layers of intertextuality which come into play when we go on to consider the form of the poem: Hopkins used as his verse form an adaptation of the Pindaric ode (the form used by the classical Greek poet Pindar), and he incorporated into this his own version of the sound patternings found in Welsh verse, especially *cynghanedd*, which makes intertwining patterns of sound in ways very much to Hopkins's taste. (At the time he wrote the poem he was at a Jesuit college in Wales and was studying Welsh poetry and experimenting with its forms.) Clearly, gaining a full-scale understanding of the intertextual affiliations of this one poem would be a challenging undertaking, and only a limited amount of the knowledge so

---

2 For the Hopkins data see *Hopkins: A Literary Biography*, by Norman White (Clarendon Press, 1992), ch. 21, pp. 250–60, 'The Wreck of the *Deutschland*'.

gained would be transferable to other aspects of our literary studies. And this is a consequence of the fact that the study of *inter*textuality has an inherent specificity which is often lacking in approaches which are primarily *con*textual. Of course, the corollary is that a good deal of contextual study *is* transferable to the study of other literary works – the Victorian social and political context which you might unearth in connection with work on a Dickens novel will probably be equally relevant when you are studying the novels of other Victorian writers.

'He could not escape those very words'

However, one advantage of studying a text from the viewpoint of inter-textuality is that it can bring in inductively those big concerns with such matters as gender, identity, and ethics which make the contextual approach so attractive to literary scholars. At the same time, this approach can give us profound insights into the nature of writing, and the sources of writers' ideas, as well as (sometimes) a strong sense of a writer's limitations. The material which follows is a kind of case study in intertextuality which asks you to consider the extent of William Wordsworth's debt to his sister, Dorothy, by making a comparative analysis of one of his poems and one of the entries from her diary, which he used as a source. In 1800, when her diary was started, William (born in 1770) and Dorothy (born in 1771) had just moved to Dove Cottage, at Grasmere in the English Lake District. Orphaned as children, they had been brought up separately by relatives; when reunited in early adult life they had determined to set up home together, and this they did in 1795. The unmarried Dorothy remained part of the household after her brother's marriage, and both lived into old age. Dorothy began to suffer from premature senility after a breakdown in 1829. William died in 1850 and Dorothy in 1855.

The opening entry in the diary explains that she first decided to keep a journal in May 1800 when her two brothers were away. But over that three-week period the journal-writing habit was established, and so continued. She says that her motive is to give William pleasure by keeping the diary, and I think she means by this that she will record for him the details of weather, nature, and scenery which he would have observed himself on their daily walks had he been present. In the interval, he will be enabled, by means of the diary, to 'see' by proxy, and she will view on his behalf. This 'proxy witness' function is an important element to keep in mind in what follows. The journal contains an amazing number of accounts of beggars, peddlars, discharged veterans, odd-jobbers, and the like who were constantly tramping the countryside in this politically troubled period, giving readers today a vivid impression of the amount of social destitution which existed in this era, eventually leading to the establishment of the hated Victorian workhouses later in the century. A typical passage in the diary begins: 'as I was going out in the morning I met a half crazy old man. He shewed me a pincushion and begged a pin, afterwards a half-penny.' Wordsworth was fascinated by these sombre outcasts, and many of his best poems tell of encounters with them. Not surprisingly, then, these are the passages from Dorothy's journal which he often uses as sources for his poetry. It is easy to see why they are so attractive to him, for they have a vivid, eyewitness quality which could never be faked, and they provide him with ready-made 'incidents from common life' of the kind he is explicitly committed to using as the basis for a new kind of poetry. Furthermore, the diary language is plain and prosaic (as is fitting for that kind of writing) and so seems to leave something for the poet to do, in terms of transforming the accounts imaginatively into something heightened and significant.

There is often a delay of a couple of years between Dorothy's diary entry and William's related poems. For example, on 3 October 1800 William and Dorothy together encountered an old man gathering leeches: during the period May to July 1802 William wrote a poem called 'The Leech Gatherer' (later renamed 'Resolution and Independence'). In the poem the meeting is presented as a *solitary* encounter between the male speaker and the old man, with Dorothy written out – 'I was a traveller then upon the moor,' the voice in the poem tells us. Another example, which is probably the best-known one, concerns a scene witnessed by brother and sister together on 15 April 1802, when they walked by the lake known as Eusemere, and came across a long belt of daffodils, which (as Dorothy describes them) 'tossed and realed and danced' in the breeze. Two years later William wrote his famous poem 'The Daffodils', using Dorothy's journal account as a source, but again writing her out of the scene – 'I wandered *lonely* as a cloud', the poem begins (my italics). Why does William omit Dorothy from these poems? (It is worth bearing in mind that there may be different reasons each time it happens.)

A final example is the one we will consider in more detail. On 27 May 1800 Dorothy opened the door of their cottage to 'a very tall woman, tall much beyond the measure of tall women', and described the ensuing encounter in her journal. There is, in fact, no indication that this person was seen at all by William, but on 13 March 1802 she read her account of the meeting to him, and (she says) 'an unlucky thing it was, *for he could not escape from those very words, and so he could not write the poem*' (my italics again). In fact, the poem *was* finished, the following day, and William's inability to escape from Dorothy's words may partly be due to the fact that he had not actually seen the woman himself. Yet once again, in the resulting poem, Dorothy is written out of the incident, and the encounter becomes a solitary one, transferred from the cottage door to the open countryside. The question for us to ponder, put bluntly, is: 'Whose poem is it?' Here is the journal entry in full, followed by the poem:

A very tall woman, tall much beyond the measure of tall women, called at the door. She had on a very long brown cloak and a very white cap, without bonnet. Her face was excessively brown, but it had plainly once been fair. She led a little bare-footed child about two years old by the hand, and said her husband, who was a tinker, was gone before with the other children. I gave her piece of bread.

Afterwards, on my way to Ambleside, beside the bridge at Rydale, I saw her husband sitting by the roadside, his two asses feeding beside him, and the two young children at play upon the grass. The man did not beg. I passed on and about a quarter of a mile further I saw two boys before me, one about 10, the other about 8 years old, at play chasing a butterfly. They were wild figures, not very ragged, but without shoes and stockings. The hat of the elder was wreathed round with yellow flowers, the younger, whose hat was only a rimless crown, had stuck it round with laurel leaves. They continued at play till I drew very near, and then they addressed me with the begging cant and the whining voice of sorrow. I said 'I served your mother this morning'. (The boys were so like the woman who had called at the door that I could not be mistaken.) 'O!' says the elder, 'you could not serve my mother for she's dead, and my father's on at the next town – he's a potter.' I persisted in my assertion, and that I would give them nothing. Says the elder 'Let's away.' And away they flew like lightning.

They had however sauntered so long in their road that they did not reach Ambleside before me, and I saw them go up to Matthew Harrison's house with their wallet upon the elder's shoulder, and creeping with a beggar's complaining foot. On my return through Ambleside I met in the street the mother driving her asses, in the two panniers of one of which were the two little children, whom she was chiding and threatening with a wand which she used to drive on her asses, while the little things hung in wantonness over the pannier's edge. The woman had told me in the morning that she was of Scotland, which her accent fully proved, but that she had lived, I think, at Wigton, that they could not keep a house and so they travelled.

BEGGARS

1

She had a tall man's height or more;
Her face from summer's noontide heat
No bonnet shaded, but she wore
A mantle, to her very feet
Descending with a graceful flow,
And on her head a cap as white as new-fallen snow.

2

Her skin was of Egyptian brown:
Haughty, as if her eye had seen
Its own light to a distance thrown,
She towered, fit person for a Queen
To lead those ancient Amazonian files;
Or ruling Bandit's wife among the Grecian isles.

3

Advancing, forth she stretched her hand
And begged an alms with doleful plea
That ceased not; on our English land
Such woes, I knew, could never be;
And yet a boon I gave her, for the creature
Was beautiful to see – a weed of glorious feature.

4

I left her, and pursued my way;
And soon before me did espy
A pair of little boys at play,
Chasing a crimson butterfly;
The taller followed with his hat in hand,
Wreathed round with yellow flowers the gayest in the land.

5

The other wore a rimless crown
With leaves of laurel stuck about;
And while both followed up and down,
Each whooping with a merry shout,
In their fraternal features I could trace
Unquestionable lines of that wild suppliant's face.

6

Yet *they*, so blythe of heart, seemed fit
For finest tasks of earth or air:
Wings let them have, and they might flit
Precursors to Aurora's car,

Scattering fresh flowers; though happier far, I ween,
To hunt their fluttering game o'er rock and level green.

7
They dart across my path – but lo,
Each ready with a plaintive whine!
Said I, 'not half an hour ago
Your Mother has had alms of mine.'
'That cannot be,' one answered – 'she is dead:' –
I looked reproof – they saw – but neither hung his head.

8
'She has been dead, Sir, many a day.' –
'Hush, boys! you're telling me a lie;
It was your Mother, as I say!'
And, in the twinkling of an eye,
'Come! come!' cried one, and without more ado
Off to some other play the joyous Vagrants flew!

How far, then, does the poet succeed in 'escaping those very words'? And just as importantly, how far is he more generally dependent on Dorothy's treatment of the subject? To answer these questions we need to consider actual verbal similarities between the two texts, as well as more general similarities (e.g. viewpoint, emphasis, progression, tone), and also significant *dis*similarities between the two (e.g. William's omissions, additions, reorderings, and alterations).

Firstly, some key differences between journal and poem concern what we might call 'gendered perspective'. Thus, William's measure of people is man ('She had a tall man's height or more') whereas Dorothy's is woman ('a very tall woman, tall much beyond the measure of tall women'). Secondly, Dorothy's setting is specific and localized ('the road to Ambleside . . . beside a bridge at Rydale', etc), whereas William's is unspecified ('I left her and pursued my way'). Thirdly, Dorothy emphasizes that the woman is 'native', part of the 'scene' – she may *look* 'foreign', but she isn't ('her face was excessively brown, but it had plainly once been fair'). William, by contrast, 'exoticizes' and 'others' the woman (*'Egyptian brown* . . . fit person for a Queen . . . *Amazonian* files . . . *Bandit's wife* among the *Grecian isles*') as all the phrases italicized here suggest. He says (presumably with a degree of irony – or not?) 'On our English land/ Such woes, I knew, could never be'. Fourthly, as already suggested, Dorothy's diary language has that 'eyewitness flatness' of tone ('about a quarter mile further I saw two boys before me, one about 10, the other about 8 years old'): William takes these details and tends to 'colourize' them, so to speak (the butterfly becomes 'crimson', the yellow flowers become 'the gayest of the land)

and, indeed, somewhat sentimentalize them ('Yet they, so blithe of heart, seemed fit/ For finest tasks of earth or air;/ Wings let them have, and they might flit/ Precursors to Aurora's car'). Fifthly (and relatedly), Dorothy's prose uses basic 'intensifiers' (as linguists call them) like 'very' or 'extremely' ('a *very* tall woman', 'a *very* white cap', 'her face was *excessively* brown': William, by contrast, often uses language based on metaphor or simile ('a cap *as white as new-fallen snow*', 'Her skin was of *Egyptian brown*' ('Egyptian' probably meaning 'like a gypsy'). Finally, and coming back to the gender issue, the contrasting attitudes of Dorothy and William reflect different assumptions about gender and power. Dorothy gives the woman bread, but doesn't give anything when asked later by the children, as she has already helped the mother ('I served your mother this morning'). She doesn't comment on the children's assertion that their mother is dead, and merely notes the tricks which they use when trying to beg ('creeping with a beggar's complaining foot'). William, by contrast, emphasizes his own generosity ('a boon I gave her', and later 'Your mother has had alms of mine') and has his own 'masculinist' reasons for being generous ('for the creature/ Was beautiful to see'). Later, when the boys pretend their mother is dead, his attitude is judgemental and authoritarian ('I looked reproof . . . you're telling me a lie'). This is not intended as a pompous rebuke of Wordsworth for being careful with his pennies – the Wordsworths were poor at the time, by genteel standards, and had just enough income to live independently in a cheap part of the country, renting an ordinary cottage, doing without a live-in servant, and getting their main entertainment from walking, reading, writing, and talking.

Intertextuality and authorship

One further advantage of taking an intertextual approach is the light it can throw upon the matter of the relationship between poetry and experience. We usually assume that poetry is about the recording of intimate personal experience, but in this poem we see a degree of 'fictionalization' of what *'actually'* happened, and the use and appropriation of another person's words and experience. Perhaps it follows from this that poems can sometimes be much more like stories than we are usually prepared to allow (that is, with invented dialogue, partly imagined situations, and strategic modifications of 'straight' factuality). After all, we don't usually assume that stories are authentic records of the author's lived experience, and yet we do often seem to expect this of poems.

The precise relationship between poetry and personal experience is a matter on which popular opinion and the views of poets themselves are often very much polarized. T. S. Eliot, in his 1922 essay 'Tradition and the Individual Talent' (included in his *Selected Essays*), insisted on the need for a separation between poem and experience. Many poets make use of a fictionalized named 'persona' in their poetry – see, for instance, the 'dramatic monologues' of Tennyson and Browning in the nineteenth century, where the speaker is an invented 'character' who is a fictionalized being, just like a character in a novel. The best-known examples of this kind of poem are Browning's 'My Last Duchess' and Tennyson's 'Ulysses'. Even when the poet is not using a persona and instead uses the first person pronoun, speaking as 'I', it is a critical convention to refer to 'the speaker' in a poem, rather than attributing the sentiments expressed directly to the author, and this recognizes the possibility of a degree of fictionalization as a legitimate proceeding in all poetry. Thus Wordsworth, as we know from our intertextual study, never did wander 'lonely as a cloud' and come across a host of daffodils, but this does not invalidate the poem.

All this, then, has a bearing on the question of the nature of authorship itself. We assume that 'authorship' means being completely responsible for both the conception and the verbal embodiment of a text, but here we see a complicated collaborative process extending over a long period of time. Dorothy's journal makes it clear just how sustained and complex that collaborative process was, and the result is that the origins (and ownership) of an idea or perception or experience become difficult to identify precisely. So the very notion of authorship is made problematic by the facts of intertextuality. One of the reasons for studying the network of intertextuality that includes Dorothy's journal and William's poems is that it shows writing *in process* – not dropping from the sky, or born in mysterious moments of inspiration, but arising from specific incidents, encounters and conversations, and ultimately proving very difficult to detach cleanly from its 'background', whether this be contextual or intertextual.

Dove Cottage, gender, and intertextuality

Of course, the gender politics of the domestic arrangements at Dove Cottage, as revealed in the diary, will now seem particularly cruel. When Dorothy says that she did 'work', or took her 'work' out into the garden, she always means *needle*work – darning and sewing socks and shirts, probably mostly William's. She bakes bread and pies and does the washing, while William composes. She writes too, but when she says 'writes' she sometimes means writing out

William's poems.[3] For her own composition she chooses the less ambitious form of the private diary. The collaborative process which produced Wordsworth's poem clearly has behind it a specific gender politics: the man uses the 'high' genre of poetry, while the woman uses the 'low' genre of the diary. The woman's data and experience are taken over by the man, so the woman is playing a 'service' role in relation to the man. We might say that the man 'appropriates the seeing' of the woman.

Dorothy freely makes her diary available to William as a quarry for the poetry which will make him famous. She also acts as his secretary, constantly writing out fair copies of all his poems – taking down his stanzas, as she puts it. For instance, on Thursday 8 July 1802: 'William was looking at "The Peddlar" when I got up. He arranged it, and after tea I wrote it out – 280 lines.' When the poems are eventually set up in print and the proofs arrive for correction, she acts as proof-reader. Her devotion to him is absolute: she lives a celibate, unmarried life, remaining a member of the household after William marries, and in due course also becoming nursemaid, babysitter, and infant-teacher to his children.

But lamenting a gender situation which then seemed 'natural', and becoming (so belatedly) angry with the poet who benefited from it, seems to me a strangely pointless process, like stoking a fire which has nothing to burn. If you believe that Dorothy was herself potentially as good a poet as her brother, and was lost to us because of gender politics, then you should read her surviving poems, and make up your own mind on the strength of the remaining evidence.[4] Personally, I see no evidence of any unusual talent

---

3 A parody in *The Virago Book of Wicked Verse* imagines the kind of difficulties Dorothy might have encountered had she gone upstairs to write the 'Daffodils' poem herself. It begins:

> *'I wandered lonely as a . . .*
> They're in the top drawer, William,
> Under your socks –
> *I wandered lonely as a –*
> Not that drawer, the top one.
> *I wandered by myself –*
> Well wear the ones you *can* find.
> No don't get overwrought my dear
> I'm coming.

4 Dorothy wrote about 40 poems between 1805 and 1840, including 'Address to a Child' and 'Floating Island', which Wordsworth included in his own books, specifying them as 'by my Sister'. For a general appraisal see Susan M. Levin, *Dorothy Wordsworth and Romanticism* (Rutgers University Press, 1987). Her poem 'Peaceful our valley, fair and green' is included in the *Norton Anthology of Literature by Women*, 2nd edn, ed. Sandra M. Gilbert and Susan Gubar (Norton, 1996), pp. 325–7.

in those poems: she was a brilliant diarist with an immensely sharp eye, and a turn of phrase which can be thrilling, and much more moving than the more high-flown poetic language of her brother. See, for instance, these descriptions in the journal of the nearby lakes, where the language swoops from the most mundane to the dramatic within a phrase or two: 'After tea went to Ambleside – a pleasant, cool but not cold evening. Rydale was very beautiful, with spear-shaped streaks of polished steel' (16 May 1800). There is a sudden epic grandeur in those 'spear-shaped streaks of polished steel', describing the appearance of the surface of the lake, before the tone immediately reverts to the mundane with 'No letters! only one newspaper.' The entry continues: 'I returned to Clappersgate. Grasmere was very solemn in the last glimpse of twilight; it calls home the heart to quietness.' Here again that last phrase suddenly hits an unforgettable intensity of tone before dropping again to the mundane. Juxtaposing the diary and the poems shows that even poetic language as self-consciously down to earth as that of the early Romantics like Wordsworth and Coleridge was still pretty elevated when looked at in comparison with the register of ordinary speech and writing, rather than in contrast with the prevailing tone of the typical poetic writing of the time.

What is also evident from the juxtaposition is a relationship of interdependency: Wordsworth as a poet needs the material which Dorothy supplies in her diaries, which is based on detailed, documented observations of people encountered in the village, and on meticulous scrutiny of such things as the effects of light on water, or the precise appearance of wild flowers against rocks. Dorothy's eye is like a microscope, scrutinizing detail in close-up: William's eye is panoramic and broad-sweeping, typically registering an overall atmospheric effect rather than a specific small detail. The two eyes need each other – the 'short-sighted' eye of Dorothy and the 'long-sighted' eye of William. Together they make a literary ecosystem, a symbiosis, a relationship of mutual dependency. Rightly or wrongly, Dorothy feels that she cannot supply the final twist needed to make her material into poetry – she needs William for that. Rightly or wrongly, William feels the need and entitlement to help himself, with her consent, to the solid, documentary observations which Dorothy supplies. We don't, today, find that very appealing, but we cannot change the past, and there is nothing we can do about it. A new approach to Romanticism is stressing notions of ecology, and it seems to me that the best way to think of Dorothy and William is as a system and a partnership which worked, an ecosystem which sustained a vital balance and did its job. Our case study of intertextuality, then, needn't end with an indignant arraignment of Wordsworth, but in an appreciation of the ploys and subterfuges by means of which writing actually gets done. And seeing *that* is one of the main benefits of an intertextual approach to literary study.

Issues of gender, finally, have been given a great deal of attention in literary studies since at least the 1970s, and this tendency is especially strong among Romanticists.[5] The study of British Romanticism was dominated until the 1980s by the male 'big five' poets (Wordsworth, Coleridge, Keats, Byron, and Shelley), but since then there has been an increasing interest in the once marginalized women members of the major groupings of romantic writers (such as Dorothy Wordsworth and Mary Shelley) and a rediscovery of the many women poets of the period (like Anna Barbauld, Joanna Bailie, Charlotte Smith, and Felicia Hemans).[6] So the irony is that increasingly figures like Dorothy, who were once on the margins of Romantic-period writing, are being seen as important figures in their own right. From the point of view of Wordsworth's many eminent visitors as his fame as a poet increased, Dorothy may have been a very minor member of his household, but that is not how she is regarded by Romantic scholars today. For them, her writing is worthy of study in its own right, and not just for the light it throws on her brother's poetry.

This section has concerned contextuality. In the next section we will broaden out to look at another example, attempting to deal with what we might grandly call 'total textuality', that is, with all the different kinds of textuality which can be seen as 'in play' (to varying extents) in works of literature. An outline sketch of 'total textuality' would include:

1. *Textuality* (also known as 'the words on the page')

2. *Intertextuality* (roughly, the words on related pages)

3. *Contextuality* (the social, cultural, and historical context of the work)

4. *Multitextuality* (the textual variants of the work itself – see Chapter 8)

5. *Peritextuality* (also known as literary criticism – the words alongside the text)

---

5 An influential book in this movement is *Romanticism and Gender*, by Anne K. Mellor (Routledge, 1993).
6 The work of some of these women poets can be found in anthologies like *Women Romantic Poets, 1785–1832*, ed. Jennifer Breen (Everyman's Library, 1992), and *Women Romantic Poets, 1770–1838*, ed. Andrew Ashfield (Manchester University Press, 1995).

6. *Metatextuality* (also known as literary theory – the text 'reconstituted' through theory)

If we call the first of these 'primary textuality' and the second 'secondary textuality', then types 3–6 are various kinds of 'extra-textuality'. The next section looks at the way these six different kinds of textuality might come into play in a reading of a well-known Victorian poem.

TOTAL TEXTUALITY: 'THE LADY OF SHALOTT'

What follows is an attempt to show the totality of the procedures which might be involved in the consideration of a specific and well-known literary text. This takes up aspects of the material on textuality set out in Chapter 2, seeking to join them up into a 'total criticism' which is informed, firstly, by the historical totality of critical responses to this text, secondly, by recent critical theories (anticipating material in Chapter 6), thirdly, by historical considerations (anticipating material in Chapter 5), and fourthly, by matters concerning textual variations (anticipating material from Chapter 8). The text is Tennyson's well-known 'The Lady of Shalott', given here in full in its later version:

Part I

On either side the river lie
Long fields of barley and of rye,
That clothe the wold and meet the sky;
And thro' the field the road runs by
      To many-tower'd Camelot;
And up and down the people go,
Gazing where the lilies blow
Round an island there below,
      The island of Shalott.

Willows whiten, aspens quiver,
Little breezes dusk and shiver
Thro' the wave that runs for ever
By the island in the river
      Flowing down to Camelot.
Four gray walls, and four gray towers,
Overlook a space of flowers,
And the silent isle imbowers
      The Lady of Shalott.

By the margin, willow veil'd,
Slide the heavy barges trail'd
By slow horses; and unhail'd
The shallop flitteth silken-sail'd
    Skimming down to Camelot:
But who hath seen her wave her hand?
Or at the casement seen her stand?
Or is she known in all the land,
    The Lady of Shalott?

Only reapers, reaping early
In among the bearded barley,
Hear a song that echoes cheerly
From the river winding clearly,
    Down to tower'd Camelot:
And by the moon the reaper weary,
Piling sheaves in uplands airy,
Listening, whispers " 'Tis the fairy
    Lady of Shalott."

Part II

There she weaves by night and day
A magic web with colours gay.
She has heard a whisper say,
A curse is on her if she stay
    To look down to Camelot.
She knows not what the curse may be,
And so she weaveth steadily,
And little other care hath she,
    The Lady of Shalott.

And moving thro' a mirror clear
That hangs before her all the year,
Shadows of the world appear.
There she sees the highway near
    Winding down to Camelot:
There the river eddy whirls,
And there the surly village-churls,
And the red cloaks of market girls,
    Pass onward from Shalott.

Sometimes a troop of damsels glad,
An abbot on an ambling pad,

Sometimes a curly shepherd-lad,
Or long-hair'd page in crimson clad,
   Goes by to tower'd Camelot;
And sometimes thro' the mirror blue
The knights come riding two and two:
She hath no loyal knight and true,
   The Lady of Shalott.

But in her web she still delights
To weave the mirror's magic sights,
For often thro' the silent nights
A funeral, with plumes and lights
   And music, went to Camelot:
Or when the moon was overhead,
Came two young lovers lately wed:
"I am half sick of shadows," said
   The Lady of Shalott.

Part III

A bow-shot from her bower-eaves,
He rode between the barley-sheaves,
The sun came dazzling thro' the leaves,
And flamed upon the brazen greaves
   Of bold Sir Lancelot.
A red-cross knight for ever kneel'd
To a lady in his shield,
That sparkled on the yellow field,
   Beside remote Shalott.

The gemmy bridle glitter'd free,
Like to some branch of stars we see
Hung in the golden Galaxy.
The bridle bells rang merrily
   As he rode down to Camelot:
And from his blazon'd baldric slung
A mighty silver bugle hung,
And as he rode his armour rung,
   Beside remote Shalott.

All in the blue unclouded weather
Thick-jewell'd shone the saddle-leather,
The helmet and the helmet-feather
Burn'd like one burning flame together,
   As he rode down to Camelot.

As often thro' the purple night,
Below the starry clusters bright,
Some bearded meteor, trailing light,
    Moves over still Shalott.

His broad clear brow in sunlight glow'd;
On burnish'd hooves his war-horse trode;
From underneath his helmet flow'd
His coal-black curls as on he rode,
    As he rode down to Camelot.
From the bank and from the river
He flash'd into the crystal mirror,
"Tirra lirra," by the river
    Sang Sir Lancelot.

She left the web, she left the loom,
She made three paces thro' the room,
She saw the water-lily bloom,
She saw the helmet and the plume,
    She look'd down to Camelot.
Out flew the web and floated wide;
The mirror crack'd from side to side;
"The curse is come upon me," cried
    The Lady of Shalott.

Part IV

In the stormy east-wind straining,
The pale yellow woods were waning,
The broad stream in his banks complaining,
Heavily the low sky raining
    Over tower'd Camelot;
Down she came and found a boat
Beneath a willow left afloat,
And round about the prow she wrote
    The Lady of Shalott.

And down the river's dim expanse
Like some bold seer in a trance,
Seeing all his own mischance—
With a glassy countenance
    Did she look to Camelot.
And at the closing of the day
She loosed the chain, and down she lay;

The broad stream bore her far away,
   The Lady of Shalott.

Lying, robed in snowy white
That loosely flew to left and right—
The leaves upon her falling light—
Thro' the noises of the night
   She floated down to Camelot:
And as the boat-head wound along
The willowy hills and fields among,
They heard her singing her last song,
   The Lady of Shalott.

Heard a carol, mournful, holy,
Chanted loudly, chanted lowly,
Till her blood was frozen slowly,
And her eyes were darken'd wholly,
   Turn'd to tower'd Camelot.
For ere she reach'd upon the tide
The first house by the water-side,
Singing in her song she died,
   The Lady of Shalott.

Under tower and balcony,
By garden-wall and gallery,
A gleaming shape she floated by,
Dead-pale between the houses high,
   Silent into Camelot.
Out upon the wharfs they came,
Knight and burgher, lord and dame,
And round the prow they read her name,
   The Lady of Shalott.

Who is this? and what is here?
And in the lighted palace near
Died the sound of royal cheer;
And they cross'd themselves for fear,
   All the knights at Camelot:
But Lancelot mused a little space;
He said, "She has a lovely face;
God in his mercy lend her grace,
   The Lady of Shalott."

Let's make some preliminary comments. Firstly, the poem is a 'multi-text', which is to say that it exists in distinctly different versions – an 1832 text and an 1842 revised version. In the earlier version one of the most striking moments in the poem is missing, for 'Lancelot does not appear in the final stanza; instead the "well-fed wits" of Camelot gather around the boat to read the puzzling parchment on the lady's breast: "The web was woven curiously,/ The charm is broken utterly,/ Draw near and fear not – This is I,/ The Lady of Shalott."'[7] Secondly, the poem is not a free-standing 'words-on-the-page' lyric poem, for it is deeply embedded in a substantial British cultural tradition of myths and legends about King Arthur and his knights, a tradition which goes back to the Middle Ages, for instance to the unknown poet who wrote *Sir Gawain and the Green Knight* in the fourteenth century, and to Sir Thomas Malory's epic poem *Morte Darthur* in the fifteenth. This tradition, then, started long before Tennyson and continued long after, with modern works like T. H. White's twentieth-century tetralogy (sequence of four novels) *The Once and Future King,* and films such as Hollywood's *The Knights of the Round Table* of 1953, the musical *Camelot* of 1967, and even *Monty Python and the Holy Grail* of 1975.

Thirdly, the poem is also embedded in Tennyson's own major contribution to this Arthurian tradition, namely his epic *The Idylls of the King* of 1859, which incorporates ten major episodes, one of which is 'Lancelot and Elaine', and it is clear that Elaine 'the lily maid of Astolat' who lives 'High in her chamber up a tower to the east', is a close analogue (or parallel) of the Lady of Shalott, for she dies of unrequited love for Lancelot and her body is placed on a barge, with the letter she has written explaining her plight, and floated down to Camelot. The image of the Astolat/Shalott lady and her barge became a major subject for Victorian painters, with notable examples by Waterhouse, Egley, Meteyard, Hughes, Grimshaw, Rossetti, and Holman Hunt).[8] There are at least three layers of 'extra-textuality' to take into account, then, these being the 'multitextuality' of the text itself, which exists in two substantially different versions, the cultural *con*textuality of the extensive 'cultural production' on Arthurian topics (poetry, fiction, paintings, and film), and the specific intertextuality of another text by Tennyson on the same material.

7   Kathy Alexis Psomiades, '"The Lady of Shalott" and the Critical Fortunes of Victorian Poetry', in *The Cambridge Companion to Victorian Poetry*, ed. Joseph Bristow (Cambridge University Press, 2000), p. 44, n. 6.

8   See *Ladies of Shalott: A Victorian Masterpiece and its Contexts*, ed. George P. Landow (Brown University Press, 1979).

4.1 *The Lady of Shalott* (1888), John William Waterhouse

Current trends in interpretation

How, then, can we come to an understanding of what the poem means? In the poem a Lady is imprisoned in a tower, which is located on an inland 'island' within the river that runs to the town of Camelot. A mysterious 'curse' prevents her looking directly out of the window of the tower, and she labours at a tapestry depicting the world beyond the tower, which she sees indirectly via a mirror on the wall. She seems to feel a longing for the bustle of life outside, and is finally tempted to look out directly when Sir Lancelot passes, an alluring object in shining armour. As soon as she looks out the curse comes into operation and she knows she is doomed to die. She places herself in a barge on the river, having painted the words 'The Lady of Shalott' on the prow, and her body drifts down to Camelot, where it is seen by 'All the knights of Camelot', and (in the 1842 version) by Sir Lancelot, who (in the final lines of the poem) 'mused a little space;/ He said, "She has a lovely face;/ God in his mercy lend her grace,/ The Lady of Shalott."' Lancelot's reaction seems perfunctory and, to modern readers, almost comically sexist, but, as Kathy

Psomiades points out, it could have been worse ('it is not, for example, as inadequate as "Can I watch the autopsy?" or "Do you think I could have the boat after we bury her?"').[9] In the parallel story in 'Lancelot and Elaine', Lancelot's indifference to Elaine's fate stems from his continuing obsession with Guinevere, which is tearing him apart and will eventually destroy Camelot and what it stands for. Should we read this back into the much shorter poem, or must we try to read the two separately, even though they are two pieces by the same author on the same theme and material?

A response to this question might be to say that, however we read the poem, our reading will be *partial*, in both senses; firstly, it will not be able to take account of every element in the poem, and secondly it will be the product of a personal predisposition or prejudice of which we ourselves must remain unaware. Thus, the most traditional readings of the poem saw it as an allegory of the necessary isolation of the artist: the Lady engages in the practice of representing life in art (through the medium of the tapestry she is weaving), but artists can only do this if they are in some measure detached from life; the detachment is represented in the poem by the tower, the island, and the prohibition on looking at life directly. But the Lady wants to be part of the flux and bustle of life, rather than being elevated beyond it in nun-like contemplation, so she is drawn to look out, thus breaking the spell, so that the tapestry flies apart ('Out flew the web and floated wide;/ The mirror crack'd from side to side').

However, this kind of interpretation (with its attribution of heroic, suprahuman qualities to the artist) is much out of favour in English Studies today, and it would be difficult to find academic critics who would take seriously the idea that artists and writers either can or should attain a kind of panoramic elevation of insight and viewpoint above and beyond life in general. It is easy, too, for them to point out the 'partiality' of the interpretation, especially the way it ignores the fact that the artist-figure in the poem is a woman. Pointing this out lays the ground for interpretations which foreground issues of gender, and these approaches are currently more highly favoured. Interpretation on these lines would see the imprisoned Lady as an emblem of the patriarchal restrictions placed on women in Victorian and later times. A general isolation from the flux of life results in a kind of vicarious or proxy living in which the woman identifies longingly with the life and achievements of husband, brothers, or children (the 'Shadows of the world', perhaps, which appear in the mirror); she is confined to activities deemed 'suitable'

---

9   *The Cambridge Companion to Victorian Poetry*, p. 29.

(here the traditional 'woman's work' of weaving), repressing many aspects of her own nature, including her sexuality, for it is the alluring figure of Lancelot which finally causes her to defy the curse and look out. The Lady, then, becomes a kind of heroic resister of these implacable patriarchal norms, and the poem a protest at the waste of human happiness and potential which they entail.

Four kinds of interpretation

Are these two basic interpretations (the one centred on notions of the artist and the one which is based on aspects of gender) mutually exclusive? The first is 'idealist' in tendency, seeing the role of the artist as requiring a stance beyond and above life, while the latter is 'materialist', in that it is rooted in notions of the earth-bound, socially determined limitations commonly placed upon a particular section of the population (here, capable and intelligent women). Do we have to choose between these two interpretations, or can they be combined in some way? Clearly, the notion of combining the two is attractive, and the argument for doing so here might be that Tennyson may well have intended the poem as an allegory of the artist, but he inadvertently produced a text in which his imprisoned muse-figure seems (to us) more obviously representative of patriarchal restrictions. This 'semi-combined' reading takes the view that the poet intended to say one thing but inadvertently expressed something else, and I call this 'semi-combined' because it makes use of both readings, but without actually reconciling them. A more truly combined reading might see the poem as exploring a notion of the artist as necessarily 'feminized' in outlook, retreating to the margins of life, in order to attain a viewpoint on it, and then observing rather than doing, characteristics of Victorian women rather than Victorian men. While he was in no sense a conventional Victorian patriarch, a Tennyson primarily intent on undermining patriarchal norms still seems to me a little implausible. True, the man who designs poems as a way of life engages in a less obviously 'manly' undertaking than one who designs battleships, like his younger relative Tennyson d'Eyncourt (even though the poems turned out to be more durable than the ships), so there is a contextual plausibility in this kind of combined idealist/materialist kind of interpretation.

All three of these levels of interpretation focus on elements which the poem itself clearly foregrounds. One further level concerns matters which the poem either does not mention at all or else features only peripherally: this seems characteristic of the 1980s, when readings were very much shaped by aspects of the literary theory then in vogue. Thus, Alan Sinfield's short book *Alfred Tennyson* (in a series called 'Re-Reading Literature', aimed at students, and featuring applications of literary theory to canonical authors) argued that 'poetry which appears to be remote from political issues is in fact involved with the political life of its society: it disseminates ideas, images, and narratives of the way the world is, and that is always a political activity'.[10] This might at first seem just another kind of 'materialist' reading, but Sinfield sees it as 'a poem about the construction of the bourgeois self, and the anxieties attendant on this construction' (*Companion*, p. 32). Seeing the poem as being about the *construction* of the social self, and its attendant anxieties, is not the same as seeing it as simply being about the social self. Sinfield isn't writing about society as an external phenomenon, but about social identity as an ongoing inner process. To repeat, the ideas he uses – 'constructing' identities, rather than just having them (such as being a Mancunian or a six-foot basketball ace), and 'entering into language', rather than just learning language and the social practices that go with it – are very distinctly ideas which derive from the literary theory of the 1980s. Thus, when the web fails to give her 'a coherent sense of herself in the world' the Lady abandons it, and sets off for Camelot in a doomed bid 'to enter language and social identity' (p. 32).

This approach takes its cue from the fact that it is impossible to use language which is 'first-hand': the words and phrases we use can never be like new-minted coins never circulated before: on the contrary, our words always have a history and a provenance. Roland Barthes in his much-quoted essay 'The Death of the Author' emphasizes this aspect of language when he writes: 'The text is a tissue of quotations drawn from the innumerable centres of culture. . . . The writer can only imitate a gesture that is always anterior [pre-existing, belated, derivative], never original.' In the case of 'The Lady of Shalott', the reflexive, theorized reading seems a natural one because the word 'text' comes from the Latin *textere*, which means to weave. The Lady is very prolific of 'texts' in the widest sense, weaving her tapestry, writing her name on the prow of the barge, singing her ceaseless songs until the breath leaves her body, and finally 'composing' her own corpse as part of a silent tableau which the onlookers seek to read and decode. This is a distinctly, then, a fourth kind of reading: it is highly theorized, reading back into the poem the theoretical concerns of the critic's own era in a manner which seems defiantly anachronistic. Sinfield's reading is applied literary theory: it bypasses a lengthy

---

10 Sinfield, *Alfred Tennyson* (Blackwell, 1986), p. 11, quoted by Psomiades, *Cambridge Companion*, p. 31.

corpus of 'peritextuality' (the many 'readings' of the poem produced over the years by the 'lit crit' industry) and draws the poem into the (then) brave new world of theorized reading, or metatextuality.

The difficulty for this kind of reading is that it seems to abandon the *overt* content of the poem altogether, and doesn't explain anything about the purpose and effect of the Arthurian and medieval setting. While it would be immediately plausible to suggest that a Victorian novel like *Middlemarch* is about 'the construction of the bourgeois self', and its attendant anxieties, nothing that is specific about this poem seems to be accounted for by this very generalized reading. The notion of 'entering language and social identity' is one which would not have been recognized by Tennyson or his readers, and, while this is not in itself enough to invalidate this kind of interpretation (after all, it is commonplace to invoke the Freudian notion of the Oedipal desires and responses in a reading of *Hamlet*), it does mean that detailed, text-specific supporting evidence is required. It is significant, too, that Sinfield ignores the gender issue – the poem for him is about 'the bourgeois self', which subsumes a specific gender politics into politics in general.

'Synoptic' interpretation

So far, then, we have looked at four kinds of interpretation – the idealist, the materialist, the combined, and the theorized. A fifth level of interpretation can be posited: a 'synoptic' approach which draws upon all four of these, aiming for what we earlier called 'total textuality'. This – exemplified by Isobel Armstrong in her book *Victorian Poetry: Poetry, Poetics and Politics* (1993) – retains the political emphasis which is an element of all but the first of these, but is much more directly keyed in to the details of the poem, trying not to lose sight of the overt content in the way that the fourth (theorized) type inevitably does. Armstrong sees the poem as one 'which has no source' and is therefore 'a modern myth' which is a 'conflation of a number of mythic structures', such as the chivalric and fairy-tale motif of the imprisoned lady in the tower, myths of the weaving lady, like Arachne and Penelope, and myths of reflection, like those of Narcissus and Echo. The Lady, she says 'dies a sacrificial death, failing to come into sexuality and language' (all these quotations from p. 83). The notion that the lady longs for inclusion in the turmoil of real life, and is tired of her isolation, is fully consonant both with the internal evidence of the poem ('I am half sick of shadows', she says at the end of Part II, as she sees in her mirror 'two young lovers lately wed'), and with Tennyson's own remarks on it, as quoted in his son's *Memoir*: 'The new-born love for something, for someone in the whole wide world from which she has been for so long secluded, takes her out of the region of shadows into that of realities.'[11]

However, it isn't quite true to say that the poem has no source: it was the first of a long succession of Arthurian works by Tennyson 'based, not on Malory's retelling of the Arthurian tales in his *Morte Darthur* (1470), but on a medieval Italian novelette entitled *"Donna di Scalotta"'*, which was reprinted in 1804 as Novella LXXXI in a collection entitled *Cento Novelle Antiche (One Hundred Ancient Novellae)*. A notebook entry of Tennyson's records this source, and he may have been introduced to this kind of Italian material by his friend Arthur Hallam.[12] Important aspects of the poem which are not found in the source are 'the mirror and the web it inspires, the curse, the geographical relationship of the island, the river and Camelot' (Staines, p. 11), and the changes between the 1832 and 1842 versions show Tennyson moving the poem further from the Italian source (Staines, p. 11). When he wrote the poem he did not know the Maid of Astolat story in Malory, which he later used in the *Idylls*, as we saw, and details which are in Malory (the barge, the letter held by the dead lady in the 1832 version, etc.) are also in the Italian source (Staines, p. 12).

Armstrong sees the Lady, who is condemned by the curse to labour ceaselessly at her weaving, as a representative of 'alienation and work' (*Victorian Poetry*, p. 85): Tennyson, she says, 'is manoeuvring together the constraints working on women and the compulsions working on other forms of labour' (p. 84), so this too has elements of the 'combined' reading, alleging that the poem combines a critique of patriarchal restraints with a kind of coded protest at the political, social, and industrial conditions which had produced widespread unrest round the time of the first Reform Bill of 1832. This interpretation involves giving considerable centrality to the agricultural workers mentioned in the poem, like the 'reapers, reaping early' in stanza 4: 'The reapers and the Cambridge rick-burners reacting to the corn laws, the starving handloom weavers who were being displaced by new industrial processes, these hover just outside the poem and become strangely aligned with the imprisoned lady' (pp. 84–5). The liminal presence in the poem of starving handloom weavers and Cambridge rick-burners (who set fire to hayricks which had been harvested with the new machinery that had made their own labour redundant – scenes Tennyson had witnessed, Sinfield, p. 30) seems to have become a widely accepted view, but the precise nature of the 'hovering' is difficult to define. The reapers in the poem are 'reaping early' and are still

---

11 Quoted in David Staines, *Tennyson's Camelot: The Idylls of the King and its Medieval Sources* (Wilfred Laurier University Press), p. 10.
12 All this information about sources is in Staines, *Tennyson's Camelot*, p. 9.

there, and 'weary', at the end of the day 'by the moon', still hearing the eerie song of the lady in the tower. She does seem to be linked with them in the next stanza as 'There she weaves by night and day/ A magic web with colours gay', but this doesn't really sound like alienated labour. Far from it, in fact, for it seems that her weaving is the one thing she finds pleasure in, for 'in her web she still delights/ To weave the mirror's magic sights', so that it is difficult to see grounds for Armstrong's statement that 'For all its magical aesthetic quality, the weaving of the web is ceaseless work without escape and without *pleasure*' (p. 84). The other peripheral female figures in the poem do not seem especially oppressed (in Part II, market girls in red cloaks, a troop of damsels glad, and the woman who is one of the 'two young lovers'), and this would seem to present another difficulty which cannot easily be disposed of. All the same, the reading is delicately poised, drawing on many different kinds of interpretive strategy: it has elements, for instance, of a 'theorized', deconstructive approach (in the way it draws peripheral details like the passers-by into a centrally signifying role in the text), it makes use of historicist data (like the plight of the hand-loom weavers), and it brings in broad layers of cultural intertextuality (for instance, weaving as a traditional literary motif).

It is not, however, an easy model to imitate, and it tends to be reproduced in cruder and more diluted form, with some elements of the synopsis ignored. In particular, the desire to read the poem as an allegory of organized labour can lead to more drastic misreadings of the text, and a recent book about university education complains about students' accounts of this poem in examinations, which seem to offer reductive versions of Armstrong's 'alienated labour' reading, attempting on spurious grounds to bring *into* the poem what Armstrong more cautiously sees as 'hovering' on the outside. Thus one student writes: 'Both the lady and the reapers are set outside the commercial capital city of Camelot, and ... indeed both may be the victims of industrial society.' On this kind of reading, Lancelot is roughly shoehorned into the role of capitalist exploiter, for 'Technology is shown as an intrusive force in the lady's life, in the form of Lancelot; she brings the curse upon herself by looking down at his shining armour and "coal-black hair"; Lancelot appears as a machine.' Finally, her abandonment of her web and loom and her sailing down to Camelot in a barge are seen as 'perhaps suggesting the weavers moving to factories in towns – urbanisation.'[13]

It may well be the case that elements authors highlight as central to a literary work may not be the real centre, and that scrutinizing the parts of the

13 These quotations from student scripts are from *The New Idea of a University*, by Duke Maskell and Ian Robinson (Haven Books, 2001), p. 152.

text which are left in shadow by the authorial spotlight may well be a good idea. But clearly, again, it has to be possible to demonstrate the centrality of these shadowed elements without implausibly ignoring, or blatantly mis-reading, aspects of the text. If the word 'coal' in the phrase 'coal-black curls' at first makes us think of coalmines, from which it is a short step to converting Lancelot into a figure like Gerald Crich (the arrogant mine-owner in D. H. Lawrence's novel *Women in Love*), then perhaps we ought to pause for second thoughts before we rush on to make something of this. The context of the phrase 'coal-black curls' is Part III, which is entirely devoted to presenting Lancelot as an alluring, sexually attractive figure, who seems brimming with all the life and vitality from which the lady feels herself excluded; he is the image which finally breaks her resolve and makes her start up from the loom. In this context his curls are called 'coal-black' because, like every other aspect of him, they shine; the phrase, therefore, designates the youthful sheen of his luxuriant black locks, a sheen which is precisely suggested by the phrase 'coal-black', for coal too has a sheen or a gloss which exactly suggests the effect Tennyson is trying to convey. Likewise, the armour obviously isn't of the kind produced by the nineteenth-century industrial workers of Vickers Armstrong (which built military tanks and turned out the battleships designed by Tennyson's cousin), but is the personal and hand-crafted kind fashioned by medieval craftsman, and therefore quite unsuited to be an emblem of nineteenth-century industrial production. As readers, then, we must find a reasonable balance between the claims of textuality on the one hand and con-textuality on the other, and we need to accept the textual restraints within which our interpretive strategies must operate. The synoptic approach, then, is our fifth kind of reading: like the third type, it is combinatory, but, whereas the 'combined' reading seeks a reconciliation between *two* opposed lines of interpretation, the synoptic combines a whole range of varied interpretive approaches.

* * *

The question we have *not* solved, however, in discussing Tennyson's poem, is the status of all that content which (in Armstrong's formulation) 'hovers' on the threshold of the poem. Bluntly, is all this 'hovering' material part of the poem or not? As I have indicated already, this question about the status of context is one of the momentous issues facing the discipline of English Studies today. It is also the subject of the next chapter.

5 English and History

At the end of the last chapter it was suggested that balancing the claims of textuality and contextuality is one of the main problems encountered in literary study today. An approach to literature which focuses primarily on textuality is often described (always disapprovingly) as 'formalism': the opposite of formalism is historicism, which we can define as the approach to literature which focuses primarily on contextuality. Currently (that is, in the early years of the twenty-first century) historicism seems to be the 'default' approach to literature, so this term is usually employed without the disapproving connotations of the word 'formalism'. You may well conclude that the historicist approach is indeed the right one, and my aim in this chapter is simply to encourage you to critique the term 'historicism', so that it becomes, at least, open to question, and is obliged to set out and defend its position in a rational manner. Our way into this topic will be to pose the question: 'How much context is there in text?' Answering it will require us to examine the basis of our critical beliefs and practices, even if we take it for granted (as we must, of course) that those beliefs are right and good.

HOW MUCH CONTEXT IS THERE IN TEXT?

To put the question this way round (rather than asking how much text there is in context) prioritizes text over context, making the assumption that our primary interest is in the text rather than the context. However, this cannot be taken for granted: for many of our most influential critics and theorists today, to be primarily interested in the text is to be guilty of 'formalism', this being a general term of disapproval for all forms of literary study which focus mainly on the formal, structural, linguistic, and generic properties of the text, rather than on its social, political, and historical contexts.

The emerging problem, however, is that outlawing formalism, and allowing contextualism a completely free rein, effectively relegates literary study to the level of a sub-branch of history, one which merely happens to have a strongly 'textual' inflection. Literary study reduced in this way can have little claim to disciplinary independence, for it will simply have become literary-flavoured history. It's rather like taking milk with coffee – if we keep adding more and more milk we eventually reach the stage where we are drinking hot milk with a slight coffee flavour. That isn't illegal, of course, and we are all at liberty to drink whatever we like, but it isn't reasonable to assume that henceforth milk is the new coffee. Getting the balance right between text and context is of fundamental importance in this regard, especially at a time when there are signs that so-called 'traditional' disciplines (like English) are coming under some pressure from supposedly more 'vocational' alternatives. Students sign up for English, by and large, because they want to study literature: the study of context is a necessary adjunct. But it is only that, and if we want it to be our main object of study (whether as students, teachers, or writers) then we ought to be in history departments.

Perhaps we can arrive at some notion of a sustainable balance between text and context by considering a well-known example of a critic 'importing' a new context into the study of a major literary work. The literary work is Jane Austen's *Mansfield Park,* and the critic is Edward Said, whose book *Culture and Imperialism* (Vintage, 1995) discusses this novel in the part-chapter 'Jane Austen and Empire' (pp. 95–116 in the original book, and much reprinted in readers on critical theory). The estate of Mansfield Park in the novel is owned by Sir Thomas Bertram, whose income is partly derived from 'his West Indian property'. At a crucial stage in the book he has to absent himself for some months to attend to problematical business affairs in Antigua, and Said's view is that 'Sir Thomas's property in the Caribbean would have had to be a sugar plantation maintained by slave labour (not abolished till the 1830s)' (p. 107). So the handsome country house in the English shires, with its surrounding park, is maintained by a far less gracious estate overseas.[1] The political, on this kind of reading, is part of private life, and the fact that 'by the early nineteenth century every Britisher used sugar' (Said, p. 108), is the invisible chain that binds the two estates together.[2] The morality of this linkage is not questioned by the novel, and the English house and its ways stand for an approach to life

---

1   The idea was first put forward in Avrom Fleishman's *A Reading of Mansfield Park: An Essay in Critical Synthesis* (Johns Hopkins University Press, 1970), but it was Said who expanded and popularized it.

2   We should add, perhaps, that not quite every Britisher used it: those who supported abolition boycotted this commodity. William and Dorothy Wordsworth sweetened their tea and porridge with honey rather than sugar as a protest against the slave trade, on which the supply of sugar to Britain depended, just as opponents of apartheid in our own time refused for many years to buy South African fruit or wine. (For the Wordsworth detail, see Penelope Hughes-Hallett, *The Immortal Dinner* (Viking, 2000), p. 227.)

which is genteel, humane, ordered and civilized, and in which due regard is given to the requirements of all the inmates. This is in contrast to the dire and cramped Portsmouth home of the heroine Fanny Price, where peevishness and selfishness rule (symbolized in the way her taciturn father selfishly positions the only candle in the room between himself and his newspaper and carries on reading while ignoring the newly arrived Fanny's presence altogether). *Mansfield Park*, then, is read by Said 'as part of the structure of an expanding imperialist venture', and, having done so, he says, 'one cannot simply restore it to the canon of "great literary masterpieces"' (p. 114).

My own experience of reading the Said piece is certainly something like that: once it has been read, the novel is changed, and can never again be viewed 'innocently'.[3] All the issues of personal conduct and social morality dramatized in the novel are recontextualized within the intimate relationship that Said shows to exist between the two contrasting estates, the elegant English country estate and the Caribbean sugar plantation. Austen does not dwell on Antigua,[4] but she does mention it a number of times, and in such a way as to justify our further enquiry into it. Said's treatment of the issue is actually quite broad-brush: only one passage in the novel is read 'closely' (the description of Sir Thomas, on his sudden return to Mansfield, putting matters to rights there like an absolute monarch, a Robinson Crusoe in total charge of his island, as Said puts it). Said mentions in passing the well-known moment in Chapter 21 when Fanny raises with Sir Thomas the topic of slavery. Sir Thomas is not generally averse to talking about the West Indies. On the contrary, Fanny tells Edmund, 'I love to hear my uncle talk of the West Indies. I could listen to him for an hour together.' Edmund tells her how well-disposed Sir Thomas is towards her, and adds, 'I only wish you would talk to him more. You are one of those who are too silent in the evening circle.' Fanny denies this with, for her, considerable warmth: 'But I do talk to him more than I used. I am sure I do. Did not you hear me ask him about the slave-trade last night?' Edmund acknowledges this: 'I did – and was in hopes the question would be followed up by others. It would have pleased your uncle to be

3 As John Wiltshire points out in *Recreating Jane Austen* (Cambridge University Press, 2001), p. 162, footnote 33, the influence of the Said reading was quite evident in the 1999 Miramax/BBC film of *Mansfield Park*. If it has reached the 'heritage' film industry, perhaps we can expect it soon to feature even on the tea towels and china mugs sold to tourists at the Jane Austen properties.
4 The final chapter has the famous opening: 'Let other pens dwell on guilt and misery. I quit such odious subjects as soon as I can, impatient to restore everybody, not greatly in fault themselves, to tolerable comfort, and to have done with all the rest.' In the present context, this may seem somewhat incriminating.

inquired of farther.' Fanny's response is to turn the accusation of silence onto her cousins:

> And I longed to do it – but there was such a dead silence! And while my cousins were sitting by without speaking a word, or seeming at all interested in the subject, I did not like – I thought it would appear as if I wanted to set myself off at their expense, by shewing a curiosity and pleasure in his information which he must wish his own daughters to feel.

The emphasis here is a little surprising: the 'dead silence' does not come from Sir Thomas's sternly indicating that the slave trade is not a suitable topic of conversation for the drawing room at Mansfield Park. On the contrary, Edmund assumes he would have been pleased to be asked more questions about this matter, and Fanny is convinced it would have gratified him if his own daughters had shown more interest than they evidently do in serious topics of this kind.

So the whole topic of silence and its interpretation is crucial here, as it so often is in matters concerning literary context. In his popular collection of literary puzzles, John Sutherland takes *Mansfield Park* and the slave trade as his first 'case'.[5] He is – at best – politely respectful but unenthusiastic about Said's thesis: he is unconvinced that Sir Thomas's Antigua 'estate' (in Said's words) 'would have had to be a sugar plantation maintained by slave labour', and points out that the novel has very little indeed to say on the subject of Antigua ('Dead silence pretty well describes *Mansfield Park's* dealings with Antigua generally', p. 4). Said, of course, sees the 'dead silence' on the matter (from nearly all previous critics, as well as from the author) as highly significant, and as indicating an aspect of colonial exploitation which is deeply ingrained in the social fabric. The English gentry of the time (the first decade of the nineteenth century) were finding that the English country estate could not yield the returns which their expectations and way of life required, especially if they had several children, so the ownership of estates in the West Indies had become a way of supplementing their incomes. This briefly enabled them to compete with the wealth of the emergent class of factory-owning industrialists whose wealth and social importance would soon leave them behind. *Mansfield Park* is poised at this moment of transition, when many social attitudes and practices are those of the residual eighteenth century, rather than the emerging nineteenth.

5   *Is Heathcliff a Murderer? Puzzles in 19th Century Fiction* (World's Classics, 1996).

But the matter is complicated by two factors. Firstly, there are a number of tricky issues concerning dating. Said says that slavery was 'not abolished until the 1830s' (p. 107). In fact, Wilberforce's bill for the abolition of slavery was passed in 1807 (Sutherland, p. 8), but slavery continued in the West Indies until 1838. Though the bill was ineffective for so long, it officially came into force in two stages, between May 1807 (when no ship could be cleared for sailing from a British port with slaves on board) and March 1808, from which date no slaves could be landed at a British port. The long period of uncertainty between 1807 and the 1830s is partly explained by the fact that the Act abolished the slave *trade*, not slavery.[6] Hence, slavery was an issue of moral and legal ambiguity for a period of 30 years in the early part of the century.

Furthermore, there is no general agreement about precisely when the novel was written and the exact years in which it is set; the earliest suggested date is 1805 and the latest 1813. For most of this period, the Abolition bill had passed into law, but Sir Thomas's ownership of slaves (if that is indeed what he did in Antigua) was not illegal, although the morality or otherwise of slave labour was a very hotly debated issue. It might be expected that after 1807 Sir Thomas would be slightly warier than before of discussing the slave trade, thus implying that the book was written *before* abolition, but other indicators in the text seem to suggest a later date. One frequently mentioned date marker is Fanny's collection of books, which includes Crabbe's *Tales*, published in September 1812 (Southam), though Sutherland suggests that possibly the initial 't' of 'Tales' is lower-case, which could mean that the texts referred to are actually the verse narratives in Crabbe's *Poems* of 1807 (Sutherland, p. 6). Another text mentioned is the *Quarterly Review* – in Chapter 10, time is passed with the help of 'sofas, chit-chat, and Quarterly Reviews': this journal was founded in 1809 (Southam, p. 13), and, he says, it carried 'the planter cause', so we might expect to find a copy lying round on the sofa in Sir Thomas's house. All the same, the pluralization is odd, and it may be that the term is being used in a loose generic sense simply to refer to journals of the kind which are published every quarter.

A second complicating factor is the precise social status of Sir Thomas, the question being, crudely: is he a representative of genteel old money or vulgar

---

6 These dates and details are taken from another essential piece on the issue, Brian Southam's 'The Silence of the Bertrams: Slavery and the Chronology of *Mansfield Park*', *TLS* (17 Feb. 1975), pp. 13–14. See also: Frank Gibbon, 'The Antiguan Connection: Some New Light on *Mansfield Park*', *Cambridge Quarterly* 11 (1982), pp. 298–305; and Moira Ferguson, '*Mansfield Park*, Colonialism, and Gender', *Oxford Literary Review* 13 (1991), pp. 118–39.

new money? Said sees him not as belonging to an ancient landed family whose income is merely supplemented by the Caribbean plantation, but as representative of 'the colonial planter class' (p. 112), whose wealth was founded on this source and who formed a distinct social group with their own well-known public activities, 'large houses, famous parties and social rituals, well-known commercial enterprises, celebrated marriages' (Said, p. 112). Southam places him socially in similar terms, remarking that 'there is something distinctly "modern-built", *nouveau*, and West-Indian about Sir Thomas and his social standing, a point worth making since some commentators wholly misplace Sir Thomas, writing about him as a member of the old and established landed gentry who bears an ancient title' (p. 14). As a 'second generation absentee [planter]' (p. 14), he is now keen to consolidate his position by giving his sons a genteel education and securing advantageous marriages for the women of the family. Hence, perhaps, his horror at the planned amateur theatricals, which he thinks likely to be talked about in the district and so to lower the tone and reputation of the household, making it seem that the family are not the real social thing after all. Sutherland, however, is inclined to question 'Said's contention that Sir Thomas's wealth comes primarily from his colonial possessions and that his social eminence in Britain is entirely dependent on revenues from Antigua' (p. 6). At this period, he says, large landowners like Sir Thomas made substantial fortunes from agriculture at home, and if everything depended on the Antigua estate we would expect Lady Bertram to show a little more concern about the situation, but, as he says, she brushes off Mrs Norris's enquiry with 'Oh! *that* will soon be settled.' This certainly undermines Said's notion of Sir Thomas being 'entirely dependent' on the Caribbean property, and implies that Sir Thomas is an English landowner of the traditional kind.

Assuming that we see the Antigua issue as an important factor in how we read the novel, perhaps the most interesting question is which side Jane Austen and Fanny Price are on – are they abolitionists or not? Sutherland sees Fanny Price as in the forefront of opposition to slavery, since in his view 'the novel contains clear indications that Fanny Price belongs to the Clapham Sect of evangelical Christianity, which hated plays and light morality only slightly less than it loathed slavery' (p. 8). Southam agrees, concluding that in spite of living in the lion's den (and looking about to inherit it) Fanny 'is unmistakably a "friend of the abolition"' (p. 14). Austen's own family had some implication in the trade ('In 1760, Jane's father, the Revd George Austen, was appointed principal trustee of a plantation in Antigua', p. 14), so that 'the Austens too had a dependence, however slight, upon the prosperity of a plantation in Antigua'. For Said, in Sutherland's view, Fanny emerges as 'a pre-Victoria, empress (and oppressor) of a dominion over which the sun never sets' (p. 2). Since the novel, says Said, is:

> part of the structure of an expanding imperialist venture, one cannot simply restore it to the canon of 'great literary masterpieces' – to which it most certainly belongs – and leave it at that. Rather, I think, the novel steadily, if unobtrusively, opens up a broad expanse of domestic imperialist culture without which Britain's subsequent acquisition of territory would not have been possible. (p. 114)

This conclusion seems to see the novel as very much implicated in the process of empire-building and exploitation, for its discreet drawing of a veil over what Antigua represents colludes with the process of simultaneously proclaiming moral human values, and seeing no contradiction between doing so and condoning slavery.

Let's now try to draw together what we have so far on the issue of contextuality, both in general and in relation to this novel. Firstly, we have followed Said in seeing Antigua as highly relevant to the novel, even though none of it is set there – indeed, it is only mentioned in passing nine times, and all the plot requires is that Sir Thomas should be absent for an extended period, not that he should be absent in this particular place. We see the novel's debate about personal morality as expanded to a political and international level by the fact of the estate in England ultimately depending (wholly or partly) on a sugar plantation in the West Indies. Secondly, we note the textual and historical precision which this kind of discussion requires – the silence at the mention of the slave trade in Chapter 21 doesn't necessarily seem to be Sir Thomas's, and we take this into account; we accept that he could conceivably have had non-slave-owning business in Antigua, and so on. Thirdly, we are highly conscious of the complicated issues surrounding the dating both of the abolition of slavery and of the novel itself (where even the matter of a 't' being lower-case or upper-case may have a bearing). Fourthly, we are aware of the ambiguity of Sir Thomas's precise social class, and how this again opens up another area of undecidability within the text. Fifthly, we reconsider both character and author in the light of the moral issues raised by the areas of context which this kind of enquiry opens up. For Said, though, the novel remains a 'great literary masterpiece', in spite of what he sees as its implication in the process of empire-building.

Where, then, does this leave us on the question of context in literary studies? I think that a way of focusing the question is to say that in literary study the problem of context in its most acute form is usually that of deciding how we interpret silence. *Mansfield Park* says almost nothing about Antigua

– it is pretty well silent on the issue, and we have to decide how to interpret that silence. Of course, it is also silent on many other issues, such as the extreme harshness of discipline in the Navy which Fanny's brother William is to join, or the conflict with the American colonies which was taking place at the time. Clearly, we cannot take just any contemporary issue on which the novel is silent and promote it to a central place in our interpretation. Somehow, the acid test is that we need to show that what we have is not just *any* contextual silence, but a *pregnant* silence. And what are the signs of the 'pregnancy', which we could look for in another instance? Well, firstly, the fact that the silence isn't *total* – Antigua *is* mentioned in the novel, and not just once. Secondly, the relevance of Antigua is *pervasive*, affecting not just a single incident, but the foregrounded moral and thematic core of the novel, which concerns issues of conduct, questions of how we can live the (morally) good life at the same time as living the (materially) good life. It is also much concerned with acknowledging and meeting the claims of others. Remember, for instance, the telling moment in Chapter 27 when Fanny decides to wear for the ball all the gifts she has recently been given, both William's cross on Edmund's chain *and* Miss Crawford's necklace, on the grounds that (although she now disapproves of Miss Crawford) 'She acknowledged it to be right. Miss Crawford had a claim.' This taking into account of everyone's claims is what Mansfield Park as a repository of moral values supposedly stands for, and this justifies our own taking into account of the claims of Antigua to due attention in the novel.

Thirdly, taking into account something the novel is largely silent about is justified also by the great weight the novel gives to the significance of silence itself. The word 'silence' or 'silenced' is used 34 times in the book, often designating moments which occur naturally in conversation as tone or implication is assimilated (Chapter 9, 'A general silence succeeded'; Chapter 10, 'This was followed by a short silence', and 'After an interval of silence'; Chapter 14, 'A short silence followed' and 'A short silence succeeded'). At other times, the silence is more momentous – the forbidding silence of Sir Thomas shortly after Fanny's first arrival at Mansfield Park, his promised silence on the matter of Mr Crawford's proposal, and the 'dead silence' which follows Fanny's mention of the slave trade. Fanny's own progress from awed silence to confident self-expression is one of the major lines of development in the book, and the related word 'quiet', and its derivatives, is even more frequently used (48 occurrences), often designating the idealized reflective calm of the place, and the way of life Mansfield Park represents. Fanny sees beyond the quality of mere 'agreeableness' (one of the attributes, inevitably, which Sir Thomas approves of in Henry Crawford), this being another much-used term in the book (73 occurrences). She demands something deeper than this, and thereby, I think, gives us licence to do the same.

These are some of the factors which enable us to admit the claims for a particular context in this case, and they may allow us to formulate criteria for assessing contextual claims in literature in general. We have looked, then, at an instance in which the claims made for the relevance of a specific context are well made and convincing. In the next section we will look at an example in which similar claims for the relevance of a specific context seem (to me) to be on weaker ground.

IS KEATS'S 'TO AUTUMN' ABOUT PETERLOO?

It was suggested in the last section that the problem of context in literary studies is really the problem of how to read silence. Indeed, John Sutherland argues that how we read what isn't there is a crucial dividing point between academic writing and 'lay' writing about literature. He cites Warren Roberts' book *Jane Austen and the French Revolution,* with the comment 'Roberts' line goes thus: as is well known, Jane Austen never mentions the French Revolution. Therefore it must be a central preoccupation, and its silent pressure can be detected at almost every point of her narratives' (*Is Heathcliff a Murderer?,* p. 5). Such assumptions, he says, mark 'a new gulf which [has] opened up between the advanced literary critics of the academic world and the intelligent lay reader' (p. 6). Roberts's book, as Sutherland says, came out 'at the high tide of the theoretic "re-reading" of classic texts' (p. 5), and deconstruction was especially keen on interrogating the 'gaps', 'lacunae', 'fault-lines', and 'slippages' in texts (all ways of denoting absences in texts). Although lay people in general probably still assume that doing English is about the close reading of 'the words on the page', the dominance of poststructuralism in the 1970s and 1980s meant that it had actually become just as interested in the words *off* the page.

But these days academic literary criticism and theory are not generally read by anybody outside the discipline, so the situation hardly ever comes to the attention of a wider public than the one which has grown quite accustomed to it. Occasionally, however, books with a hybrid readership (part 'lay', part academic) bring the issue into the open, and, since literary biography comes into this category, the publication of major biographies sometimes has this effect. When Andrew Motion's biography of Keats appeared,[7] in 1997, reviewers

7 *Keats* (Faber & Faber, 1997).

seemed shocked at the extent to which the poet was seen so much in terms of the politics, and the cultural politics, of his day. Motion's discussion of 'To Autumn', Keats's most celebrated poem, seemed to cause particular affront. Perhaps reviewers had expected that a fellow poet would praise the 'balance' and 'perfection' of the work, and Motion does at first seem to be taking this line, as he informs us that 'Because "To Autumn" holds its balances so expertly, it has often been called Keats's "most . . . untroubled poem". This, combined with its great fame and familiarity, can make it seem unassailable' (p. 461). He then begins to assail it, for balance, expertness, and untroubledness had become suspect qualities in the critical climate of the 1990s: 'The surfaces of the poem might seem painterly and therefore static,' he assures us, 'but in fact they too are disturbed' (p. 462). Some of the disturbing factors are 'the social anxieties which had dogged him all his adult life', now unexpectedly in crisis since his recent visit to London (see below). Then came the lines which reviewers found especially shocking, as Motion linked the poem to a political event which had happened the month before it was written, when soldiers killed 11 people at a political demonstration at St Peter's Fields, Manchester, an event immediately dubbed (in mocking reference to the then recent Battle of Waterloo) the 'Peterloo Massacre':

> It would oversimplify the case to say that because the poem was written in the aftermath of Peterloo, it is precisely concerned with the Massacre. . . . At the same time, it cannot and does not want to escape its context – which it registers in a number of subtle but significant ways. It has been suggested that the word 'conspiring', in the third line, both embraces and deflects the plotting that Keats knew surrounded Henry Hunt's recent activities [The soldiers' attempts to reach 'Orator Hunt' and prevent him speaking had led to the Peterloo Massacre in August: Keats was present a fortnight later, in a crowd of about 30,000, at Hunt's triumphal arrival in London.] The reference to the gleaner is more certainly charged with contemporary references. Gleaning [the practice of gathering in stray ears of corn left by the reapers – a traditional perk for locals] had been made illegal in 1818 . . . and . . . the figure . . . also refers to his sympathy for the denied and the dispossessed. So does his description of the bees. They are a reminder of the miserable facts of labour that Keats had condemned during his walking tour in Scotland . . . (p. 462)

The whole poem, then, is turned into a kind of encrypted political statement, and all its favourite features – the 'conspiring' mists, the bees, the gleaner, and so on – acquire hidden political meanings. Somehow, the exercise was all the more galling for being couched in Motion's characteristically suave prose style,

rather than in the more openly provocative verbal complexities of deconstruction.

Yet, from within the discipline, Motion's political reading of the poem in
1997 seemed almost routine, for it had long been taken for granted that those
'stubble-plains' touched with 'rosy hue' represent not the fields Keats saw while
walking by the Water Meadows in Winchester but the blood-stained ground of
the previous month at St Peter's Fields in Manchester, whether or not it would
'oversimplify the case' to say so. Though the poem is in fact silent about the
Massacre and the 'miserable facts of labour', an 'interpretive tradition' had
grown up from the 1980s onwards which reads a poem's silences as highly
significant – 'it cannot and does not want to escape its context', says Motion
of 'To Autumn'. In effect, though poets have the theoretical right to remain
silent, anything they *don't* say may well be taken down and used against them.

A more uncompromising version of the Motion reading of 'To Autumn'
appeared in Andrew Bennett's *Keats, Narrative and Audience*.[8] Bennett
bypasses the poet's silence on political matters at the start: 'The *apparent*
silence of "To Autumn" on the subject of politics tends to be read as evidence
of a Keatsian desire to abstract poetic language from history' (p. 159, my
italics). He follows the lead of Jerome McGann, who 'has analysed "To
Autumn" as "an attempt to 'escape' the period which provides the poem with
its context"'. He again spells it out: 'To historicize Keats's poem . . . would be
. . . to listen to the fractious intertextual cacophony of history, politics,
economics, noises which "To Autumn" *seems* to silence' (p. 161, my italics).
What follows in the essay is an elaborate reading of a poem which (in my view)
isn't there, a poem about the repeatedly mentioned topics of the essay –
'history', 'politics', 'economics', 'agrarian politics', the 'topographical violation
of boundaries', 'agricultural labour relations', 'financial accumulation',
'subtextual economics', the 'legal limitations of enclosure', the 'discourse of
gleaning'. In place of Keats's poem, the critic stages a melodrama about
'fracturing', 'suppression', 'illicit incursions', 'transgression', 'repression',
'invasion', 'violation', and 'intrusion'. And whatever *isn't* in the poem counts as
further evidence against it: it is a poem which 'suppresses the cacophonous
noises of history' (p. 160): the goddess Ceres isn't mentioned in it either, yet
'Ceres is the pervasive unstated presence in "To Autumn"' (p. 164) and 'the
unstated figure of the goddess Ceres activates the discourses of labour,
property, lawful exchange, and legal boundaries, it is possible to hear in "To
Autumn"' (p. 165): there is also 'a displaced representation of financial
accumulation' which 'activates the subtextual economics' of the poem (p. 166),

8 *Keats, Narrative and Audience: The Posthumous Life of Writing* (Cambridge
   University Press, 1994), ch. 9.

this being part of the 'silent barring of money from "To Autumn"' (p. 167); furthermore 'the stanza's silence over the political question of gleaning' (p. 169) is yet another offence which must be taken into account.

The critic says that 'we must refuse to be figured within, or by, the bounds of the text', and he certainly practises what he preaches. He is eminent, and work like his is widely emulated and admired, but it demonstrates (in my view) the dangers of professing our determination to read literature 'in context', and then admitting no *textual* restraints in deciding what the *con*text is. If we truly desire to be literary critics and literary theorists, rather than speculative historians, then we *must* do precisely what Bennett says we *mustn't*: we must 'agree to be figured within, or by, the bounds of the text'. Otherwise (and in spite of the heavy-industrial scholarship which historicist readings require), there can be little skill, or intellectual challenge (or fun, even) in doing literary criticism and theory. Such writing (which allows the text no voice, except for the one the critic hears in its silences) is not the same thing as doing criticism, just as repeatedly kicking a football into an empty goal-net is not the same as playing football.

One other striking aspect of such readings of Keats's poem is the dislike and distrust they express for the qualities which so many poets strive hard to achieve: Bennett writes, oddly, of the poem's '*notoriously* mellifluous harmonics' (p. 167, my italics), and is suspicious of the line 'barred clouds bloom the soft-dying day', because in the draft the wording is 'a gold cloud gilds the soft-dying day'. This mediocre line was rejected by Keats in favour of words which are vivid, accurate, tough, concise, and innovative, and instantly recognizable as the real poetic thing. But, for Bennett, changing the line is merely part of the psychic melodrama of concealment, and the poet makes the change because of his 'silent barring of money from "To Autumn"'.

I should add that I am not arguing that poems exist in a vacuum separated from all else a poet may be experiencing. On the contrary, I don't doubt that there are some links between aspects of the poem and the post-Peterloo social agitation. For instance, the surprising word 'conspiring' near the start of the poem was quite probably put into Keats's mind (subliminally or otherwise) by the intense discussion of conspirators and conspiracy in connection with 'Orator Hunt' and others, in the weeks after Peterloo.[9] But this is quite different from saying that the poem is really about Peterloo and social injustice, or that

9   The same point is made by Vincent Newey in his essay 'Keats, History, and the Poets', in *Keats and History*, ed. Nicholas Roe (Cambridge University Press, 1995), p. 186. Newey writes that if we accept the 'Peterloo' reading of 'To Autumn' (which he traces back to Jerome McGann's essay 'Keats and the Historical Method' in his (McGann's) *The Beauty of Inflections: Literary Investigations in Historical Method and Theory*, Clarendon Press, 1988) we 'collude in making of Romanticism a bankrupt ideology of evasion'.

Keats culpably tried to evade these matters by writing about an 'innocent' topic like the changing seasons and so was constantly 'ambushed' psychologically as he wrote the poem by the return of what he was trying to repress.

You will have noticed, finally, that we have now considered two examples of historicist readings of literary texts, and have found Said's 'slavery' reading of *Mansfield Park* broadly acceptable, while rejecting the 'Peterloo' reading of 'To Autumn'. Are we, then, applying inconsistent standards and just picking and choosing on personal whim? I hope not, but you will have to make a decision on this point for yourself. For the record, in my view, some of the main differences between the two cases are these. Firstly, *Mansfield Park* isn't *completely* silent on the topic of Antigua and slavery – they are mentioned in the text – whereas 'To Autumn' is completely so on the matter of Peterloo and labour relations. Those topics have therefore to be *read into* the text by the critic. Secondly, in the case of *Mansfield Park* the slavery issue and the matter of the West Indies estate have an evident relevance to the issues of morality, conduct, and silence which are the overt themes of the novel, whereas in the case of 'To Autumn' it is difficult to see any such 'fit' between the claimed content (social unrest and injustice) and the overt matter of the poem (seasonal transition, coming to terms with loss and change, and so on). Finally, the Said reading of *Mansfield Park* explicitly does not accuse the literary work of being culpably evasive and attempting to disguise the socially unacceptable by dressing it in high art. It *adds* a dimension to the work, whereas the 'Peterloo' reading seeks to *subtract* from the work's standing and is dismissive of the qualities readers have previously admired in it, reducing it to a new mono-dimensionality. Something like these three grounds, suitably adapted, ought to provide a general basis for evaluating historicist readings of literary texts.

IS HISTORY THE NEW ENGLISH?

The problem illustrated by the case of 'To Autumn' is the problem not just of how to identify context but of what to do with it when we have identified it. The approach we have been critiquing originated in McGann's work (as already mentioned) and in that of other major figures (such as Marilyn Butler[10] and Marjorie Levinson[11]) and it is usually described as 'New Historicist'. In

10 *Romantics, Rebels and Reactionaries: English Literature and its Background* (Oxford University Press, 1981).
11 See her co-edited collection *Rethinking Historicism: Critical Readings in Romantic History* (Basil Blackwell, 1988).

these heavily historicized approaches, context tends to overwhelm text, so that we begin to find that historical work progressively replaces textual work. The text is disenfranchised (we refuse to be figured by its bounds), and our standards and procedures become those of history. This is fine if we believe that History is the new English, but not otherwise.

One thing we need is clear terminology which can highlight the nature of the dilemma for us, and perhaps useful terms can be found in Stephen Greenblatt's essay 'Resonance and Wonder'. Greenblatt (a scholar of Early modern literature, not Romanticism) is the founder of New Historicism, and what was new about the New Historicism when it started in the early 1980s was its way of making vivid and thought-provoking juxtapositions between a literary text and a contemporary (or near-contemporary) historical document of some kind. The document might be a personal memoir, part of a travel narrative, or an account of court proceedings. The document would be closely discussed for the light it throws upon (say) the attitudes of its era towards notions of personal or national identity, or sexuality. The reading of the document might take up over half the essay, and the findings would then be used to illuminate a key aspect of a Renaissance play.[12] Work like this at its best had an exciting specificity and freshness, but this fascinating essay captures the moment when Greenblatt begins to pull back a little from the current of the movement he himself founded.

In the essay he tries to explain his own approach to works of art by using these central concepts of 'resonance' and 'wonder': 'by resonance I mean the power of the object displayed to reach out beyond its formal boundaries to a larger world, to evoke in the viewer the complex, dynamic cultural forces from which it has emerged and for which ... it may be taken to stand (p. 276). So the 'resonance' of a work of art is an echo within it of the 'cultural forces from which it has emerged'. 'Resonance' is the quality that connects the art object to the social and political world. Thus, for example, a stylized and formally staged scene in a play may evoke formally staged events in politics (like the inauguration of a president or a state opening of parliament) or in religious

12 For work in this style see Greenblatt's book *Shakespearean Negotiations* (Clarendon Press, 1990). Greenblatt's anecdotal 'co-texts' often have the effect (or is it the side-effect?) of 'Americanizing' the Shakespeare text under discussion. For instance, in the famous essay 'Invisible Bullets' (the second chapter of the book), Shakespeare's *Henry IV* and *Henry V* are read in the context of Thomas Harriot's *A Brief and True Report of the New Found Land of Virginia*; in another influential essay, 'The Cultivation of Anxiety: King Lear and His Heirs' (in Greenblatt's *Learning to Curse: Essays in Early Modern Culture*, Routledge, 1990), the anecdotal co-text is a piece about dealing with a difficult child, from the *American Baptist Magazine* of 1831.

ritual (like the formal procession to the altar for a High Mass). This kind of juxtaposition makes us see all three areas (theatre, politics, and religion) as part of the same cultural 'economy'. We are aware that these procedures are intended to evoke a kind of awe in us, to impress upon us an image of power, and to think in this archetypally New Historical way is to become aware of the play's 'resonance' – its 'active context', in other words.

'Wonder', by contrast, is the power of the art object in itself, in isolation, so to speak, 'the power to evoke an exalted attention' ('Resonance and Wonder', p. 277). To expand this a little: all works of art have an enclosing 'frame' of some kind which *separates* them from the world – there is a literal frame around a picture; there is white space on the page around the words of a poem; there is a proscenium arch (or some equivalent) around the staged play. The 'exalted attention' which the work of art is able to evoke is partly the product of the frame. Of course, the frame is porous – the resonance operates through it – but it is always there, and should not be wished away by ditching formalism and 'wonder' and opting for contextualism and resonance.

New Historicism's concern has been very much with 'resonance'; it has wanted to 'reduce the isolation of individual "masterpieces"', says Greenblatt (p. 277). But Greenblatt seems to feel in this essay that the 'resonance' approach has now gone a little too far ('textual contextualism has its limits', p. 278), and he wants to give a slight steer towards 'wonder'. He uses the example of museums and galleries, and the parallel is a fruitful one: imagine, for instance, the display of a major painting like Monet's *Water Lilies*: a display format based on principles of resonance might juxtapose with the picture such items as photographs of the place depicted, contemporary descriptions of the place (a gardener's, a relative's, and so on), other paintings of the same scene, the artist's own account of the painting, contrasting views of other kinds of garden (a medieval garden, a Japanese garden, and so on). All this contextualizing, of course, would make us think about the work as an object of representation *within* the world, rather than as an object that *transcends* the world. On the other hand, to display the work with the emphasis on 'wonder' it would probably be isolated from other pictures, perhaps on a plain white wall, maybe visible down a vista from adjoining rooms, and with nothing to accompany it but a discreet label giving the artist's name, the title of the painting, and the year it was completed. This form of presentation emphasizes purely formal properties – size, the massing of shapes within the composition, the disposition of colours across the canvas, and so on. It is not striving to tell us anything at all about the social conditions of privilege that produce art, or about the sources of an artist's ideas or methods of working, or whatever an artist might be thought to be (sub)consciously avoiding by painting massive pictures of gardens all the time.

New Historicism turned us towards 'resonant contextualism' so decisively, Greenblatt fears, that we may be losing the capacity of wonder altogether – we seem to be interested in nothing but social conditions, and methods of working, suffused by a kind of retrospective resentment of the social privileges enjoyed by the artist. But, if we are not interested in shapes, colours, and composition *at all* for their own sakes (which is to say, if we have cast off formalism without even a twinge of regret), then the whole process of discussing the poem (or any other art object) is curiously pointless, since ultimately it won't really matter what we have to say about all the rest. Context, then, has its claims; but if we allow its unlimited expansion, without ever formulating criteria which put *its* claims in context, then we may find that little is left which can properly be called literary studies.

* * *

It may seem a little mysterious that literary studies has made such major U-turns as that represented by the shift from nearly exclusive formalism to nearly exclusive historicism. It seems like switching from one extreme position to its opposed extreme without passing through any intermediate state (as if St Francis were suddenly to become Vlad the Impaler). In order to get some understanding of the processes involved, we need to consider the history and development of the various critical and theoretical positions which, in the end, constitute English Studies. This is what the next chapter attempts to do.

6 Literary Criticism and Literary Theory

A BRIEF HISTORY OF CRITICISM

Let's begin by underlining a broad distinction between literary theory and literary criticism. The former asks questions about literature in very broad terms – questions like 'What is it?' 'How does it work?' 'What is it for?' Literary criticism, on the other hand, is about the interpretation and appreciation of individual literary works, so these larger questions (necessarily) are often left in abeyance by its practitioners. Contrary to general belief in Britain and America, literary theory came before literary criticism. That is, since ancient times, literature has more usually been thought of from a broad theoretical perspective, rather than in critical (that is, text-specific) terms. The heyday of criticism is really just a brief 'window' of about 50 years in the twentieth century (roughly 1920–70), interrupting a tradition of critical theory which had started with Aristotle's *Poetics*, in Ancient Greek times, and includes: Longinus *On the Sublime* in the Roman period; Sidney's 'Apology for Poetry' in the Renaissance; Shelley's 'Defence of Poetry' in the Romantic period; and T. S. Eliot's essay 'Tradition and the Individual Talent' in the twentieth century. All these are representative of a kind of writing which is best described as 'literary theoretical' rather than 'literary critical', since they discuss ideas about literature's purposes, effects, procedures, and status, but without primary focus on the interpretation of individual literary texts. However, in Britain and America in the period roughly from the 1920s to the 1970s literary debate was dominated (though to a greater extent in the former than the latter) by the interpretive discussion of individual literary works, in other words by literary criticism. Then from the 1970s onwards, the dominance in professional discussions of literature again shifted back to the theoretical, in debates instigated by such figures as Roland Barthes, Michel Foucault, and Jacques Derrida, which tended to centre upon questions of a philosophical, historical, or linguistic nature.

British and American criticism: key differences

The earliest examples of the literary-critical, or text-based, approach were Samuel Johnson's *Lives of the Poets* and *Prefaces to Shakespeare* in the eighteenth century, and Coleridge's discussion of Wordsworth's writing in *Biographia Literaria* in the early part of the nineteenth. It is usual to distinguish two main varieties of criticism in the 50-year 'window' when criticism was dominant, these being British 'close reading' (also called 'practical criticism') and American 'New Criticism'. The British practice stemmed from empirical work on the evaluation of literary texts at Cambridge in the 1920s, as described in I. A. Richards's *Practical Criticism: A Study of Literary Judgement* (1929). Richards's pupil William Empson, in his book *Seven Types of Ambiguity* (1930), exemplified the practice of minute verbal scrutiny of literary texts, while T. S. Eliot's *The Varieties of Metaphysical Poetry* (the Clark Lectures at Cambridge, 1926–7), and F. R. Leavis's *New Bearings in English Poetry* (1932) began the process of revising and supplementing the existing canon of literary works on the basis of detailed textual reassessments. The British variant of literary criticism, then, was characterized by: firstly, a predominant interest in the *evaluation* of literary texts; secondly, by its methodological *implicitness* – that is, it refused to spell out as general principles the reasons for its exclusion from consideration of matters concerned with historical or biographical contexts, or with the reader's response to the text; and thirdly, by its *moralism* – that is, it valued a literary work primarily for its embodiment of humane values, rather than for aesthetic qualities in the narrow sense.

The American version of literary criticism, known as the 'New Criticism', takes its name from John Crowe Ransom's book *The New Criticism* (1941), and is also seen in Cleanth Brooks's *The Well Wrought Urn: Studies in the Structure of Poetry* (1949), and in W. K. Wimsatt's *The Verbal Icon: Studies in the Meaning of Poetry* (1954). It was characterized by the opposite of the British qualities: firstly, it was predominantly interested in the *interpretation* of literary texts; secondly, it was methodologically *explicit*, that is, it valued explicit programmatic statements about method (such as notions like 'The Intentional Fallacy' and 'The Affective Fallacy' (see the essays with these titles in *The Verbal Icon*) which laid out the grounds for excluding from consideration the author's intentions and biography, or the reader's reactions to the text); thirdly, it valued a literary work primarily for formal and aesthetic reasons, such as the extent to which it maintained a fine balance of opposed qualities and brought them into a unity of synthesis.

The British interest in textual *evaluation* meant that key essays frequently took the form of comparisons between two texts which dealt with similar subject matter, the purpose of the comparison being to establish grounds for ranking one text as superior to the other. Well-known examples include Leavis's essay comparing Shakespeare's *Antony and Cleopatra* with Dryden's version of the same story, *All for Love* (in his book *The Living Principle*, 1975) and the essay 'Reality and Sincerity: Notes in the Analysis of Poetry' (1952–3), in which he compares poems by Emily Brontë and Thomas Hardy on bereavement. Likewise, the original experiments recorded in I. A. Richard's *Practical Criticism* were designed to expose the uncertainty with which even well-educated readers make such comparative literary 'judgements' (a key word for the British practitioners of criticism).

What Leavis as a critic most valued in literature was the quality of 'enactment', in which the words 'embodied' the sense, rather than simply indicating or 'describing' it. In the *Antony and Cleopatra* essay he asserts that 'Shakespeare's verse seems to enact its meaning . . . while Dryden's is merely descriptive eloquence', and the same distinction is used to delineate the difference between Donne and the Romantics on the one hand and the work of the Victorian poets on the other. He praises Donne and Keats in *Revaluation* (1936) for 'the liveliness of enactment – something fairly to be called dramatic', contrasting this quality with the 'decorative-descriptive' style of Tennyson. But, for Leavis, it should be emphasized, 'enactment' is a linguistic strength with a *moral* foundation, for it is a matter not merely of technique, but of a lived and 'felt life' embodied in the very texture of the language. Thus, it is because Hardy has *been* bereaved, combined with his excellence as a poet, that his poetic language has this quality – the latter alone could not ensure it. Thus (in 'Reality and Sincerity') 'Hardy's poem is seen to have a great advantage in *reality* [which is to say] that it represents a profounder and completer sincerity.' By contrast, Brontë is 'dramatizing herself in a situation such as she has clearly not known in actual experience'. Yet the piece also illustrates the characteristic weaknesses of the 'closed' close reading approach (see below), for Leavis ignores contextualizing issues, treating the two poems as if both were personal lyrics, whereas Brontë's is actually part of a historical saga, spoken by a 'character', and written in a manner appropriate to formal public declamation, rather than being presented as the product of private, meditative inwardness.

'Intrinsic' and 'extrinsic' criticism

The American tendency towards greater explicitness of methodological principle led to a number of useful distinctions, such as that between 'intrinsic' and 'extrinsic' criticism. The former is text-based, intensive, and analytical, while the latter is context-based, extensive, and discursive, making use of (for instance) historical information, knowledge of generic conventions, and biographical data. F. W. Bateson's notion of 'contextual reading' (in opposition to 'close reading') aimed to synthesize the two modes of intrinsic and extrinsic approaches. A more recent formulation along similar lines distinguishes between 'unseen close reading' (or '*closed* close reading', as we might call it), and 'seen close reading' (or '*open* close reading'). The former is the textual practice that rules out of play the use of any external data, and limits the critic strictly to 'the words on the page'. The latter, by contrast, reads the text closely, but alongside, and open to, a range of necessary reference material. This formulation attempts to cope with the paradox that the interdict placed by dominant critical practice on the use of 'external' data took root at precisely the time when the most prestigious literature (Eliot, Pound, Joyce) increasingly required copious 'external' annotation to explain the significance of allusions, proper names, mentions of historical figures, mythological parallels, and so on.

Other objections to the critical practice of minute and intense verbal scrutiny might be listed as follows. Firstly, it really only works at its best for the short lyric poem – it cannot do so, even for poetry, when the scale is epic and the mode primarily narrative. Secondly, for obvious reasons, it can never be a sufficient tool for the novel, given the vast scale of the text in comparison with the nature of the critical method – a close reading of the average Victorian novel would be like trying to bring in a grain harvest using only a pair of nail scissors. In practice, the main critical resource of close readers of novels is to 'poeticize' the text, giving exaggerated importance, for instance, to the novelist's use of verbal imagery. Thirdly, the method is inappropriate to drama, except verse drama, but even here the 'poeticization' of the text is, again, often very marked, so that plays tend to become a static tableau of images – Leavis's praise of *Antony and Cleopatra* involves (again) treating famous speeches as if they were free-standing lyric poems, rather than moments in a drama. Fourthly, the linguistic data identified in the close reading process often remains less than convincingly integrated into the flow of critical argument. Identifying an assonantal pattern in a poem is the easy part; linking this convincingly to a reading and interpretation of the poem as a whole is the real challenge.

'THEORY HAS LANDED'

'Literary theory', or just 'theory', is a loose portmanteau term for a series of new approaches to literature which emerged strongly in the USA, Britain, and elsewhere from the 1970s onwards, challenging the dominance of both UK 'practical criticism' and American 'New Criticism'. The term 'theory', when used in connection with literature, includes structuralism, poststructuralism, deconstruction, feminism, Marxism, New Historicism, Postcolonialism, Postmodernism, literary linguistics, 'Queer Theory', and ecocriticism.[1] By the 1990s the study of theory had become the main topic on English degree courses; but how exactly did this spectacular rise come about? Because several of the major literary theorists are French (by nationality and/or culture), literary theory is usually regarded as a kind of French 'invasion' of lands which had hitherto been content to practise literary criticism and close reading, without ever raising their heads from the 'words on the page' to look around at the wider intellectual and social context of literature and literary study. But this view is, at best, a caricature of the real situation, since before the outbreak of continental theory in the 1970s there already existed well-established alternatives to the dominant forms of criticism consolidated in both countries.

In the UK in the late 1950s, for instance, Richard Hoggart's seminal (and still fascinating) book *The Uses of Literacy* (1957) and Raymond Williams's *Culture and Society* (1958) offered broader notions of culture than Leavisite approaches to literary study allowed, and these concerns became the focus of the influential Centre for Contemporary Cultural Studies at Birmingham University, which had been founded by Hoggart in 1963. Other prominent UK critics of the time whose work was in broad alignment with that of Hoggart and Williams included Alan Swingewood (of the LSE), whose book *The Sociology of Literature* (written with Diana Laurenson) was published in 1972, and David Craig (of Lancaster University), author of *The Real Foundations: Literature and Social Change* (1973), another key work which challenged Leavis's resistance to the broader social contextualization of literature. This kind of material overlaps chronologically with the arrival of the work of continental theorists in the early 1970s.

In the USA, a similar situation existed, though the actors and factors are very different, of course. A simple way of expressing the difference is to say that, whereas in the UK the initial interest was chiefly in structuralism, in the USA it was chiefly in poststructuralism. The long dominance of New Critical methods in America was no longer assured: New Criticism was like a huge ice floe which seemed intact, but in reality had already been fatally eroded and undermined by climate changes, and was in fact ready to break up. Jacques

1 This book does not aim to provide you with a systematic introduction to literary theory, but the bibliography entry for this chapter has five books suitable for students seeking information on the topic for the first time.

Derrida, the foremost theorist of deconstruction, was invited to Yale and became a leading member of Yale's 'famous five' (Harold Bloom, Paul de Man, Geoffrey Hartman, and J. Hillis Miller were the others, and they are the collective authors of the definitive collection of essays *Deconstruction and Criticism*, 1979). The five became the spearhead of deconstruction and post-structuralism in the USA. Hillis Miller (b. 1928) had already, from the 1960s, explored beyond the limits of New Criticism, showing a strong interest in European approaches which emphasized consciousness rather than form, while de Man (1919–83), even before the final 'deconstruction' period of his career, always emphasized 'rhetoric' above 'reference' in the literary work. Bloom (b. 1930), brought up, like Derrida, in the ambience of Talmudic scholarship (that is, in the Jewish tradition of biblical interpretation), had a strong interest in broad-scale, neo-Freudian approaches to literature, and had always been a high theorist whose intellectual ambitions were as great as those of Derrida himself. Hartman (b. 1929), finally, had been one of the first to question the 'formalist' exclusivity of the New Criticism, he too arguing for the relevance of the Jewish rabbinic tradition of interpretation, and of psycho-analytic approaches (see his book *Beyond Formalism: Literary Essays 1958–1970*, published in 1970). Again, then, the simplistic notion of literary theory as an alien or external force challenging the native American and British traditions of exclusively formalist literary criticism is clearly untenable.

In the earliest 1970s period of theory, key texts were often only available in extracted or translated form, so the work of intellectual 'mediators' was crucial. One of the most effective of these is Jonathan Culler, author of *Structuralist Poetics* (1975). The uncompromising central point of Culler's book is its insistence that the proper object of literary study is not the appreciation and enjoyment of individual works of literature, but the quest for an under-standing of what constitutes literature and 'literariness'. This recipe for a change of emphasis in literary studies might not have seemed terribly promising at first, but the appeal of such an approach to postgraduates and to younger academics was considerable, for general ideas had been artificially suppressed in English Studies for a long time, thereby inevitably creating a strong appetite for them. Thus, a whole range of questions were never touched upon at all – questions, for instance, concerning the purpose and potential of literature itself, the nature of literary language and literary representation, the role of the reader in the creation of literary canons, and so on. Theory offered to release this hidden, repressed 'subconscious' of English Studies, breaking the widespread taboo on ideas and generalizations which many decades of practical criticism had effectively imposed. Now 'close reading' was replaced by 'theorized reading', and 'critical practice' (the term derives from Catherine

Belsey's highly successful *Critical Practice* of 1980) became the catchphrase for an approach to literature which involved a newly theorized way of reading which aimed to replace the old method of 'practical criticism'. Belsey's book insisted that there is a single system of cultural meanings and representations, with no privileged literary realm operating by separate rules and norms. Thus (to put it crudely) gold-rimmed glasses signify the intellectual in Hollywood movies *and* in highbrow Russian novels. It is, for Belsey, merely 'bourgeois mystification' to suggest that language and representation work in a special way in literature. All the same, a particular kind of writing, classic literary realism, is especially to be condemned, since it fraudulently pretends to present reality 'straight'. The task of the reader of such works is constantly to resist the illusion of reality they create, avoiding, for instance, any discussion of 'characters', imagined as if they were real people. Instead, the book urges us to concentrate on identifying and decoding the techniques and structures of *representation* (a key term and concept of theorized reading).

As this stage (that is, by the early 1980s) theory began to popularize its basic beliefs, and there was a more general shift of interest from structuralism to poststructuralism, that is, from early Roland Barthes to early Jacques Derrida, so that, instead of seeing verbal structures as intimidatingly ordered and rule-based, we begin to see them as (thrillingly, subversively) anarchic and unpredictable. This stage of literary theory is also the period of the 'theory wars', a time of bad-tempered rows between theorists and non-theorists at conferences and meetings, and on TV and radio programmes. It was a strangely fraught time, dominated politically by Reaganism in the USA and Thatcherism in the UK, with the frustrations induced by the political scene spilling over into the academic sphere. The crude extremism encapsulated in a notorious remark (attributed to the British Tory prime minister Margaret Thatcher) that 'there is no such thing as society' generated its equally reductive counter-slogan in English Studies, which increasingly insisted that 'everything is socially constructed', which is to say, in effect, that 'there is no such thing as the individual'. The characteristics of the 1980s phase of theory, then, are: firstly, prolonged and bitter hostilities between traditional approaches to literary study (usually called 'liberal humanism') and 'theory'; secondly, the continuation of the shift from structuralism to poststructuralism; and, thirdly, the growing confidence of theorists through a vigorous culture of conferences and dedicated journals, leading to the spread of theory, till it became established at the heart of the undergraduate syllabus.

Since then, in the 1990s and beyond, the white heat of the 'Copernican revolution' of theory (to use Catherine Belsey's term) has undeniably cooled, for it is evident that the inevitable post-revolutionary 'Reign of Terror' (the period which brooked no revisionist alternatives) has long been over, and it is common to describe the late twentieth- and early twenty-first-century phase of English Studies as the 'post-theory' era. This new era is characterized by (among other things) an apparent return to the view that every degree-level teacher of literature is primarily a period specialist (a medievalist, an early modernist, a Romanticist, and so on), rather than primarily a poststructuralist, or a Marxist, or a feminist – a very significant shift. Whereas in the 1980s the 'default' approach to literary study was broadly poststructuralist or deconstructionist, today (which is to say in the first decade of the twenty-first century) it tends to be broadly 'historicist', as already argued, and committed to the endeavour of reconstructing the cultural and historical moment of a work's first appearance.

SEVEN TYPES OF CONTINUITY

So far in this chapter we have had a brief 'history' of literary criticism, followed by an account of the spread of literary theory since the 1960s. Did theory, then, really sweep away that old world of criticism and ring in a brave new theoretical world of English reborn? As we saw, theory *is* often spoken of in this way, for terms like 'the theory revolution' are often heard. I must confess that I have used this kind of terminology myself, but I have increasingly come to believe that we can only make sense of the recent history of English Studies by seeing theory as 'evolutionary' rather than revolutionary. Theory succeeded so well because it reinforced views already widely held within the discipline (not just by the specific British and American 'transitional' figures mentioned in the last section), but at the same time it restated them in dramatic, extreme, and glamorous ways. So if we look closely (and looking closely is what English Studies is about), we can see many lines of continuity between 'criticism' (a term used here as a rough and ready label for the reading practices dominant in Anglo-American literary studies from the 1920s to the 1970s) and 'theory' (used as another rough label for the range of theories which dominated literary studies from the 1970s to the 1990s). Criticism and theory are usually taken to be out-and-out opposites, but my point here is to see them as a pairing, like Jekyll and Hyde, for those two apparently contradictory figures in Robert Louis Stevenson's story 'Doctor Jekyll and Mr Hyde' are actually the same person, albeit in different moods and guises. My suggestion, then, is that there are in particular 'seven types of continuity' between criticism and theory, making a series of bridges between the two worlds. Thus, the main content of theory, in spite of its elaborate and exotic dress, is not really so very revolutionary within the British and American context. In fact, it is striking that theory very often dealt with problems which had frequently been examined before in the course of British and American literary and critical history.

The first type of continuity concerns the attitude to authors. One of the most dramatic interventions of theory is its proclamation of the demise of the author, as set out in Roland Barthes's 1968 essay 'The Death of the Author' (reprinted in Stephen Heath's Barthes reader, *Image, Music, Text*) and also in Foucault's 1969 piece 'What is an Author?' (in Paul Rabinow's *The Foucault Reader*, 1986). Barthes and Foucault, in these essays, see texts as primarily the products of (respectively) 'language' and 'discourse', thus dethroning the author as the independent source of what they produce. So Barthes writes: 'the removal of the Author utterly transforms the modern text; the text is henceforth made and read in such a way that at all its levels its author is absent.' This is the crucial point of an essay widely taken to have revolutionary implications; yet such radical downgrading of authors had long been a commonplace of English criticism. Rather surprisingly, perhaps, it is often the view held by critics who were also novelists or poets. Shelley, for instance, writes: 'The poet and the man are different natures, though they exist together. They may be unconscious of each other and incapable of deciding on each other's powers and efforts.' That phrase 'they may be unconscious of each other' has profound implications, for it suggests that the poet as a conscious individual being is not entirely in control during the act of composition; if this is so, then what *could* be in control if not something we might think of as 'language' or 'discourse'? And T. S. Eliot is equally explicit 100 years later in his essay 'Tradition and the individual Talent' when he writes: 'The emotion of art is impersonal; the more perfect the artist the more completely separate in him will be the man who suffers and the mind which creates.'

'The death of the author' is also implicit in the kind of practical criticism instigated by I. A. Richards in the 1920s, which detaches the text not only from its author's name but also from the conditions and circumstances of its production. But, even then, in the 1920s, anti-authorism and anti-contextualism (and the two always go together) were not new, for the literary 'touchstones' of Matthew Arnold in the previous century operated in the same way, using a passage of long-attested worth as a kind of litmus paper to test the value of newer works by comparison, a process which divorces works of literature from their genesis and context and appeals instead to the intrinsic and ahistorical qualities of the writing itself. By the 1960s anti-authorism was so entrenched in Anglo-American criticism that it took either courage or eccentricity to protest against it. When William Empson entitled a 1970 essay '*Ulysses:* Joyce's Intentions' this was an act of defiance of an already long-standing tradition that the intentions of an author in writing a work were inadmissible evidence in literary studies, since even when they had been expressed and recorded in writing by the author it did not follow that these intentions had actually been realized in the resulting literary work. When Empson's essay on Joyce later appeared in a book called *Using Biography* the sin was compounded, since the purpose of ruling out any appeal to authorial intention had been to counteract what critics saw as an unhealthy interest in authors' lives at the expense of their works. By 1968/9, then, authors had been long absent in British critical thinking, and the step from the author's absence to the author's death was a fairly small one to take.

A second area of continuity between criticism and theory is a consequence of the 'de-authorization' which is seen in both, namely the empowerment of readers (or critics). For Barthes, the consequence of the death of the author is the birth of the reader, for, with the author dead, readers are liberated from the second-order task of interpretation (which Barthes seems to see as passively scanning the text in order to decode the author's intended meaning), for 'once the author is removed, the claim to decipher a text becomes quite futile'. So 'refusing to assign a "secret", an ultimate meaning to the text' 'liberates what may be called an anti-theological activity that is truly revolutionary since to refuse to fix meaning is, in the end, to refuse God . . . reason, science, law'. To challenge the author, then, is to challenge all authority. It is a universal proclamation: 'I will not serve.' Having made this defiant proclamation, the reader is then licensed, on every new act of reading, to enjoy for ever the exhilarating post-revolutionary moment of overrunning the czar's palace, enjoying the sense of being liberated from his tyrannical rule, but without ever having the responsibility of moving on to the next stage and working out how to construct an alternative society, an alternative set of meanings.

For Foucault, too, authors were czarist authority figures whose sole purpose had been to prevent the reading proletariat from discovering its subversive power: as he says at the end of 'What is an Author?' 'the author is therefore the ideological figure by which one marks the manner in which we fear the proliferation of meaning.' He doesn't explain what is inherently fearsome about multiple meanings, or why the czarist controllers wouldn't be perfectly happy to have readers harmlessly engrossed in turning the textual kaleido-scope and generating endlessly proliferating meanings. But the point to emphasize is the clarity of the pattern: Barthes and Foucault both want to disempower authors and empower readers, and they take it for granted that doing so has revolutionary potential. The same kind of 'pro-reader' tenden-cies are self-evidently present in criticism, which also licensed readers to discover textual worlds of ambiguity, paradox, and even contradiction. Thus, in William Empson's seminal book *Seven Types of Ambiguity* of 1930, readers are shown how to discover all these varieties of ambiguity within texts, the culminating kind being when there is an 'irreconcilable contradiction between elements of the text'.[2] Criticism and theory alike are fixated on those 'proliferating meanings', and therein lies a third element of continuity between them.

Closely related to the dethronement of the author is a fourth continuity, the belief that the world of the text is self-contained, a view encapsulated in Derrida's remark that 'there is nothing outside the text'. Although a long history of contention now surrounds this remark, it seems to assert the independent existence of the text; the text is not validated with reference to an external reality which it reflects, but rather exists in and for itself. If it is not the creation of an author or God figure, then the text must always have existed, and it cannot be understood with reference to any prior events, or anything outside itself. But this, again, is a position which had been implicit in Anglo-American criticism, which had always worked on the assumption that 'there is nothing outside the text', confining its attention to the 'words on the page' and not looking beyond them to (for instance) matters of history or contextuality. Again, what the theory provides is not a new thought or a new practice, but simply a very dramatic statement of the assumption which underlies a wide-spread practice. The high linguistic drama of statements like that proclaiming the death of the author and the view that there is nothing outside the text have an 'in your face', attention-getting quality which are typical of theory, and this again helps to explain the impact theory had on literary studies when it came on the scene in the 1970s.

Closely related to this is a fifth element of continuity: the view that the real is the product of language, a view which is sometimes called 'linguistic determinism'. To exemplify this: we might usually (and reasonably) think that the word 'spring' denotes an actual annual event in nature, but a linguistic determinist could assert that 'spring' is really a linguistic construct, since the year does not fall 'naturally' into four demarcated seasonal segments (like a

2   It might be counter-argued that W. K. Wimsatt's essay 'The Affective Fallacy' actually attempts to impose very severe restrictions on readers, which it does; but it does not condemn the discovery of multiple meanings, which are held to be *intrinsic* to the text – what it condemns is the mistaken concentration on *extrinsic* factors, such as 'the psychological effects of the poem' (e.g. making us feel sad, or happy, or both at the same time, or reminding us of Great Uncle Wilbur). At such moments (that is, when they turn their attention to such things) readers cease to be readers and restrict *their own* interpretive freedoms.

pre-cut 'Four Seasons' pizza); rather, it runs continually without a break, and the four seasons are indeed a human imposition on, or a reading of, the year, so this is an example of the way our language builds our world for us. But, in criticism, this 'constituting' aspect of language had long been recognized, and indeed this 'performative' quality was often seen as characteristic of the highest type of literary language. Thus, for instance, F. R. Leavis (as mentioned earlier) saw linguistic 'enactment' as the supreme virtue in literature, and what distinguished Romantic poets from Victorians was that Victorian poets like Tennyson were only able to *designate* or *describe* things in language, whereas Keats could make his poetic language *enact* the sense. Notions of 'enactment' are also implicit (in the theory of fiction put forward by Henry James, Percy Lubbock,[3] and others) in the distinction between 'saying' and 'showing', where the latter does more than just *tell* us the events in words and seems rather to *embody* them. In all these cases, language is transcending itself in various ways – creating the real, and making the absent present. Hence the supercharged notions of language which are pervasive in literary theory have plenty of precursors in literary criticism. What was lacking, again, in the earlier period was the philosophical boldness required to make dramatic and generalized focal statements about this aspect of language.

A sixth element of continuity between criticism and theory concerns the assertion that texts have multiple meanings, a notion of texts which sees them as 'polyvalent' shifting skeins of multiple meanings.[4] Theory's view of criticism is that it had believed in the possibility and desirability of pinning each text down to an agreed single meaning. But, firstly, it is difficult to find many critics making such an assertion, and secondly, criticism has in practice generated a bewildering array of competing readings of canonical literary texts. It is true that the New Critics of the older generation were always keen to demonstrate the underlying 'unity' of the text, but this presupposed a surface on which meanings were multiple, competing, and diverse. Critics did not envisage that a demonstration of the nature of the underlying unity would be universally accepted and would bring critical debate to an end – on the contrary, Leavis's well-known model of the typical form of critical exchange envisaged an infinite prolongation which would never reach a conclusion, since he saw the typical critical response by one critic to another as being 'Yes, but . . .'. Indeed, it has

3   Henry James, *Theory of Fiction*, ed. James E. Miller Jr (University of Nebraska Press, 1972); Percy Lubbock, *The Craft of Fiction* (Jonathan Cape, 1921).
4   I am making a slightly tenuous distinction (in the second and sixth points of continuity) between empowering readers to discover multiplicities of meanings, and asserting that the possession of multiplicities of meanings is characteristic of literary texts (or of textuality in general).

been theorists who have postulated terminal consensus, leading to an apocalyptic end of criticism, and their actual readings of literary works have been far more uniform and homogeneous than those of literary critics, since their readings almost invariably show literary language itself to be under terminal pressure or in a state of unsolvable crisis, irrespective of the work's overt content.

A seventh element of continuity between criticism and theory is a certain negative attitude to philosophy which they have in common. French theory, on its emergence in the 1960s, presented itself as a breaking-free from the narrow and debilitating rationalism of the traditional French academic training. Though it drew heavily upon philosophy, this took the form of radical rereadings of classic philosophers – they were 'deconstructed' and 'read against the grain' in senses which were (and remain) quite unacceptable to the orthodox philosophical tradition. But intellectual life in Britain never had any particular reverence for philosophy in the first place, so it was no challenge to British critics to go along with the French theorists' disparagement of traditional schools of philosophy. In fact, no aspect of intellectual life could be more marginal and more generally disdained in Britain than philosophy. 'Philosophizing' is usually taken as almost synonymous with straying off the point and entering a realm of tedious abstraction and pedantry. As far as English Studies were concerned, the matter had been decisively settled in the 1930s when F. R. Leavis's debate with René Wellek resulted in a comprehensive victory for Leavis in which it was established – to Leavis's own satisfaction, at least – that philosophy had nothing at all to do with literary criticism, and could only be a fatal interference between the critic and the literary text. The culture in which Leavis's crudely asserted empiricism could carry such weight was obviously not one in which the so-called 'queen of the sciences' had ever been accorded much respect by non-philosophers. Hence, we were perfectly happy to go along with Derrida's wholesale junking of 'Western metaphysics', to which we had never been wedded in the first place. Indeed, the British education in which the mere names of Aristotle, Plato, Locke, and Descartes were ever even once mentioned would be quite exceptional.

SONNET 73: READING WITH THEORY

Criticism and theory, then, share a range of self-evident affinities or continuities. Some of the procedures of critical close reading were set out in the first part of Chapter 2, as ten frequently seen reading 'moves' or procedures. These, we said, are indispensable yet insufficient. So what is it that literary theory can provide? What is missing? Well, the ten 'moves' mostly look inwards into the text itself, and we also need to look outwards. This necessary looking outwards from the text is why we have and why we need literary theory. The textual principles do not contain much that would focus us, for instance, on the cultural contexts and intertextual connections of a literary work. Theory can help us, especially, in considering four major aspects of the relationship between literature and the world beyond, these being, firstly, literature and history, secondly, literature and language, thirdly, literature and gender, and, finally, literature and psychoanalysis. These will now be considered in turn, using the example of Shakespeare's Sonnet 73:

> That time of year thou mayst in me behold
> When yellow leaves, or none, or few, do hang
> Upon those boughs which shake against the cold,
> Bare ruined choirs, where late the sweet birds sang.
> In me thou see'st the twilight of such day
> As after sunset fadeth in the west;
> Which by and by black night doth take away,
> Death's second self, that seals up all in rest.
> In me thou see'st the glowing of such fire,
> That on the ashes of his youth doth lie,
> As the deathbed whereon it must expire,
> Consumed with that which it was nourished by.
> This thou perceiv'st, which makes thy love more strong,
> To love that well which thou must leave ere long.

History

The speaker in the poem, to put it delicately, is not as young as he was, and he ingeniously uses this fact to place a kind of scarcity value on himself. He is not going to be around long, so she (or he) had better love him well while he is. There is something very odd about that second line, but for the moment it's the fourth line I want to concentrate on. What does it mean? At one level, the general meaning is clear. The speaker is old. He is like a bare tree in winter. The birds of summer which used to sit upon those boughs and sing have now gone. It's all very sad. He is feeling sorry for himself, and he wants his lover to feel the same. But that word 'choirs' is like the bullet that grows (as discussed under the ten starter points in Chapter 2). It's the point in the poem where the literal and the metaphorical begin to 'deconstruct' each other. For it isn't just a pretty way of referring to birds: it also means, literally, the choir-stalls in which the monks used to sing Vespers. And those choirs are indeed bare and ruined now, because the monasteries were closed at the Reformation by Henry VIII and the buildings were abandoned. All this happened not very long ago (the word 'late' means 'recently'), and the metaphor chosen by the poet (the branches of the trees on which the birds used to sing in summer being like the wooden choir-stalls where the monks once sang) evokes all this recent and highly contentious history. Is it a coded reference, a line in which a secret recusant – that is, a closet Catholic – signals regret for the suppression of the old Catholic religion? This would be a very fashionable interpretation today, for there are theories that the young Shakespeare spent part of his youth with a noble Catholic family in Lancashire.[5]

Things are now becoming complicated. Instead of being a free-standing literary jewel which we can hold up to the light and scrutinize with our ten principles of interpretation, this little poem suddenly seems to be deeply enmeshed in the history of its time. Of course, we could take a course in Reformation history and find out all about the monasteries. But it isn't so simple. It isn't just a matter of acquiring knowledge: if the allusion is actually there, it teaches us that we do not understand what the relationship is between literature and history, for, if it is an allusion, then it is very difficult to work out precisely what it is doing in the poem: I mean this literally – not just how and why it got there, but what *effect* it has on the poem. Baffling yet fascinating questions of this kind are one of the reasons for using literary theory. Here, then, is a whole area much in need of discussion in broad theoretical terms. This, surely, is the kind of gap in our understanding which theory can attempt to fill.

Language

I said a moment ago that there is something odd about the second line of Sonnet 73, and investigating that oddity brings us to the issue of literature and language. What is odd about the line, of course, is the peculiar order in which

5   This line from the sonnet was discussed by William Empson as the first literary example in *Seven Types of Ambiguity*. Empson (in 1930) saw in it 'ruined monastery choirs' (among much else), and the line had already been read in the nineteenth century as evidencing a nostalgia, at least, for Catholicism. More recently, Shakespeare's Catholic and Lancashire connections were discussed in E. A. J. Honigmann's *Shakespeare: the Lost Years* (Manchester University Press, 1985, 2nd edn 1998), and developed in a *TLS* article entitled 'Shakespeare and the Jesuits' by Richard Wilson (19 Dec. 1997). Park Honan's biography *Shakespeare: A Life* (Oxford University Press, 1998) accepts and incorporates these findings. (I am grateful to my colleague Andrew Hadfield for help with these details.)

the words occur. In the memory (in my experience), the line is nearly always 'yellow leaves, or few, or none' but Shakespeare actually says 'yellow leaves, or none, or few'. This seems to violate the natural word order, which would follow the logic of a phrase like 'going, going, gone' where a process of gradual diminishing is followed through until there is nothing left at all. This is one example of the way English words occur in a predetermined order; we put the 'knives and forks' on the table, not the 'forks and knives'. A phrase like 'going, going, gone' has the logic of a countdown – 'three, two, one, zero'. That is the way the words 'collocate', as a linguist would say; so the phrase 'yellow leaves, or none, or few' violates an expected and logical pattern. And, of course, it isn't done to accommodate rhyme or metre, since neither 'none' nor 'few' is a rhyme word and both have a single syllable, so swapping them round doesn't make any difference to the metrical structure of the line. So it seems that what is happening is that underneath the main current of the language another current is running in the opposite direction. The speaker is *saying* that he is sexually 'past it', but then hints, with a nudge and a wink, that he isn't, quite, and this is indicated by the unexpected order of the words.

This underlying counter-current of language can often be sensed. Language seems to have a natural tendency to undermine and contradict itself, to be one thing on the surface and another beneath. When a teacher says to a child 'Is that your coat on the floor?', it isn't a question, in spite of its surface form, it's a command: it means 'Pick it up.' Reading literature well is often a matter of picking up these counter-currents, these points where language undermines itself, runs against its own grain, carries along its own opposite in its slipstream. An example I am reminded of is when the Duke of Edinburgh recently withdrew his royal patronage from Harrods department store. I'm told that the sign in the shoe department which used to say 'Shoe-makers to His Royal Highness the Duke of Edinburgh' was altered to read 'Cobblers to Prince Philip'. That phrase *says* one thing, but, of course, *means* something else. Beneath the surface current of its meaning (which is respectful and reverential) another current runs in the opposite direction. Deconstructive reading is a kind of dowsing tool designed to pick up that counter-current that runs beneath the linguistic surface. In the first line of the poem, then, the speaker says: 'That time of year thou mayst in me behold'. Is there a hint of optionality, as it has been called, in that word 'mayst', so that he is saying, in a sceptical way, 'Well, you *could* look at me like that'?[6] This

---

6 My reading is indebted to Roger Fowler's chapter 'Language and the Reader: Shakespeare's Sonnet 73' in his book *Style and Structure in Literature* (Basil Blackwell, 1975).

notion of the undercurrents and crosscurrents of language, then, opens up another area where we seem to need theory; it is the area of the investigation of the relationship between literature and language, and the often strange characteristics of language itself.

Gender

Another area for theory is that of the relationship between literature and gender. In the case of this poem, the gender issue is pretty stark. We might ask the question: what are the signs in this poem that it is written by a man rather than a woman? (This is often a very good question to ask of a literary text.) One sign, I think, is the fact that as a ploy in the seduction process the speaker draws attention to his relatively advanced age. Could a woman speaker in a love poem associate herself with images of late autumn, sunset, approaching death, and dying embers? It seems unlikely. The male speaker takes advantage of a set of implicit cultural stereotypes whereby age in men connotes experience, man-of-the-world ease, and notions of depth of character. No such positive stereotypical associations would be available to an ageing woman speaker. Once again, the problem of the precise nature of the relationship between literature and society – word and world – is problematized, in this case concerning how literature relates to gendered social norms. But, clearly, there is a relationship of *some* kind and it is active in this poem. In this regard, we again seem to need theory, a theory which can look at the relation between literature and gender, and explicate (meaning, literally, to unfold) some aspects of the connections between them.

Psychoanalysis

The final area is the relationship between literature and psychoanalysis, which we can open up by asking what exactly the speaker's strategy of seduction is in this poem. The answer, I think, is that the strategy seems to be what we might call 'pre-emptive': he himself says that he is getting old, to pre-empt anybody else saying it, boldly bringing the tricky question of age into full view himself. He does this especially in the dark and gloomy image of approaching night in the second quatrain, which mentions twilight, then 'after sunset', then the last glow removed by 'black night', then death sealing everything up as in a tomb. Surely, we think, it's all over for this man. But in the next quatrain (lines 9–12) he draws back from this sombre image of total extinction, and suddenly we have images which suggest a rekindling – a glowing fire, youth, being consumed by something. Suddenly the deathbed is suffused by images of residual passion, residual potency – and remember that for the Elizabethans the words 'death' and 'dying' often carried a secondary sexual meaning connected with orgasm. The 'going, gone, going' pattern of line 2 is repeated in the larger pattern made by the three quatrains, where the last one actually steps back from the extreme statement of the second-to-last.

What is working here, then, is a psychological process: often, the best way to conceal something is to reveal it, to hide it in the open, as is sometimes said.[7] If both parties to an exchange are aware that something is being left unsaid, then it will appear in everything which *is* said. The addressee of the poem, whether it's male or female, is thinking: 'But he's too old for me.' The speaker knows this, so *he* speaks that thought, and then he plants a little doubt about the truth of it, with his suggestive references to the few leaves which still remain, the sap which still flows, the fire which still glows, the passion which still consumes. These mental processes are ones which psychoanalysis knows all about, and here again is another area in which theory can operate, that of the relationship between literature and psychoanalysis.

DOING IT DECONSTRUCTIVELY: 'HD' AND ADRIENNE RICH

So far in this chapter I have made a general case for using literary theory, arguing its compatibility with many elements of our traditional literary training. I'd like to look at another example now, and take just one of the four categories in more detail, namely the second, concerning the relationship between literature and language. The reason for taking this one is that it enables us to think about deconstructive reading, which on the one hand has been a powerful tool in literary theory, but on the other has clear affinities with the kind of intensive close reading which we have always practised (as already argued, there are many continuities between them).

So, what *is* deconstruction? In general terms, it can be thought of as a kind of anti-reading, originating in the work of Jacques Derrida in the late 1960s,

---

7   This paradoxical trope (of concealment by non-concealment) is the driving force of Edgar Allan Poe's famous detective story 'The Purloined Letter', a tale which fascinated Derrida and Lacan, and on which the literary theory establishment developed something of a fixation in the 1980s. See *The Purloined Poe: Lacan, Derrida and Psychoanalytic Reading*, ed. John P. Muller and William J. Richardson (Johns Hopkins University Press, 1988), which usefully rounds up and comments on this material.

the aim of which is to expose the meanings which the text never intended itself to bear. In Terry Eagleton's well-known definition, it is 'reading the text against itself' or 'reading against the grain', 'knowing the text as it cannot know itself' (see *Literary Theory: An Introduction*), thereby revealing fault-lines (a favoured term) of doubt and contradiction within it. For Barbara Johnson, in another often-quoted description, deconstruction is 'the careful teasing out of the warring forces of signification within the text' (see her book *The Critical Difference*, 1980). As J. A. Cuddon suggests, in *A Dictionary of Literary Terms* (4th edn, 1998), this may result in the discovery of multiple and contradictory meanings, so that a text 'may betray itself', to use the emotive, hyped-up language which is often found in deconstruction. Other terms which are often used to describe deconstruction are 'textual harassment', and 'oppositional reading'. The process of deconstructing a text often involves fixing on what looks like an incidental detail – a particular word, or a particular metaphor – and then bringing it in from the margin of the text to the centre. In this way the text is 'decentred' by the reading process, and the overall effect is often perverse, obsessive, manic, or even apparently malevolent towards author and text, reader and literature. If we think of the text as a cat, then old-style close reading involves stroking the cat so that it purrs and curls in upon itself contentedly, feeling good. Deconstructive reading is like stroking the cat the wrong way, against the grain of the textual fur, so that the cat bristles and hisses, and the whole situation becomes less predictable. The close reader of old aimed to show a unity of purpose within the text: the text knows what it wants to do, and, having directed all its means towards this end, it is at peace with itself. By contrast, the deconstructor aims to show that the text is at war with itself, and that it is characterized by disunity rather than unity. So the deconstructor looks for such things as, firstly, *contradictions*, secondly, *linguistic quirks and aporia*, thirdly, *shifts or breaks (in tone, viewpoint, tense, person, attitude, etc.)*, and, finally, *absences or omissions*.

So how does this kind of reading look in practice? I will give a mini-example and a longer example. 'Oread' is a tiny poem by the American imagist poet 'HD' (Hilda Doolittle, 1886–1961). It reads in full:

> Whirl up, sea –
> whirl your pointed pines,
> splash your great pines
> on our rocks,
> hurl your green over us,
> cover us with your pools of fir.

COURTESY OF PERDITA SCHAFFNER AND NEW DIRECTIONS PUBLISHING CORP

6.1 HD (Hilda Doolittle)

'Oread' is a poem which has already deconstructed itself. The title word, 'Oread', means a wood nymph, but the poem is an emblem of the impossibility of reading, and an embodiment of the Derridean dictum that there is nothing outside the text. The deconstructive malevolence splits the title thus: 'O/Read' and then shows that it is impossible to say *what* we are reading. Is it a description of a stormy sea which presents that sea through the metaphor of a wind-tossed pine forest? Or is it a poem about a wind-tossed pine forest which describes it using the metaphor of a stormy sea? It's impossible to say.

Or, rather, it's about neither. It's about an object which is pure textuality, which only exists in language; it's a sea/pine forest, or a pine forest/sea. Here is a poem, then, which actively *resists* reading.

For a more sustained example of the 'resistant' poem we can take Adrienne Rich's poem 'Transit':

> When I meet the skier she is always
> walking, skis and poles shouldered, toward the mountain,
> free-swinging in worn boots
> over the path new-sifted with fresh snow
> her graying dark hair almost hidden by   5
> a cap of many colors
> her fifty-year-old, strong, impatient body
> dressed for cold and speed
> her eyes level with mine
>
> And when we pass each other I look into her face   10
> wondering what we have in common
> where our minds converge
> for we do not pass each other, she passes me
> as I halt beside the fence tangled in snow,
> she passes me as I shall never pass her   15
> in this life
>
> Yet I remember us together
> climbing Chocorua, summer nineteen-forty-five
> details of vegetation beyond the timberline
> lichens, wildflowers, birds,   20
> amazement when the trail broke out onto the granite ledge
> sloped over blue lakes, green pines, giddy air
> like dreams of flying
>
> When sisters separate they haunt each other
> as she, who I might once have been, haunts me   25
> or is it I who do the haunting
> halting and watching on the path
> how she appears again through lightly-blowing
> crystals, how her strong knees carry her,
> how unaware she is, how simple   30
> this is for her, how without let or hindrance
> she travels in her body
> until the point of passing, where the skier
> and the cripple must decide
> to recognise each other?   35

Contradictions

Some *contradictions*, firstly, are easily picked out: there is a literal flat contradiction between line 10, 'when we pass each other', and line 13, 'we do not pass each other'. There is a perceptual contradiction in the 'graying dark hair' of line 5 – can it really be both at the same time, and, in any case, if it's almost hidden by a cap how can the speaker know either way? In line 7 the 'fifty-year-old, strong, impatient body' again seems a perceptual contradiction, for the image of youthfulness implied by the 'strong, impatient body' sets up contradictory connotations to those of the phrase 'fifty-year-old'.

Linguistic quirks and aporia

Secondly, the *linguistic quirks and aporia* are those points in the poem where the language itself (rather than the perceptions) seems to be behaving oddly. For instance, in line 9, is 'level' an adjective or a verb? If the former, the meaning is fairly mundane – the two figures are roughly the same height; if the latter, the effect is more dramatic – the other's eyes level and lock with those of the speaker, tracking and maintaining the eye contact as she moves. In lines 24–5, are the two figures sisters or not? The line seems to mean that they are paired *like* sisters, but they are *not* sisters. The speaker's reference to 'she, who I might once have been' is also ambiguous; it could mean 'she, whom I once had the potential to become, or to be like', or 'she whom I might have been like, had I chosen to be'. On the other hand, it could mean 'she, who I perhaps once was (or once was like)'. Then, in line 34, the phrase 'must decide' is a linguistic *non sequitur*: 'must' implies obligation and 'decide' implies choice. It makes sense to say 'You must decide' or 'You must leave him', but it doesn't make sense to say 'You must decide to leave him'. This is indicative of a deeper confusion in the poem between obligation and choice, which is compounded at the end of the poem by placing a question mark after something which isn't a question. Further, is the cripple in line 34 literal or metaphorical? The speaker is moving along paths on and by the ski slopes, 'halt(ing)' in lines 14 and 27, which, of course, implies movement. In what sense, then, is the speaker to be thought of as a cripple?

Shifts

Moving now to the *shifts in person, attitude*, etc., in the first two stanzas the figure described seems to be a stranger to the speaker, someone unknown ('the skier'), though strangely the speaker knows her precise age and knows the colour of her hair even though she is wearing a cap. The speaker speculates about her, as one might about a stranger ('wondering what we have in common', line 11). In the third stanza, however, she seems to become a remembered person ('Yet I remember us together', line 17), with whom the speaker has shared significant moments in the past. Then in the final stanza she seems to have become an apparition, associated with haunting, and materializing in a quasi-mystical way through the snow ('she appears again through lightly-blowing/ crystals', lines 28–9). The differences between these three versions of the skier are so fundamental that the word 'shifts' hardly does them justice.

Absences and omissions

Finally, the *absences and omissions*. Again, these are fundamental. Who *is* the skier? We are never told. At the centre of the poem, then, is something left out, something withheld? Are these two roles ('the skier' and 'the cripple', lines 33–4) two aspects of the same person? The reader should resist the temptation to 'recuperate', or 'narrativize', or opt for the simplest reading, in which two sisters' lives move onto different 'paths' when one is crippled in a climbing accident and her subsequent life is poisoned by sibling envy. The skier seems to connote an alternative self, a self-that-might-have-been, by whom the real self is haunted. The potential self seems to have a degree of hostility towards the actual self (also the scenario of Henry James's ghost story 'The Jolly Corner'), and the self's awareness of this being seems to deconstruct the confident boundaries of her own subjectivity. The deconstructive reading, then, seems to enhance the perceived strangeness of this remarkable poem.

We are left, then, with a poem that seems to be fighting a civil war with itself. There is no secure, overarching vantage point from which it all makes sense. The cat of signification isn't purring any more. Deconstruction, of course, believes that it is characteristic of all language to fight itself in this way, so that any poem, when subject to deconstructive enquiry, would reveal such symptoms to some degree (though obviously not to the same dramatic extent as 'Transit', a poem I chose as my example because it lends itself so well to this approach).

* * *

We started this chapter by tracing the development of criticism and theory, and concluded it by looking at examples of the difference theory can make to textual practice. But the development of criticism and theory is embedded within a broader institutional history – it isn't practised by lone individuals living a high intellectual life in lofty isolation. On the contrary, it is the business, mainly, of people who go into work every day to do it, and who daily swap ideas, gossip, prejudices, and scare stories with fellow workers over coffee, just as they would if they worked in a firm of merchant bankers, or in a department store. 'English Studies', then, has an institutional history, in the same way that the civil aviation industry or income tax collection have. To understand the development of literary theory, and the resulting variety of textual practices, then, we need to place it within the context of the discipline's own institutional history. So that history is the topic of the next chapter.

7 English Now and Then

Studying English seems to us such a natural thing to do that we probably never pause to ask ourselves when it started, or how recently it came to be as it is now. There is, indeed, no reason why the history and development of our own discipline should be a constant preoccupation, but it is a distinct liability to be completely unaware of its history, if only because such unawareness would limit the scope of what we might conceive ourselves as doing when we do English. There is also the real danger that our ignorance might lead us to imagine that present disagreements are entirely new, whereas they are, quite often, replays of past conflicts, so that some knowledge of that past can be immensely useful in understanding the roots of our own disagreements. The view of 'early English' offered here first considers the USA and the UK separately in the nineteenth century, and then conflates the two from the post-First World War period onwards. This joint national focus necessarily entails some neglect of the specific lines of development of the subject elsewhere, particularly in British Commonwealth countries, and in non-Anglophone countries in and beyond Europe. Also, the 'UK' view offered here is really the view from England, and there are different readings of this history from elsewhere within Britain. Robert Crawford, for instance, in *The Scottish Invention of English Literature* (1998), argues that English Studies (which we can roughly define as the formal study of vernacular literature) began in eighteenth-century Scottish universities (with the appointment of professors of Rhetoric), and was exported during the next century to the United States and elsewhere. His book, and those listed in footnote 1 below, will help to provide a broader national and institutional perspective on these issues.[1]

---

1 Gauri Viswanathan, *Masks of Conquest: Literary Study and British Rule in India* (Columbia University Press, 1989); Rajeswari Sunder Rajan, ed., *The Lie of the Land: English Literary Studies in India* (Oxford University Press, 1992); Balz Engler and Renate Haas, *European English Studies: Contributions towards the History of a Discipline* (The English Association, for ESSE, 2000).

EARLY ENGLISH IN AMERICA

In the United States 'English' became a distinct academic discipline towards the end of the nineteenth century.[2] In the earlier part of the century the 'Humanities' section of the college curriculum was based on the study of Latin and Greek, taught by daily 'recitations' in which brief passages were set for study and individual students were called on in class to translate a few sentences and answer questions about any grammatical difficulties contained in the passage. Courses were taught from a single textbook, and 'classes' and 'recitations' were the whole of it – there were no lectures in which a broader view of the literature and culture under study might be offered, and no seminars in which the meaning and significance of the set texts could be discussed. Graduate study in the mid-century period was virtually nonexistent (there were said to be only eight graduate students in the whole of the USA in 1850), and the idea of 'majoring' in a discipline did not exist, so there were no 'electives' (or options), this being a later Harvard innovation. As Gerald Graff remarks, when lectures and written examinations were introduced later in the century at Harvard and Cornell, they were regarded as dangerous innovations, not as the essence of conservative pedagogy which they would be taken as today.

As the century progressed, literature in English was allowed a peripheral presence on the curriculum, and the method of study was directly based upon the 'philological' model imported from German universities, which is to say that it was heavily language-based, involving the teasing out of the grammar of the text, the etymology of the words used in it, the provenance of its images, and the naming and classification of the literary tropes and devices employed by the authors. Highly specialist and scholarly though this kind of thing is, as pedagogy it is more a protracted form of aversion therapy to literature than a way of interesting undergraduates in reading and enjoying major authors. By the 1880s there were annotated editions of major writers – Shakespeare, Spenser, Bunyan, and so on – to cater for this dreary market. But a different approach to literature teaching was also developing, one based on 'rhetoric' rather than philology. These courses would be taught from a reader containing extracts of famous passages from major writers. Students would read them aloud and be coached in doing so with suitable weight and expression, or would memorize them for public performance. From this approach evolved

---

2   I am drawing in this sub-section on Gerald Graff's fascinating and definitive book *Professing Literature: An Institutional History* (University of Chicago Press, 1987).

the Harvard Composition course, in which students would write their own pieces on the same themes, putting into practice the lessons learned from the models. This, of course, is useful vocational training for the professions which many of the male students would later take up, as politicians in local, state, or federal government, as attorneys, or as ministers of religion. But the 'rhetorical' approach, and the emphasis on public speaking, fell out of favour as the century progressed, as it was seen as stimulating a rather vacuous and tricksy style of public speaking; so the Harvard Composition course lost its oral element in 1873 and became a course in writing.

The 'rhetorical' (or non-philological) mantle was inherited by the 'generalists', as Graff calls them, teachers like Henry Wadsworth Longfellow, Charles Eliot Norton, and James Russell Lowell at Harvard, who taught a much more generalized kind of literary appreciation. Generalists and philologists often coexisted uneasily in the same department (a familiar situation), but the drive towards the professionalization of the discipline was already well under way, and the generalists, in spite of their often charismatic and popular lecturing style, were too methodless to prevail in the era of the MLA (the Modern Language Association, founded in 1883, which became the discipline's main professional body in the USA). So the balance was finally tipped against philology only after the First World War, when an upsurge of patriotism inaugurated the formal study of American literature, and the emergent New Critics established for the first time a coherent rationale for the study of literature 'as literature', rather than as language.

EARLY ENGLISH IN THE UK

At Oxford and Cambridge, the UK's only universities in the early nineteenth century, the syllabus was dominated by the study of Latin and Greek, just as in the American colleges. When University College London was founded in 1828, a professor of English Language and Literature was appointed, and likewise at King's College, London, founded the following year, where a professorial appointment was made in 1835 (it was the same person, Thomas Dale, who moved from one to the other). This meant that English could be studied at the new London University, though not as a separate degree subject until 1859. So began the spread of university English nationwide and beyond, as London's degrees could also be taken externally at university colleges (the predecessors of today's large civic universities), in many of the large industrial cities throughout Britain, and overseas in countries under British influence or control.

In many ways, these new English degrees can be seen as part of a move-ment against elitism, for they were a form of education available to those not born into the privileged upper classes whose male members would study Latin and Greek at their public schools, and then go on to Oxford and Cambridge before sliding into comfortable careers in government, the judiciary, the armed forces, or the universities themselves. English degrees were available to women, to those who were not members of the Anglican Church, and to those whose background, while not being impoverished, was not privileged either. This is the heroic 'humanist' story of English Studies which is told in the few sources available until, roughly, the early 1980s.[3] An opposing view, which became dominant in the 1980s during the 'theory wars', sees the spread of English as a middle-class conspiracy to maintain social stability by duping the aspirant lower middle classes into acquiescence with the system that oppresses them. Rather than being given a share in the material wealth to which they are entitled, they are offered cultural 'wealth' instead, in the form of access to Shakespeare, Milton, and similar cultural 'capital', duping them into a belief that they are thereby becoming stakeholders in society as currently structured.[4]

When the subject of English was belatedly established at Oxford in the 1870s, the price exacted by the university was that it should be accompanied by systematic study of the history of the English language and its antecedents – Old English, Middle English, Old Norse, and so on. This form of study included the translation by students of major Old English texts like the epic poem *Beowulf*, and the assumption was that 'hard' content like this would prevent English degrees from becoming a 'soft option' that involved little more than mere 'chatter about Shelley', in the notorious phrase used in the faculty debates by Edward Freeman, an Oxford professor of history.[5] Clearly, close textual study for its own sake was not then envisaged or imagined; this could

---

3   Such as Stephen Potter's *The Muse in Chains* (Cape, 1937, repr. Folcroft, 1973): E. M. W. Tillyard's *The Muse Unchained* (Bowes & Bowes, 1958), and D. J. Palmer's *The Rise of English Studies* (Oxford University Press, 1965).

4   For this version of the history of English, see Brian Doyle, 'The Hidden History of English Studies' in *Re-Reading English*, ed. Peter Widdowson (Methuen, 1982); Terry Eagleton's chapter 'The Rise of English' in his *Literary Theory: An Introduction* (Blackwell, 1983); and Chris Baldick, *The Social Mission of English Studies* (Oxford University Press, 1983).

5   In an article in the *Contemporary Review* in 1887, Freeman explained that what he meant was speculative biographical chatter about *Harriet* Shelley, Shelley's first wife (who drowned herself in the Serpentine in Hyde Park when he abandoned her). Freeman's article is reprinted in a fascinating collection of key documents on 'early English' in the UK, *The Nineteenth-Century History of English Studies*, ed. Alan Bacon (Ashgate, 1998).

hardly be necessary, the assumption was, since the texts were in the student's own language.

All this, it should be added, gives a strictly university perspective on the UK history of English. But it should be emphasized that English had long been an important part of the higher education curriculum outside universities, for instance, at institutes for the part-time education of working people, and at training colleges for teachers. The 1870 Education Act, which established a national system of compulsory elementary education, also provided for the setting up of colleges to train teachers for these new state schools, and English was from the start a major subject on the syllabus at these. Whereas English was only grudgingly accepted onto the university syllabus, at the training colleges it immediately assumed what we would see as something like its mature twentieth-century character, with the emphasis on literary criticism and close reading. As David Shayer writes, in a valuable book about the history of English teaching, 'in fact from 1905 until the mid-twenties, when the universities caught up with them, one can say that for scope, variety, correct priorities and proper study attitudes, the training colleges were offering some of the best English courses in the country.'[6]

EARLY ENGLISH IN PRACTICE

Early English degrees did involve (among other things) close work on literary texts, but in a form which would probably seem rather puzzling to a modern student; for this *is* English, but not as we know it, and the object of attention in close textual study was the language of the text *as language* (that is, as simile, metaphor, rhetorical device, and so on) rather than its literary and thematic significance: in other words, the approach was very much influenced by philology. The following example of a set of model questions about a poem gives us a glimpse into the discipline in the first decade of the twentieth century, when it was in a hybrid or transitional phase. These questions show evident unease about merely philological text work, but the compiler obviously has no very clear idea of what should be offered instead. The example is from David Shayer's book (p. 34), and the questions are actually being recommended for the teaching of literature in schools rather than universities; but they are indicative of a period of uncertainty about how to teach literature in the gap between the growing disillusionment (from the turn of the century onwards) with the old historical-biographical-grammatical approach of the nineteenth century, and the arrival of the 'close reading' pedagogy in the 1920s

6   *The Teaching of English in Schools*, RKP, 1972, p. 31.

and 1930s. For a class on Tennyson's poem 'Break, break, break' the following questions are recommended:

1. Give the derivation and etymology of the word 'break' as used in the poem.

2. Scan the line 'Break, break, break' and compare the metrical effect of 'Ding, dong, bell'.

3. Discuss the influence of geological strata on poetry.

4. Express in good prose the thought that the poet would fain have uttered, and indicate the reason of his disability.

This confusing set of questions is indicative of a desire to move away from talking about authors rather than texts – there is no question here about Tennyson's life, nothing about how the poem was 'made in a Lincolnshire lane at five o'clock in the morning, between blossoming hedges' in 1842 (as Tennyson himself had helpfully explained), nor anything about the unstated subject of the poem, the poet's friend Arthur Hallam, who had died in 1833. Instead, the poem is to be treated more or less 'on the page', so this session is, albeit confusingly, about 'reading literature as literature', with (for instance) attention drawn to the effects of the poem's rhythm and imagery (the 'geological strata').

On the other hand, looking at the etymology of a key word in the poem (as required by the first question) is very much a residual element, harking back to an approach which is essentially philological and obsessed with 'the naming of linguistic parts' in literary texts. All the close work demanded of students and pupils in the nineteenth century (and lingering on in many places into the second half of the twentieth) amounted to this, with the meaning and significance of the lines taken for granted. The bizarre third question about rock strata is prompted, presumably, by the mention of the 'cold grey stones' on which the sea breaks in the poem – but this is clearly either the subject for a PhD thesis or else no subject at all. But perhaps even this question shows a desire to focus 'internally' on what the poem is *about*, rather than (for instance) on what prompted it. The final question (about what the poet would fain express if he could) manifests the same desire, but anyone who could answer it would have the answer to life, the universe, and everything, and would obviously have no need of poetry. (I am reminded of a friend's embarrassment when she was asked, during an English class at school, to explain exactly what Cleopatra meant, in Shakespeare's *Antony and Cleopatra*, when she said, 'Oh, my oblivion is a very Antony'.) Such direct demands upon us to unscrew the inscrutable were explicitly condemned by the American New Critics in their doctrine of the 'heresy of paraphrase', which held that the sentiments expressed in a poem were not usually precisely expressible in any other medium, not even 'good prose'.

TWO REVOLUTIONS AND A 'TURN'

From the period after the First World War onwards, it is possible to see a major convergence in the course of the discipline on the two sides of the Atlantic. Though with different inflections, the discipline is radically reshaped by two revolutionary breaks with its own past; the first, starting in the 1920s in the UK and the 1930s in the USA, involves a new kind of radically text-based study, and the second, about 50 years later, during the 1970s, involves a radical shift to literary theory. In the UK, in the 'Cambridge revolution' of the 1920s, the discipline (to put it crudely) junked much of its own past, a past which had been about such things as the lives of authors, the literary history of genres and 'influences', the quasi-nationalistic celebration of the literary canon as the 'soul' of the nation, and the rhetorical analysis of devices such as metaphor, simile, and allusion within texts. This range of concerns had amounted to a kind of conflation of the American 'philological' and 'generalist' approaches. Instead, under the crucial influence of Cambridge figures like F. R. Leavis, I. A. Richards, and William Empson, it now turned to a rather more austere mode of study, condemning most of the approaches previously available as (in various ways) 'external' to the text, because they studied primarily the political and social context from which the writing emerged, or the philosophical positions embodied in it, or the genre history of which it is a part. The 'Cambridge' mode of thinking radically sidelined all this and sought to focus exclusively on the text itself. The text became, as it were, an object caught in a searchlight, plunging its surrounding contextuality into darkness, a darkness which the very presence of the searchlight rendered all the more impenetrable. The key books which set out the new approach were Richards's *Principles of Literary Criticism* (1924) and *Practical Criticism* (1929), and Empson's *Seven Types of Ambiguity* (1930).

The New Critical revolution of the 1930s in the USA had essentially the same aims and effects, insisting upon a rigorous, text-based focus for literary study, the key books being John Crowe Ransom's *The New Criticism* (1941) and *Understanding Poetry* (1938), by Cleanth Brooks and Robert Penn Warren, who had been students of Ransom's. The effect upon students of literature classes taught in this new way could be immensely powerful, producing a never-forgotten classroom experience, which those who subsequently became teachers themselves often sought to reproduce for their own students. Here, for instance, is an account of the impact of this kind of teaching (the writer has just asked himself the question 'Where did the New Critical revolution take place?'):

> As far as I am concerned the revolution took place in a classroom during my sophomore year. A man walked in and suddenly, instead of taking notes on [Robert] Frost's trip to England, we were asking why 'nothing gold can stay' – in the poem, in our lives, everywhere. He was a new critic. The old critics had talked about history or biography or the sources, without ever getting into the stories and poems. They were dull. The new man offered us live reading. He was not dull. What kept him from being dull (outside of his natural talents) was his motto: read literature as literature. The motto, we heard later, came from something called the New Criticism. It was forcing a change in classroom after classroom, not only on our floor but up on the graduate floor.[7]

Pedagogic revolutions begin like this, when a teacher walks into a classroom and does something different, and the effects on those in the room can last a lifetime.[8]

The second revolution which followed in both countries roughly 50 years later was the arrival of literary theory of the 1970s (as discussed in the previous chapter), and it represented another radical shift by the discipline onto new ground (though, as we saw, the shift was sometimes just a restatement of long-held views in startlingly new terms). The ground in question is the fourth area in the following list of five possible areas of primary interest within English Studies:

1. Traditional scholarship – historical, biographical, linguistic.

2. Close reading, with an implicit human value discovered in the act of reading.

3. The study of literature in its social and cultural contexts.

---

7   From Harold Swardson, *Fighting for Words: Life in the Postmodern University* (Verlag Die Blaue Eule, Essen, Germany, 1999), pp. 42–3. The quoted passage is in ch. 2, 'The Heritage of the New Criticism'.

8   Of course, these procedures too could degenerate into routine, as Valentine Cunningham notes: 'Anyone who was a student in the early 1960s (like me)', he writes, 'will recall the sheer dullness of the by-then established New Critical routines suffocating readings in their affectionate but strangulating grip' (*Reading After Theory*, Blackwell, 2002, p. 38).

4. An 'international' approach to literary study, invoking structuralist, poststructuralist and other foreign critical modes.

5. The aligning of literature with other, more popular modes of signification, notably television and films.[9]

Of course, this kind of model has to leave out all the fine shading: for instance, the traditional scholarship of area 1 obviously did not stop dead in the 1920s, when area 2 became the dominant, but continued to be a force, which is now often called the 'old historicism', as represented in such books as E. M. W. Tillyard's *The Elizabethan World Picture* and Basil Willey's *The Seventeenth-Century Background*. Likewise, the precise relationship between this 'old' historicism of then and the 'new' historicism of today, and between the traditional study of 'sources and influences' on the one hand and current interests in forms of intertextuality on the other, are matters which are difficult to tease out, and cannot be addressed at all in such a broad-scale model. All the same, the model does give us a useful large-scale map of the shifting territory of English Studies, and it has the virtue of highlighting the simplicity of the 'two revolutions' notion of the twentieth-century disciplinary history. Using the model, we can say that 'English' begins with a focus on area 1 ('traditional scholarship'), the 1920s and 1930s revolution switches it to area 2 ('text'), and the 1970s revolution to area 4. Since those two revolutions, the discipline has taken a 'turn' to history again. So, in its current 'double revisionist' phase (that is post-textual revolution and post-theoretical revolution), it favours the 'new historicism' of area 3, but with strong elements of the traditional, or 'old historicist', contextualism of the area 1 focus with which it began its career. Area 5 (for the record) has tended to drift out of the English Studies area and into a realm of Cultural Studies, which is loosely affiliated with Media Studies, Communications Studies, and Sociology. It is easy to say, and easy to see, that a fully adequate study of literature in an ideal world would need to combine elements from areas 1–4. It is equally obvious that this simply cannot be done on an undergraduate syllabus, and that is the source of nearly all the shifts and disagreements which have occurred throughout the history of the discipline.

My argument in Chapter 6 was that the 'theory re-revolution' of the 1970s had many elements of continuity with 'close reading' and New Criticism. In

---

9   This useful list (attributed to John Beer) is given in Bernard Bergonzi's account of the 'theory wars' of the 1980s, pp. 15–16 in the chapter 'Bitterness in the Eighties' in his book *Exploding English: Criticism, Theory, Culture* (Oxford University Press, 1990).

other words, the two major revolutions are, as it happens, related: close readers are always closet theorists, and theorists always closet close readers, each belonging to the Devil's party without knowing it (as Blake said of the Milton of *Paradise Lost*). In textual terms, both tended to find 'infinite riches in a little room' (to use Marlowe's familiar phrase from *The Jew of Malta*): they both home in on specific verbal details of a text and extrapolate from them large areas of (often counter-intuitive) significance, often suspended outside any immediate contextual or historical associations. The effect of this is, however, deeply democratizing, in the sense that once the method has been grasped its effectiveness depends primarily on the mental acumen and ingenuity of the user. A professor might enter the classroom with a vast array of literary-historical knowledge which no student (undergraduate or post-graduate) could hope to emulate, but that intellectual armoury cannot easily be brought to bear on the target, which is often (so to speak) too close for these huge-calibre guns to be trained upon it. Hence, the pedagogic potential of the close reading method is very considerable: everything is brought back to basics, reduced from scholarly high-tech to pedagogic low-tech, and dependent once again on the good teacher's ability to walk into a room, take the most familiar of texts, and say something different about it. Yet the demands of that kind of pedagogy are both exhausting and exhaustible, and it was inevitable that sooner or later we would begin once again to talk about Frost's trip to England, not to mention Shelley's first wife, the problem of the succession in Elizabethan England, the cultural effects of the Exclusion Crisis after the Restoration, and the plight of the Victorian handloom weavers. All these except the first two are very typical of the topics on which much energy is currently expended in English departments. The text, it seems, is like a bright light, which we cannot go on looking at for long without needing to turn away and focus for a while on something a bit easier on the eye. That is one of the reasons behind the 'turn' to history which took place in the 1990s.

CODA: ENGLISH HERE AND THERE

English degree courses today are not, of course, the same worldwide, and being aware of the range and diversity of English degrees can help us to under-stand and appreciate the special characteristics of our own local version of English. Potentially, the differences are infinite, but these are some of the main ones. Firstly, if you take an English degree in a country where English is a foreign language (rather than in Anglophone countries like the USA, the UK, or Australia), then 'English' will mean language study as well as literary study, probably in more or less equal measure, with courses in phonetics, semantics, grammar, contemporary usage, and so on. So your study will be multi-disciplinary, in the sense that you will be studying both literature and language in a sustained way. Whether it will also be *inter*disciplinary – that is, with real integration of the language and literature elements – will depend on where you are studying, and where your teachers did their own training.

Secondly, if you take your degree in the USA, then you will receive systematic training in writing technique (in courses with titles like 'Freshman Composition') to a far greater extent than anywhere else in the world. This will mostly occur in the early, pre-specialist stages of the degree, when you will also be taking introductory courses in other disciplines. These pre-specialist stages are also more extended in Scottish universities, and to a lesser extent in Wales, than they are in England. Thirdly, opportunities to do your own original creative writing as part of an English degree will be much greater in the USA, and more recently in the UK, than elsewhere in the world. In Europe outside the UK, the distinction between critical and creative work remains very firm, and the kind of writing students are required to undertake often places more emphasis on acquiring sound scholarly procedures of research and applica-tion than on the encouragement of independent critical judgement. Likewise, the style of teaching in the UK tends towards the 'dialogic', placing open seminar discussion at the centre of the syllabus, whereas elsewhere the tendency is often towards the 'monologic' or 'transmission' model of teaching, with lectures being seen as the key element in the learning process. This can sometimes have the result that, to overseas eyes, the UK student can seem bizarrely ungrounded in some of the basics. These differing cultural practices can become matters of great importance if you take part (as many students do today) in exchange semesters at universities abroad. Fourthly, the course itself will be longer 'elsewhere' than the standard three-year length of the British undergraduate degree. Finally, the inner canon of writers regarded as the cornerstones of the syllabus will vary greatly across the globe, with black and women writers, for instance, being given a much more prominent place in the USA than elsewhere, and the syllabus in Europe tending to give more emphasis to the British writers of the 'realist' school from the 1950s and 1960s (Graham Greene, John Braine, Kingsley Amis, for instance) than is currently the case in the UK, where many courses seem to jump straight from modernism to postmodernism, that is, from (say) Joyce, Woolf, and Eliot to Toni Morrison, Angela Carter, and Hanif Kureishi.

* * *

So far in this book, we have, for the most part, referred to the novels and poems under discussion in a brisk and confident fashion, as if there could never be any doubt about what we mean when we say (for example) *King Lear* or 'Frost at Midnight'. Of course, it would be difficult to undertake the kind of broad, general discussion of literature featured in this book if we remained perpetually conscious of the fact that these textual entities always have a degree of instability, in spite of their prominence as literary classics which most educated people have seen, or read, or at least know about. For the literary theories discussed in the previous chapter have radically 'destabilized' the notion of what a literary work is, and these textual instabilities are often highlighted, too, even by the more traditional forms of literary history. So the next chapter is about the question of the literary text itself, and the various processes of mediation it passes through before it reaches the reader. In particular, the chapter considers the role of the textual editor, who is often responsible for the precise form in which the author's words finally reach us. Authors seldom publish their own work, and once they put down their pens (or switch off their word processors) the work enters a complex process of transmission before it finally reaches the scholar's desk, or the reader's bedside table. That is the process we look at in the next chapter.

8 The Text as Text

ON AVOIDING TEXTUAL EMBARRASSMENT

It's not unusual to pick up a book and read it, taking it for granted that what you are reading is (uniquely) the text named on the cover. You might, for instance, be asked to read Henry James's famous 'novella' (short novel) 'Daisy Miller' for a seminar. This is currently available in paperback from Penguin, Wordsworth Classics, Dover Thrift Editions, and Oxford Paperbacks. There are also several expensive scholarly editions, plus an audio-book edition, and a downloadable 'e-book' version from Amazon. However, you may notice during the seminar that when tutor or other students quote from the text the wording in your own edition is not always the same, and that sometimes the differences even seem quite significant. Why is this? Ultimately, it is because (unlike the birth of a baby or the launching of a ship) the writing of a book is not a once-and-for-all event. On the contrary, it may take years; and in the author's eyes the book may never be a finished and closed account at all, so that each reprint or new edition may be seen as an opportunity for further revisions. Perhaps it is sometimes literally the case (as Ecclesiastes says) that 'of the making of many books there is no end'.

'Daisy Miller' is a good example of a book whose writing never really had an end, for James first published it in the *Cornhill Magazine* of June–July 1878, when he was 35. It was revised for its first appearance in book form in England in the following year, and it was given its final substantial revision for the collected New York Edition of James's work, which appeared in 1909, when the writer was an eminent man of letters of 66. So the writing of 'Daisy Miller' is an 'event' which lasts for 30 years. This story was James's only popular 'hit' – the American book edition which appeared later in 1878 (a few months after the story's first publication in the *Cornhill*) sold 20,000 copies in a couple of weeks. It is probably because of its very success that it is 'one of the most extensively revised of all James's works for the New York Edition. (It has been estimated that 90 per cent of the sentences were altered in some way and some 15 per cent more material added.)'[1]

Yet will it matter, really, which text of 'Daisy Miller' you have taken into the seminar with you? Perhaps a discussion develops about the characterization of Daisy: one group sees her as a kind of proto-feminist who disdainfully rejects the codes of behaviour considered appropriate at the time for 'nice girls'; in evidence they quote Giovanelli's remark at the end (referring to the fatal visit to the Coliseum) that 'she did what she liked'. But this group have a text based on the New York Edition (probably Jean Gooder's Oxford paper-back): yours (probably the Penguin) is based on the 1879 text, which doesn't contain that line: in your text Giovanelli just says 'she wanted to go', which is quite different in tone and implication.[2] If the seminar registers the difference, and begins to spend a little time on the textual question, you may look down Gooder's list of variant readings. An obvious task for a tutor to set would be to ask you to try to describe any patterns or tendencies you can detect in the changes – what is it that James was seeking to achieve by making them?

One answer would be that he often seems to be aiming for 'retrospective thematization', that is, he is belatedly heightening what was widely perceived to be the central conflict in the story, that between American 'nature' and European 'culture'. Daisy is the 'natural' American whose free and open behaviour is untainted by over-conventionalized European norms: hence, several of the changes made for the New York Edition introduce words like 'native' or 'natural' into descriptions of Daisy: in 1879 Giovanelli (with whom the scandalized high-class, American expatriate society in Rome had assumed she could be having an affair) says of Daisy (in the same passage at the end of the story) that of all the women he has met 'she was the most innocent'. In 1909 this becomes 'Also – naturally! – the most innocent.' In 1879, earlier in the story, 'Daisy turned to Winterbourne, beginning to smile again', whereas in 1909 this becomes 'Daisy at last turned on Winterbourne a more natural and calculable light.' The older James must have thought this an improvement, or he wouldn't have made the change, but I don't want to evoke the contrast (which Horne gently parodies) between a youthful 'freshness' of style and the more orotund

1   Quoted from the 'Note on the Texts' (p. xxix) in *Daisy Miller and Other Stories*, ed. Jean Gooder (Oxford University Press, 1985). This excellent edition contains a list of variant readings, so that some of the main differences between the 1879 and 1909 texts can be seen at a glance.

2   I am drawing quite closely here on Phillip Horne's chapter 'Henry James at Work: The Question of Our Texts', pp. 63–78, in *The Cambridge Companion to Henry James* (Cambridge University Press, 1998). Horne's chapter is about 'Daisy Miller', and he is the author of *Henry James and Revision: The New York Edition* (Oxford University Press, 1990). In thesis form, this was one of the sources used in Gooder's Oxford paperback.

phraseology of James's 'maturity'. Frequently the later Jamesian style works well for the often older characters of the later fiction, but it seems (to me) less appropriate to a character as young as Daisy. In any case, it is notoriously easy, in the case of a writer who was a heavy reviser, to get our prose stereotypes mixed up, as a critic as eminent as F. R. Leavis did, when he inadvertently quoted the revised 1907 text of an 1875 Henry James novel to illustrate the superior 'freshness' of James's *early* style. Leavis (it should be said in mitigation) made his mistake only in a review, and later admitted his error, though in a form which evidences a very high level of what might now be called spin-doctoring: Leavis admits that the bits of James that strike us as 'characteristic felicities' are often late revisions, but the point is that the late revisions aren't needed to 'make the writing wonderfully intelligent, brilliant and sensitive'.[3]

The general point being made here, then, is that the text often has a double, and that it *does* matter which one we read. At the very least, in order to save ourselves possible textual embarrassment, we should make a point of knowing the source of the text we are reading (which will nearly always be indicated in a 'Note on the text' printed after the introduction), and we should also be aware of the existence of any alternative versions. Thus, there are Quarto and Folio versions of *Lear* and *Hamlet*; there are different endings for well-known Romantic and Victorian poems like Coleridge's 'Frost at Midnight' and Tennyson's 'The Lady of Shalott'; there are significant differences between the magazine and the book versions of controversial novels like Hardy's *Tess of the d'Urbervilles*; and T. S. Eliot's *The Waste Land*, a key modernist work, exists in two very different versions.[4] These are matters which must concern

3 Quoted by Horne, p. 72. Leavis's error was discussed by John Butt in *Art and Error: Modern Textual Editing*, ed. Ronald Gottesman and Scott Bennett (Methuen, 1970), and is mentioned from time to time in discussions of Leavis (e.g. in George Watson's *Never Ones for Theory: England and the War of Ideas*, Lutterworth Press, 2000, p. 76).

4 Most general books on Shakespeare have a chapter on the question of the text: for an excellent example see Russ McDonald, ch. 6, 'What is your Text?', in *The Bedford Companion to Shakespeare: An Introduction with Documents*, 2nd edn (Bedford St Martin's, 2001). The different versions of 'Frost at Midnight' are discussed in the chapter 'The Politics of "Frost at Midnight"', in Paul Magnuson's *Reading Public Romanticism* (Princeton University Press, 1998), though this more extreme style of discussion represents the kind of 'textual anxiety' which I am not recommending here. For 'The Lady of Shalott' see Chapter 4 of the present book, and for *Tess of the D'Urbervilles* see J. T. Laird's compact and fascinating book *The Shaping of 'Tess of the D'Urbervilles'* (Oxford University Press, 1975). To compare the original *Waste Land* with the published text see *The Waste Land*, ed. Valerie Eliot, a facsimile and transcript of the original drafts, including the annotations of Ezra Pound (Faber & Faber, 1971). To read about the rediscovery of the original manuscripts of this poem as the story first broke, see Donald Gallop. 'The "Lost" Manuscripts of T. S. Eliot', *TLS* (7 Nov. 1968), pp. 1238–40.

us as English specialists, even though it is very far from my purpose to provoke a debilitating 'textual anxiety' of the kind which is sometimes evident at conferences and graduate seminars. Rather, my emphasis is on how much can be learned from some consideration of 'textual variants' and the issues they raise. This is the focus of the next section.

'IN TWO MINDS': BLAKE AND KEATS

Some kinds of reading feel like trespassing. Sometimes this can be a pleasurable thrill, as when we read the published letters or diaries of well-known writers. Even when these have been written with half an eye on publication, they still offer a special sense of intimacy with the author which other kinds of writing do not provide. But when we read the unpublished manuscript drafts of well-known poems, then the sense that we shouldn't really be there at all is stronger still, for we are looking at what the author explicitly rejected as wrong, or inadequate, or clumsy. We know that authors didn't want us to see these lines because they were not the lines which they published. Of course, this fact gives these authorial rejections an irresistible fascination. In them we see the great author groping in the dark towards the light-switch of inspiration, and often just missing. It is sometimes rather like that famous Heineken lager advert seen on TV in the 1980s which showed William Wordsworth beginning to compose a poem, and starting with the rather flat line: 'I used to walk about a lot on my own.' It clearly wasn't quite right, so he screwed up the paper and tried again, this time producing the line: 'I used to wander around the countryside by myself.' Still no good, so he takes a long draught of Heineken (which reaches the poets other beers can't reach), and then, with immense confidence, rolls out the line: 'I wandered lonely as a cloud/ That floats on high o'er vale and hill.'

Well, in poets' drafts we often find lines which, in their self-evident inadequacy, can be surprisingly like 'I used to walk about a lot on my own'. Sometimes the difference between the published lines and the lines in draft is only a matter of a single word, but it can be the crucial word, the one which seems most characteristic of the whole poem. This, for instance, is the start of William Blake's famous poem 'London' as published:

> I wander through each chartered street,
> Near where the chartered Thames does flow,
> And mark in every face I meet
> Marks of weakness, marks of woe.

These lines seem to have a kind of majestic inevitability, as if they had always existed, and the voice has an unmistakable air of poetic confidence and authority. Perhaps we could all imagine ourselves being William Blake, but surely we *couldn't* quite imagine ourselves writing those lines. There is something about that strange word 'chartered' that (I take it) you just couldn't ever imagine yourself choosing. What does 'chartered' mean, precisely? Critics have never really agreed. The streets are owned by the corporations of the City of London; they are the mortgaged territory of proto-capitalism which generates both great wealth and great poverty, and the word 'chartered' seems to hint at this trumping of the human by the legalistic – but there is surely more to it than that. And, anyway, even if we *could* imagine ourselves using the word 'chartered' once, we could never imagine repeating it immediately in the next line. This word 'chartered', in fact, seems to encapsulate the sombre individuality of Blake's poetic vision, and it's impossible to imagine the poem without it. But hang on. This isn't what Blake first wrote. Behind these mesmeric lines there is an equivalent to 'I used to walk about a lot on my own', for this is what Blake first wrote:

> I wander through each dirty street,
> Near where the dirty Thames does flow,
> And mark in every face I meet
> Marks of weakness, marks of woe.

It's quite a shock, isn't it? If we can imagine ourselves being Blake – an impoverished, passionately left-wing poet – then these are exactly the lines we *can* imagine ourselves writing. These lines seem to be produced almost on poetic auto-pilot: they are the kind of poetic language which the Victorian poet Gerard Manley Hopkins called 'Parnassian', which is a high poetic diction of a type which can be rolled out by poets who have learned the craft. Parnassian is not ridiculous or despicable; on the contrary, it is often dignified and competent. It has the characteristic tone and timbre of a particular poet; but it lacks that additional twist of strangeness, or hauntingness, or some such extra quality. Hopkins realized, with a sudden loss of faith, that his great contemporary Tennyson wrote in Parnassian most of the time. He defines it in a letter to his friend Baillie (10 September 1864):

> Now it is a mark of Parnassian that one could conceive oneself writing
> it if one were the poet. Do not say that *if* you were Shakespeare you can
> imagine yourself writing *Hamlet,* because that is just what I think you
> *cannot* conceive.[5]

It is very curious too, that eminent people can be taken in by Parnassian. The
major critic F. W. Bateson (whom I greatly admire, in spite of his occasional
critical aberrations) actually believed that the original version was better than
the final one. He writes in his book *The Scholar Critic* (1972) that 'the explicit
"dirty" seems better to me than the more pretentious and obscure "chartered"'.
Be that as it may, what we see in poets' manuscripts is how very thin the line
can be which divides the production of routine Parnassian from that something more which poets can produce at the height of their powers. But, when
we look at poets' drafts, it is often striking that the routine and the mundane
lie so close to what seems a universe of quality beyond them.

I'm going to look now at another manuscript example from another
Romantic poet – John Keats and his famous narrative poem 'The Eve of St
Agnes'. This poem, as you will probably remember, is a retelling of a medieval
tale. The young man Porphyro has hidden himself in Isabella's bedroom
because he wants to be there when she wakes up. There is a legend which says
that young women dream of their future husbands (or husband) on the Eve
of St Agnes. He hopes that his hidden presence on this night in the room of
his beloved Isabella will influence her into dreaming about *him.* At least, that's
his excuse. Verse 26 is the one in which Keats describes the unsuspecting
Isabella undressing for bed, watched by the hidden Porphyro. As you might
be able to imagine (whether or not you can imagine yourself being Keats) this
verse presents the writer with a number of serious difficulties. For many
readers, this is the verse for which they have been waiting impatiently all the
way through the previous 25 stanzas. But, clearly, it has to be done tastefully,
otherwise it might seem like a deliberately titillating soft-porn scenario. Not
surprisingly, therefore, Keats's manuscript shows him experiencing some
difficulty with this stanza, and there are crossings out and fresh starts in
abundance. Below is a printed representation of these handwritten sheets (as
they are reproduced in the section called 'Poems in Process' at the back of the
fifth edition of the *Norton Anthology of English Literature: The Major Authors,*
1987). Words which were different in the first draft are italicized, and the
original word or phrase is given in square brackets at the end of the line.

5   Hopkins's letter to Baillie is discussed by Christopher Ricks in his essay
    'Literary Principles as Against Theory' in his book *Essays in Appreciation*
    (Oxford University Press, 1998). Ricks sees it as an example of using a literary
    principle, rather than a literary *theory.*

'THE EVE OF ST AGNES', STANZA 26

1. *Anon* his heart revives: her *vespers* done,	[But soon] [prayers]
2. Of all its wreathéd pearls her hair she *frees*;	[strips]
3. Unclasps her *warméd* jewels one by one	[bosom]
4. Loosens her *fragrant* bodice; by degrees	[bursting]
5. Her *rich* attire *creeps rustling* to her knees:	[sweet] [falls light]
6. Half-hidden, like *a mermaid in sea-weed*,	[a Syren of the sea]
7. *Pensive awhile she dreams awake*, and sees,	
	[She stands awhile in dreaming thought]
8. In fancy, fair St Agnes in her bed,	
9. But dares not look behind, or all the charm is *fled*.	[dead]

The questions I would I ask about this stanza are these:

- Can we detect any patterns in these changes?
- If so, do they give us any clues about the kind of effect Keats is aiming for?
- Are all these changes for the better?
- If not, in which cases were first thoughts better?

I will incorporate tentative answers to the questions in my own comments on Keats's manuscript changes. One evident pattern is that the second thoughts tend to prefer a word or form which is antique or 'medieval' in tone, so that, in the first line, 'Anon' is preferred to 'But soon', and 'vespers' to 'prayers'. This seems to fit the evoked atmosphere, which is mystical and mysterious, and hence suited to the retelling of a romantic legend. In the second line the word 'frees' seems more in keeping with this dreamy atmosphere than 'strips', which would suggest a much more brisk and purposeful undressing. 'Frees' implies both the thickness of the hair and the elaborateness of the coiffure, which has richly intertwined it with adornments. The word 'frees' is similar in implied pace and mood to 'unclasps' in line 3, which again suggests an unhurried, musing atmosphere. 'Warméd' in the same line (pronounced as two syllables) replaces 'bosom': the former is vividly sensuous without being explicit, whereas the latter is crudely explicit, but without any particular force. Exactly the same could be said about the rejected 'bursting' bodice in line 4 – it is almost comically explicit, evoking at best a snigger, like the comic sexuality of the British 'Carry On' films of the 1960s; by contrast, 'fragrant' is strongly sensuous, and it is interesting how both these words ('warméd' and 'fragrant') evoke by implication the intense arousal of the hidden observer, rather than the sensibility of Isabella, since neither of these qualities would be particularly apparent or remarkable to the wearer herself.

The rejected 'sweet' in line 5 would have done the same, but Keats prefers 'rich' (an objective rather than a subjective description) to enhance the sound effect which is the main quality of line 5. The sound depicted is the rustle of the heavy, layered material of the dress as it is gradually removed: the effect is to emphasize, again, the antique, medieval setting, and perhaps the restrictions and conventionalities from which the couple wish to escape. The escape from the garments is gradual, not an instant floating free, as would be implied by 'falls light', and this allows the 'freeze-frame' effect in line 6, as the moment when the garment is half on and half off suggests the image of a mermaid half-hidden in seaweed. This is preferred to the 'Syren of the sea', which would suggest a malign female force (the Sirens, in classical mythology, enticed sailors by their haunting singing, bringing them in too close to the shore, and thus to shipwreck). The implication of using the word 'Syren' would be almost that Isabella is deliberately enticing Porphyro to his ruin; so Keats switches the image to the mermaid, sometimes reputed to be the rescuers of shipwrecked mariners.

The freeze-frame effect continues in line 7, as Isabella pauses, half in the dress and half out of it, momentarily lost in thought, but this line is more completely recast than any other in the stanza, though the resulting shift in meaning is very slight. 'Pensive' has a slight 'soft focus' effect in comparison with 'thought', but Keats seems mainly to be 'braking' the stanza before its climactic moment of the mental vision of St Agnes in the bed. The slowing is achieved by varying the metrical regularity of the stress pattern. In the draft, the iambic beat has its regular alternation, which can be represented by showing the stressed syllables in bold, and breaking the line into its iambic feet:

She **stands** / a **while** / in **dream** / ing **thought** / and **sees**

This is a completely regular iambic pentameter line, which is to say that it has five feet, each foot having two stresses, the heavy stress coming after the light one. This is the metre of vast amounts of English verse, and the iambic drum beats with complete regularity through the first five lines of the stanza, so that you can take any of them and mark the stress pattern in exactly the same way ('Of **all**/ its **wreath**/ed **pearls**/ her **hair**/ she **frees**', and so on). But the pattern shifts in line 6, so that we could not stress it in this way without making it sound ridiculous. Without getting over-technical about it, we can say that the effect of breaking (and braking) the iambic pattern in lines 7 and 8 is to focus on, and increase the impact of, the vision of St Agnes, and this seems to be the reason why Keats makes a major reshaping of line 7 without otherwise altering the sense or feel of the line to any great extent.

The final change in line 9 (of 'dead' to 'fled'), by contrast, has no bearing on the form of the verse at all, since one monosyllabic word is substituted for another which has the same rhyme. But 'fled', again, has a softer and more evocative tone, helping to maintain the romantic, suspended atmosphere which culminates with Keats's famous line representing the sexual consummation in words which are erotic without, again, being sexually explicit, for as she lies in bed dreaming of her future husband, 'into her dream he melted'. Looking at a poet's drafts, then, can give us a remarkable insight into the workings of the poetic process, so that we seem to be colluding in the dilemmas and verbal choices which are the essence of the art and craft of poetry itself.

SEARCHING FOR THE ONE TRUE TEXT

But which one, we might ask ourselves, is the 'true' text of Keats's stanza? How much should an editor of a text tell us about the composition process we have just been examining? Let's start our consideration of this question with a discussion exercise, one which takes up issues already raised implicitly during this chapter. The case is hypothetical, but the issues are fundamental. Imagine that you are editing a definitive critical edition of the stories of Ima Jeenius (1880–1956). The first story in the collection was written when Jeenius was 23. The question is, which of the available versions of this story will you use as your copy-text (that is, the one which will provide the basis of your printed edition)? In other words, which, in your view, is the 'true' text? Here are your choices:

Text 1. This is a handwritten manuscript (a 'holograph'), signed, and dated '1903', by Jeenius. It is the earliest known version of the story. It contains deletions and substitutions, and it is possible in these cases to read both what Jeenius first wrote and what Jeenius later decided was better.

Text 2. This is also a holograph. It is the manuscript which Jeenius sent to the magazine which first published it. Essentially, it is a fair copy of Text 1, usually with the substitutions from that text preferred, but occasionally with the original deleted wording restored. There are also some changes entered in a different handwriting, known from external evidence to be that of the magazine's editor.

Text 3. This is an office-made typescript on the magazine's headed paper. It is essentially the same as Text 2, but there are some corrections and changes made in the handwriting of the author. The alterations in another's hand from that text have been incorporated, and none of these has been altered back.

Text 4. This is a set of corrected printer's proofs for the version printed in the magazine. The proof corrections are in the author's hand, and contain further deletions and substitutions, mostly very minor, except for an added paragraph.

Text 5. This is the version actually printed in the magazine. There are a few minor changes which were not indicated in Text 4; it is not known whether or not these were instigated by the author. (They *may* have been; the author would have received one proof copy to retain and one to return, and might have reread the retained copy after returning the corrections and subsequently sent a telegram (let's say) with further changes.)

Text 6. In 1923, 20 years after its first magazine publication, the story appeared in book form in a collection of Jeenius's stories. This version makes some further changes from the magazine version, all presumed to have been instigated by the author. Generally, they tend towards greater detail and explicitness on sexual matters, enabled partly by the greater broad-mindedness of the 1920s. In this book the story has a certain title, and contains a line which was widely quoted, and indeed became virtually synonymous with Jeenius in the public mind. No other new version of the text published in Jeenius's lifetime used this title or this line, but this edition was *reprinted* many times over the next quarter-century, and indeed became the main source of Jeenius's considerable income and status. In the 1953 lecture (see below, *Text 8*) Jeenius expressed dislike for both the well-known title and the famous line. All the same, critics have always referred to the story by this title, and most critical discussions of Jeenius have something to say about this line.

Text 7. In 1950, to mark the 70th birthday of the now famous Jeenius, a collected edition of the works was published. Jeenius revised many of the stories for this edition, and this one contains an unusually high number of changes. Jeenius reversed some of the changes made in the 1920s published version, partly in response to critics' tendency to prefer the earlier (less sexually explicit) version (on the grounds that it was more subtle). This is the last version of the text actually seen through the press by Jeenius.

Text 8. In 1953, in a British Academy lecture, Jeenius reminisced about the publication of this first story and indicated some dissatisfaction with *all* the published versions of the tale. The author's ideal version, it was indicated, would probably contain elements from all seven of these versions. The author was specific about some of these elements and vague about others. (So 'Text 8' is a notional text, not a physical text, but an editor might aim to construct it, following Jeenius's hints.)

Text 9. After Jeenius's death there was a demand for new editions of the works, which were now set texts on English courses. The story was republished in a collection called *The Portable Jeenius*, using Text 7 as the basic copy text, but incorporating the preferences which Jeenius had been explicit about in the lecture description of Text 8.

As a first step in thinking about the problems of textual editing, as exemplified in this imaginary (but not untypical) case, you might try to decide upon your general editorial approach: here are some broad options for you to consider.

Editorial primitivism

As 'primitivist' editors, we would try to reconstruct the story as it was in Jeenius's original conception of it, before it became 'contaminated' by the editorial process, by contact with the 'market', by the tastes of a readership that has specific culturally constructed preferences and prejudices, and by the later tinkerings of an older and established author keen to present a certain self-image, a certain 'narrative' for the career as a whole. So our overriding aim as primitivists would be 'authenticity', to restore the tale to its original state, in the form in which it first flowed from the pen of Jeenius. If Jeenius, being young, and desperate for publication, was persuaded by editors to make changes or additions, for whatever reason (perhaps because the editor thought readers too prudish to accept certain incidents or phrases, or too dim to pick up anything not spelled out for them), then we will aim to remove these alterations and restore what Jeenius first wrote. We will even seek to save Jeenius from the later authorial self, whom we instinctively stereotype as a conservative compromiser, rather than an artist whose technique was constantly being refined as the career went on. The text which results from our editorial efforts may well please nobody at all except other editors, being, perhaps, clumsier and cruder than we had ever thought of Jeenius as being, and perhaps even lacking the parts which readers came to see as most typical of Jeenius's genius. Lovers of Jeenius may even be rather scandalized at what we have done to the text, rather as the most recent 'restoration' of

Leonardo da Vinci's painting *The Last Supper* has produced a (to many) shockingly pale and patchy image, which, it is true, has been freed of all the work of past restorers, but now seems hardly to be a painting at all.[6]

The procedures of primitivist editing are highly technical and meticulous, but the approach seems to rest on very familiar attitudes to creativity which are rooted in ideas which go back to the Romantic period. The primitivist seems to believe that literary creativity is essentially about the lone, talented individual conceiving thoughts in isolation. It can never have a social dimension (in which friends, editors, readers, and so on might play a part); it happens in an instant, not over an extended period of time, and it believes that only first thoughts are real thoughts, just as the romantic novelists of the late eighteenth century (whom Jane Austen challenged in her novel *Persuasion*) believed that only first loves ('first attachments') are real, and that only young love is true love. Of course, the editorial primitivist would indignantly deny believing any such thing as this implies about creativity, but these are surely the attitudes which the primitivist editorial endeavour embodies. Another name for it might be 'first intentionalism', since it strives to uncover the text which resulted from the first intentions of its author.

Last intentionalism

The opposite editorial approach might be called 'last intentionalism'. As editors of this persuasion, we would regard the creative process as something cumulative and sustained over many years. We will seek to construct a text which incorporates the *culmination* of the author's work upon it; our ideal will be to offer the latest version of the text which had authorial approval and which incorporates the author's mature thoughts upon it. Here the underlying assumptions is that artists grow, and that those whom the gods love don't

6   See *Leonardo: The Last Supper,* by Harlow Tighe (University of Chicago Press, 2001), discussed in the *New York Review of Books* (9 Aug. 2001). The main aim of the year 2000 restoration of the painting was to remove the work of previous restorers, so that all the paint which remains to be seen is paint applied by Leonardo. The result is to reduce a famous image to a ruin, because the original work began to deteriorate almost as soon as it was completed. Since previous restorers could see more of Leonardo's work than we can now, and presumably attempted to reproduce it, the process of removing what they did may seem arrogantly misguided. Likewise, the greater closeness of earlier editors to the author of the text should make us cautious about deleting their work. At any rate, it is helpful to think of textual editing as 'restoration' work which has many ethical problems in common with what happens in the art world.

always die young. Most writers reserve the right to revise works when they are being republished, so that an individual poem (for instance) may have subtle differences between a first magazine appearance, its appearance in a first collection, its appearance in a mid-career *Selected Poems,* and its appearance in a definitive *Collected Poems.* If the latter came out during the poet's lifetime, and was seen through the press by the poet (meaning that the poet saw and corrected the proofs), then we can assume that this version represents final thoughts, and completes the creative process as far as that poem is concerned. We may not feel ourselves that it is necessarily the best version, and it may well be that at some point in the process of revisiting the poem over the years the poet lost touch with the original impulse that brought it into being. But, all the same, if we think the poet a great poet (or even just a good one), then we may decide to allow the poet's judgement to override our own. This strategy, though, does seem to be especially fraught in the case of poets who lived long lives and whose political views shifted during that time. Two well-known cases are William Wordsworth and W. H. Auden. In Wordsworth's case, the straight-down-the-line 'last intentionalist' editor would have to prefer the 1850 text of *The Prelude* to the original which Wordsworth wrote as a young man, and which readers have overwhelmingly preferred. In the case of Auden, we would have to accept the old Auden's repudiation of 'September 1st 1939', one of his best and best known poems, and not print it at all, since Auden in his later years wanted to suppress it entirely, or at least emend the famous line 'We must love one another or die' to 'We must love one another *and* die', for, as Auden said (in effect), not dying is not an option. It is perhaps becoming obvious, then, that neither first nor last intentionalism, pursued in exclusion of every other consideration, is likely to produce the best possible all-round text – so what other options are there?

Syncretism

Some editorial situations, by contrast, are fairly straightforward: Keats, for instance, was dead at the age of 26, so did not live to revisit 'The Eve of St Agnes' as an eminent middle-aged poet who might want to shift the emphasis of the material. It seems to me self-evident that his second thoughts (in the 'Eve of St Agnes' example just considered) usually refine the project and make the lines more effective, but the matter would become more difficult to decide as second thoughts become nineteenth and twentieth thoughts at an increasing distance from the original conception. Yet, *sometimes,* much later thoughts are indeed improvements, and as an editor we might want to incorporate these into our text, even though we would not want to adopt either the full-scale 'last intentionalist' or 'first intentionalist' position. If we decide that our editorial aim will be to avoid privileging either the 'early' author or the 'late' author, while wanting to remain open to both 'early' and 'late' insights, then we might opt for 'syncretism'. As syncretist editors our aim would be to produce an 'ideal' text of this story. The version we print would incorporate early and late thoughts judiciously, using whatever external evidence is available, and extrapolating from this where necessary. Once again, the possibility of pleasing everybody with a syncretist text is remote, and, while the aims seem logical and laudable, the outcome may well provoke some unease. For one thing, the text we produce will never have appeared under the author's name during the author's lifetime, so that it may well seem to be under the ownership not of its author but of its editor, who may indeed then possess copyright of this new text (through the publishers), and expect to be asked for permission by scholars who wish to quote from it. This will seem an anomaly to most readers, and to many scholars, for how can an editor *own* a text? Yet something like this is the present situation with texts of James Joyce's *Ulysses*, a seminal modernist novel which, in the 1990s, generated competing and combative editorial teams, each dedicated to the goal of producing the definitive text. Editors of the competing texts point out that the original texts of the novel (which avoided prosecution for obscenity by being typeset in France by printers who did not read English) contained innumerable errors, but we might feel, all the same, that this error-ridden text is the one which made Joyce famous, and that that text, strictly speaking, *is* the 'true' *Ulysses*, and therefore the one which should serve as the base text for modern reprints. But at this point the problem begins to seem deeply philosophical – is the 'real' *Ulysses* the text which Joyce had in mind and had *meant* to give the public, or is it the text which the public actually received, with all its imperfections and accidents?

Populism

If you believe as an editor that the true text is the one actually received by the readership at the end of the publication process, then you might want to subscribe to the editorial principle of 'populism'. As populists, we will prioritize the text which has been 'canonized' by 'use and custom'. To publish means to give a piece of writing to the public. Neither author nor critic has the right to take back the gift, we would argue, even for the purpose of making a series of adjustments before returning it to its rightful owners. In the main, we would want to accept the book in the form in which it had its most definitive success, even if, for instance, its author had given it a different title, or no title at all, or had placed the material it contains in a different order. This is the case with D. H. Lawrence's first collection of stories, which appeared in 1915 under the title *'The Prussian Officer' and Other Stories*. Lawrence did not call any of his stories 'The Prussian Officer', and he did not intend the one to which the publisher gave this name to be the 'flagship' story of the volume. His publisher, however, felt that, with the outbreak of the war, he could cash in on the widespread interest in German militarism by using this title, and he also changed Lawrence's proposed ordering of the tales so that this one became the culmination of the volume. Should a modern editor repudiate all this and aim to reproduce the manuscript as it was when Lawrence sent it to the publisher? Obviously, that manuscript is of great interest, and we want to know about it, and about how Lawrence had intended the book to be. But we cannot reverse literary history and wish *'The Prussian Officer' and Other Stories* out of existence, for that book is what *actually* happened, and not the one which Lawrence had in mind. We cannot expect, surely, that readers can be corrected belatedly and begin to call it by a different name. To think otherwise would be to concede to editors not just the copyright and ownership of texts but the overlordship of literary history itself. As with every other sphere of life, the events of literary history are sometimes the result of accident, and writers, just like the rest of us, have to accept that.

I hope that the above discussion of some of the problems faced by textual editors will not result in the generation of pointless 'textual anxiety' in readers. Its purpose is simply to show that what we refer to without a second thought as (say) *The Great Gatsby* or 'Frost at Midnight' may in fact exist in several different versions, all of which have their claims, and between which editors have to adjudicate. I have tried to indicate in a generalized way the grounds and principles on which editors base their choices. It is possible, in the case of major writers, to consult variorum editions, which record all the different extant versions of every line or sentence. Naturally, these editions are massive, cumbersome and expensive (they often occupy teams of textual scholars for their entire careers). They are designed for 'consultation', rather than for reading, and they don't solve the problem of which text to supply for modern readers in general (rather than for scholars and critics). The important thing is that as students of literature we should be aware of the layers of editorial mediation which often lie between ourselves and the text we read.

* * *

When we think of reading literary texts, our primary image is still that of holding a bound book, with pages we can flick through. If a passage seems important we might underline it, or turn down the corner of the page, or write something in the margin. If interrupted, we can drop in a bookmark, or a supermarket till receipt, and slip the book into a pocket or handbag. Books, especially paperbacks, are the most portable and humane of objects, so endearingly 'user-friendly', in fact, that the subjects of old-fashioned auto-biographies and memoirs often speak of their books as their 'friends'. Increasingly, though, our 'bookmarks' are electronic, and an ever greater proportion of our reading is done on the screen rather than the page. Such reading is, however, almost by definition, 'work' rather than leisure – I don't know anyone who reads online books in bed. But doing English today means not just reading the words on the page but scrutinizing the script on the screen as well. These online resources are the subject of the next chapter.

9 Online English

BOOTING UP

The concern of this chapter is to show how using online resources can enrich the way we think and write about literature. It does not aim to provide a comprehensive guide – it's more illustration than exhortation, and it discusses only resources which are freely available, and available free – that is, without subscription or password. If you are currently taking a degree in English there will be plenty of other material which you can access via your academic library. Some of this will be in the form of CD-ROMs, and some will require you to enter your user ID and a password supplied by the library. This procedure will give you access to specialized databases to which your own institution will have paid the (often quite substantial) subscription fees. But what is available will, of course, differ widely from one institution to another, and it therefore seems inappropriate to discuss those materials here. Your own library or subject department will doubtless have a help-sheet (or several) giving you details of the sources available to you locally. Indeed, well-endowed institutions will have vast amounts of specialized online data on tap for their students, but there is an even vaster array which has the kind of global accessibility which is the essence of the internet. The availability of these electronic archives can to some extent counter the effects of overstretched institutional budgets, of remoteness from major copyright libraries, and even of differences in wealth between nations, giving many of us some of the privileges once enjoyed only by the best-placed and most successful scholars.

Because the huge volume of material available online can be so overwhelming, I have tried to formulate a simple 'map' (Figure 9.1) which identifies some major categories of material. I see two important kinds. Firstly, 'full-text databases' (as the name implies) mainly offer complete texts of literary works online, sometimes with appended critical and contextualizing material. Secondly, there are 'topic and period' web sites, in which the emphasis is the other way round. That is, they mainly supply contextualizing and critical materials, but sometimes with appended texts. In my basic map, each of these two main categories has two sub-divisions: the databases, firstly,

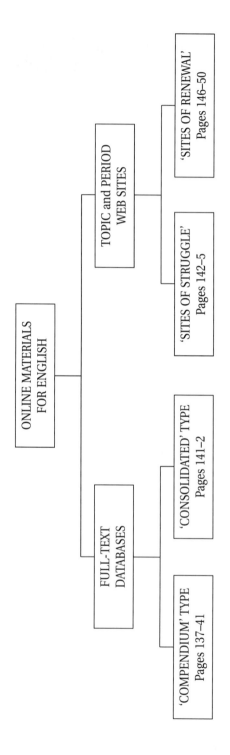

9.1 Four kinds of online materials for English

can be of either the 'compendium' or the 'consolidated' kind. In the former, we are offered online all the books or plays by a given author, each work having a separate searchable file, meaning that the file for each book is a separate document, so that to look at usage of a given word or feature across the whole *œuvre* you would have to search each file in turn. In the 'consolidated' kind of site, by contrast, there is (as well as the files for individual texts) a 'consolidated' file containing all the books as a single searchable document, which can be used like a concordance (see below) to search for (say) individual words right through the whole of the author's works. These, then, are the two main kinds of full-text database.

For the topic and period web sites, the sub-division is into what I call (a bit more fancifully) 'sites of struggle' and 'sites of renewal'. The former emphasize materials which aim to *broaden* the scope of literary study, introducing texts and materials on neglected, non-canonical writers, and/or providing a wider range of historical, theoretical, and contextualizing data than was hitherto widely available for the literary study of a given topic or period. The latter, by contrast, focus on the major canonical authors who have long formed the bedrock of literary studies, but aiming to *deepen* our study by providing radical and innovative materials for teaching and studying them. Typically, they exploit the technical range and capabilities of the internet to the full, often with a multimedia element (using sound, photographs, facsimiles, film clips, multiple texts, and so on). The bulk of the present chapter is a discussion of these four different kinds of online material – but, firstly, some friendly words of warning.

BEING CHOOSY ONLINE

The quality of open-access materials varies a great deal. I would recommend that you always look these gift horses in the mouth. Some attractive-looking sites will have been set up by naïvely enthusiastic amateurs whose knowledge and understanding may be limited. In general, it isn't difficult to distinguish the good from the less good, and a touch of 'internet snobbery' can be helpful in doing so. In other words, if a site is maintained by an internationally recognized cultural institution (the Folger Library, let's say, or the British Council, or a well-known university) then it is worth making the assumption that the material is probably going to be useful and reliable. On the other hand, sites with the words 'my' or 'favourite' (or both) in the title are often bad news, and should be treated with caution ('My Edgar Allan Poe Page', 'My Favourite Romantic Poems', and the like). Misspellings, colloquial English, and erratic punctuation are always danger signals (you see how snobbish I am suggesting you should be). Be cautious, in any case (that is, no matter how illustrious the source), when downloading quoted material from sites, whether the material be poems, stories, or quotations from critics. If you intend to write about a downloaded poem or story in an essay, then you should, where possible (which is to say usually in the case of major canonical authors), check the text for accuracy against the most recent critical edition of the author available in your university or college library. If the site doesn't indicate which edition of (say) a Coleridge, Wordsworth or Tennyson text is being reproduced, then you should assume that an out-of-copyright nineteenth-century printing is probably being used to reduce costs. This *may* differ slightly from the text in an up-to-date modern edition, and it will be without any of the new insights and discoveries which modern textual scholarship may have supplied.

Be warned, too, that while web pages of the 'My Favourite Romantic Poems' type often reproduce poems in full, they are nearly always transcribed inaccurately and should not be relied upon. The inaccuracies may seem minor: for example, capitalization may not be faithfully followed; punctuation may be randomly modernized or ignored; spellings may be inconsistently modernized, elisions expanded ('o'er' rendered as 'over', and so on), and stanza numbers switched from roman (iv) to arabic (4). All these inaccuracies are individually minor, perhaps, but cumulatively they mean that you are not reading the poem the author published. In these matters, nothing less than pure, 100 per cent pedantry will do.

The online version of a poem or other literary text may be accompanied by notes supplied in hypertext form, which is to say that when you click on a particular word or phrase in the text you are taken to an explanatory note. If the site is reputable, these may well be useful and authoritative. Obviously, though, if you make use of the annotation you should also credit the source. Generally, it is worth noting, the reputable sites tend to provide mainly *scholarly* material of various kinds, rather than just *critical* material (or, at least, they use the latter predominantly to complement the former). For instance, a site might make available a range of poetry and documents from a given historical period which are not published in modern reprints: or it might present data on manuscript variations in the writings of a well-known author, perhaps using actual facsimiles of the author's handwritten originals. A site which simply provided critical essays and opinion on (let's say) Coleridge or Shakespeare would not be offering anything different from what is widely available in academic books and journals, and we might wonder why the author hadn't sought that form of publication. There is some risk, too, that such material might seem to invite being lifted at the click of a button into one's own essays. There are, it is true, eminent scholars whose web sites include some of their own complete critical essays. Usually these essays are subsequently included in books, so the author's aim is presumably to make them available in the public domain in the (often) two- or three-year gap between composition and appearance in book form. All the same, doubts have been expressed about the wisdom of this practice, in the light of widespread anxieties about possible plagiarism in assessed work on English courses. So I will emphasize here that the rule for web material is the same as that for printed materials – you need to acknowledge the source of anything you make use of.

Increasingly, tutors are asked what form the citation of web material should take. The best source of guidance is the web site of the MLA, the Modern Language Association, which issues internationally accepted guidelines on style for books, articles, and essays. Enter the MLA site, at <http://www.mla.org/>, click on 'MLA Style' in the list of options, then on 'Frequently asked questions about MLA Style', and scroll down to 'How do I document sources from the World Wide Web in my works-cited list?' When you click on this you are taken to a succinct page which gives step-by-step guidance and examples. This is how a reference should look for the site called the 'Victorian Women Writers Project', which is referred to later in this chapter:

> *Victorian Women Writers Project.* Ed. Perry Willett.
> 19 Jan. 2001. Indiana U. 10 Apr. 2002
> <http://www.indiana.edu/~letrs/vwwp/>

So the basic convention is that you should give: the title of the site, underlined or italicized, and the name of the person responsible for the site (all in the first line); the date of latest modification, the source, and the date you last accessed the site (all in the second line); and, finally, in the third line, the web address, enclosed in angled brackets (that is, '<' and '>'). All the information you require should be on the site's entry page, but if any of these items are missing don't worry; just record what you can, keeping this basic shape. The person here designated 'Ed.' may be variously described as the Director, the Project Manager, and so on.

To repeat, in keeping with the spirit of this book, the emphasis in what follows is practical: I try to illustrate the use of online materials in the context of the kind of problems and opportunities which occur when we are writing and thinking about literature. At the end of the chapter you will find a cumulative list of the sites discussed.

GOING THROUGH THE GATE

To get a general sense of what databases are available, you need to use one of the main 'gateway' sites which contain links to large numbers of domains. Perhaps the most widely used of these for Humanities subjects is 'The Voice of the Shuttle' <http://vos.ucsb.edu/index.asp>, which was started in 1994, and is headed by Romantics scholar Alan Liu from the English Department of the University of California, Santa Barbara. 'VoS', as everyone calls it, is without rival for its ultra-clear structure and its range of coverage. It was recently rebuilt (October 2001), and (the entry page says) is best viewed in its new form with Internet Explorer 5+ and Netscape 6+. The intellectual depth of the site is partly due to the fact that those contributing links have a degree of independence: a free 'account' is opened, enabling unvetted links to be added and maintained, and these can subsequently be upgraded to full link status after being reviewed by VoS editors. This gives an ideal combination of, on the one hand, the freedom and openness which is the essence of the internet, and, on the other, the guarantees of quality which students and academics need if they are to use electronic resources with confidence.

On arriving at the VoS entry page you will see the scope of the enterprise from the three lists running down the left-hand side of the page, headed respectively 'Contents', 'Resources', and 'Guide to VoS'. Under 'Contents' there is a succinct list of broad headings for the whole range of Humanities disciplines, from Archaeology to Religious Studies. The most useful ones from the English Studies viewpoint are 'General Humanities Resources', at the head of the list, the 'mega-heading' 'Literature (in English)', and the much-used 'Literary Theory' link (so much used that some have imagined that VoS is solely a dedicated literary theory site). If you click on 'Literature (in English)' you have the options of either using the very broad literary categories in the summary panel at the top right of the page ('Anglo-Saxon and Medieval', 'Romantics', 'Victorian', 'Contemporary (British and American)', 'Minority Literatures', and so on), or else browsing your way down the main list. If you click on (say) 'Victorian' in the summary panel you will be taken to another vast list, including both broad, generic sites (such as 'The Victorian Sonnet', 'The Victorian Women Writers Project') and specific sites on individual writers from Arnold to Wilde. If we go back to the entry page and briefly explore the 'Literary Theory' resources, we see that the head item is Dino F. Felluga's popular 'Undergraduate Introduction to Literary Theory' <http://omni.cc.purdue.edu/~felluga/theory2.html>. I have found this a useful item, even though it seems to have been suspended in an incomplete state since 1998, covering only New Historicism, Cultural Materialism, Feminism, and Psychoanalysis. However, plans for expansion have been announced (April 2002). The virtue of the site is that it is based upon the simple, practical, and effective formula of using the theoretical ideas in relation to two short literary texts (these being a pair of sonnets from Edmund Spenser's *Amoretti* sequence). Go back to the main sub-category of 'Literary Theory', which is 'General Theory Resources': click on 'On-line Literary Resources: Theory' (a list maintained by Jack Lynch of Rutgers University), and then click on 'Modern Literary Theory', which takes you to a site called 'Introduction to Modern Literary Theory', <http://www.geocities.com/kristisiegel/theory.htm>, a useful site set up by Kristi Siegel of Mount Mary College, Milwaukee. This is another undergraduate introduction to literary theory, and it too has the virtue of simplicity and good design. It doesn't do applications, but the coverage is broader than Felluga's current range, and it offers clear definitions, a basic bibliography on each theory, and a series of further links. In my experience, material of this kind, which is actually written for students, is far more useful than the massive readers on which many literary theory courses are based. Sites like these show the advantages of clarity and good design over the gimmicky, graphic-heavy presentations which the very capabilities of the web itself often seem to stimulate.[1]

Other countries tend to have their own smaller-scale equivalents of VoS. I frequently use the 'Literary Links' list in the English Department at Dundee University, UK <http://www.dundee.ac.uk/english/>. Also in the UK is the *Humbul Humanities Hub* <http://www.humbul.ac.uk>, which 'aims to be UK higher and further education's first choice for accessing online humanities resources'. Enter the site and click on 'English Language and Literature', then click on 'Primary Sources'. One hundred and twenty of these are described in alphabetical order over nine pages.

'COMPENDIUM' DATABASES

In Chapter 5, I said that the word 'silence', or 'silenced', is used 34 times in Jane Austen's *Mansfield Park*. It would have been naïve of me to hope that you were amazed at my industry and dedication to duty in rereading the novel from cover to cover listing occurrences of this single word in my notebook:

---

1   In terms of the classification used in this chapter, both Felluga and Siegel can be called 'sites of struggle', since they seek to advance the pedagogic status of literary theory, which is still, notionally, an oppositional force in the discipline.

Search Results

Terms entered: **silence**

34 Matches

Chapter	Line	Text
2	96	Bertram's **silence**, awed by Sir Thomas's grave looks,
6	206	It did not suit his sense of propriety, and he was **silence**d,
6	297	but his determined **silence** obliged her to relate her
9	197	The chapel was soon afterwards left to the **silence** and stillness
9	374	A general **silence** succeeded. Each was thoughtful.
10	64	This was followed by a short **silence**. Miss Bertram
10	177	After an interval of **silence**, "I think they might as well
10	181	This could not be denied, and Fanny was **silence**d.
13	304	And Edmund, **silence**d, was obliged to acknowledge that the
14	125	A short **silence** followed. Each sister looked anxious;
14	243	A short **silence** succeeded her leaving them; but her brother
15	265	Miss Crawford was **silence**d, and with some feelings of resentment
17	95	She either sat in gloomy **silence**, wrapt in such gravity
18	147	but her diligence and her **silence** concealed a very absent,
19	195	where nothing was wanted but tranquillity and **silence**.
20	44	**silence**d as ever she had been in her life; for she
21	90	"And I longed to do it—but there was such a dead **silence**!
25	88	contrast to the steady sobriety and orderly **silence** of
26	36	some minutes' **silence** to be settled into composure.
28	251	want to be talked to. Let us have the luxury of **silence**."
30	105	As soon as her eagerness could rest in **silence**,
30	234	They will be angry," he added, after a moment's **silence**,
32	168	**silence**, "that you mean to refuse Mr. Crawford?"
33	214	In spite of his intended **silence**, Sir Thomas found himself
33	234	for the strictest forbearance and **silence** towards

33	281	in the course of eight years and a half. It **silence**d her.
34	351	hoped to **silence** him by such an extremity of reproof,
35	238	**silence** and abstraction. Edmund first began again—
37	141	a great talker, she was always more inclined to **silence**
41	4	his **silence**, between which her mind was in fluctuation;
41	259	Fanny was doubly **silence**d here; though when the moment
44	11	and persuaded myself that you would understand my **silence**.
45	164	long **silence**, and behave as if you could forgive me directly.
47	119	was not to be **silence**d. The two ladies, even in the short

34 Matches found.

9.2 Occurrences of the word 'silence' in *Mansfield Park* by Jane Austen

As I am sure you realized, I obtained the information by looking up the novel in a full-text online database. I simply entered the word 'silence' in the search box, and seconds later a list of the 34 occurrences came up on the screen, each complete with chapter and line number. I could then see whether there was any pattern in the occurrences – for example, were they clustered in particular parts of the book? (They didn't seem to be – it looked like a fairly even spread.) To look closely at any specific example, I had merely to click on that example in the list and the screen would then show the word, highlighted in its textual context, so that I could look for any peculiarities or special features in the way the word was being used. I used the *Electronic Literature Foundation (ELF)* version of *Mansfield Park*, which is in the 'Works of Jane Austen' section of the site <http://elf.chaoscafe.com/austen/mansfield/>. The statement on the entry page for the *ELF* proclaims that its mission is:

> to produce advanced electronic texts to be used by students, scholars, and admirers of literature around the world. Our goal is to provide free access to a variety of texts from world literature available in several languages and/or editions, with forums for communication regarding these works, for all types of readers.

Works available (early 2002) include the whole of Shakespeare, Chaucer, Dante, Poe, etc. *ELF* is a good example of the 'compendium' kind of database, in which each of the specified author's works is a separate file.

For major authors like Austen, comprehensive textual data had often already been available in the days before Information Technology, in the form of massive volumes called 'concordances'. A concordance of Shakespeare, for instance, would list all occurrences of specific words right across the Shakespeare canon. Concordances required massive labour to produce, of course, and they only existed for the most major writers and texts (Shakespeare, the Bible, Tennyson, and so on). Their great size and unwieldiness made them library-only items, and years of usage reduced them to a sorry state of dilapidation. Their limitations were, in summary, their great cost, their zero portability, the difficulty of correcting or updating them for many years once they had been published, and their general inflexibility – they could only supply the needs which their compilers had anticipated.[2]

The most frequently used full-text database is the *Oxford Text Archive*, at <http://ota.ahds.ac.uk/>, which was founded in 1976. This has international coverage of texts, and is free to users (you are asked to give your e-mail). The *OTA* is a little old-fashioned, and heavy usage means that access is often rather slow. For modern authors, too, the coverage is patchy and eccentric – you could, in 2001, access Sylvia Plath, but only *The Bell Jar*, not the poetry. For D. H. Lawrence you have only *Women in Love*, for George Orwell only *1984*, and for John Osborne only *West of Suez*. The *OTA* is a 'compendium' type of database – though it has the whole of Shakespeare, each play is a separate file.

As another excellent example of a single-author, 'compendium' type full-text database we can take the *Internet Shakespeare Editions* site <http://web.uvic.ca/shakespeare/index.html>, which is run by the University of Victoria, Canada, and provides scholarly, fully edited and fully refereed texts of Shakespeare's plays and poems. Each play, however, is a separate file – there isn't a consolidated file of all the plays and poems which would enable you to track occurrences of a given word right across the canon. Nor is there any specific search apparatus. However, working on the vocabulary of (say) *Troilus and Cressida* we can simply use the 'Edit' menu of *Windows*; we click on 'Find', and then insert (let's say) the word 'war' in the dialogue box: then clicking on 'Find Next' we quickly discover that 'warre' or 'warres' occurs 19 times in this play.[3]

2   As an example, see John Barlett's *A Complete Concordance to Shakespeare*. This is published by Palgrave, and was last reprinted in 1997. At a little under 2,000 pages, it has remained in print for over a century (original publication was in 1894), and was priced at £185 in 2001.

3   The advantage of using a 'non-case-sensitive' search for 'war' is that versions of the word with a different spelling are also picked up. A site with its own search engine and an old-spelling text might give a zero return for 'war' if the spelling used throughout the online text is 'warre'.

But this is just raw data: what, you might ask, is the point of doing such a search (other than because we can)? How could data like this be used in the course of an actual critical argument about the play? Well, we could go on, for instance, to look for patternings within the list of uses – which character is the most frequent user of the word, and is it always used with reference to military matters, or are there cases where it is used metaphorically, for instance, with love being seen as a kind of warfare? Hence, we would be using the full-text database to provide data for a critical and interpretive argument. Of course, this could have been done by a diligent reader using a printed text, but it would have taken much longer, and perhaps, having expended so much time on it, we would be tempted to over-invest in the results of the search. It would be interesting, too, to know whether the word 'warre' is used as frequently in other Shakespeare plays which entwine the love and war themes, for example, *Othello* and *Antony and Cleopatra*. The answer (which takes less than five minutes to determine on the same site) is that it is used 15 times in the former and 37 times in the latter. Is the difference significant? Well, it may be, although one factor we would need to remember is that *Antony and Cleopatra* is the longest of the three, so we might expect more occurrences of the word in it. To reach any useful conclusion, it might be necessary to refine the search further: for instance, perhaps the really significant count in each play is the ratio between uses of the word 'love' and uses of the word 'warre', this being an element which would eliminate the factor of the length of play.

'CONSOLIDATED' DATABASES

The exemplification so far has mainly concerned the tracking of single words, and it is clear, as we have said, that this could be undertaken either with a printed concordance, or, more rapidly, with a consolidated full-text database. If we were intrigued, for instance, by the mass of commentary on the famous line in which Hamlet speaks (in i.ii.130) of his 'too too sullied flesh' ('solid' in the Folio, 'sallied' in the two Quartos), then we could look in the concordance to find a list of all other uses of 'sallied/sullied/solid' by Shakespeare. But we might decide instead that we wanted to know how many times Shakespeare uses the phrase form 'too too'. In his extended note (pp. 436–8) on 'too too sullied flesh', Harold Jenkins, editor of the Arden second edition of *Hamlet* (1982), notes that 'too too' followed by an adjective was a common Elizabethan turn of phrase, and this is borne out by a search on *The Works of the Bard* database <http://www.it.usyd.edu.au/~matty/Shakespeare/test.html>. This is a 'consolidated' database, so that when we insert the form 'too too' in the search box it gives examples of 'too too' in six other Shakespeare plays ('I love this lady too too much' in *Two Gentlemen of Verona*, and so on). By contrast, with a concordance, we would have to trawl through all the entries on 'too', checking to see if any contained the double 'too' form. The consolidated full-text database, then, is a kind of super-charged, open-ended version of the old concordance. Good scholarly practice (my colleagues tell me) is always to make the same search in two different databases, checking out any discrepancies, and then cross-checking the results in a printed concordance if one is available.[4] This is, I suppose, a two-belts-and-a-pair-of-braces principle. In the case of Shakespeare this double-check process will probably highlight differences between Folio and Quarto versions of the plays, which is an important matter, and one which is properly antecedent to any significant critical discussion at a text-specific level.[5]

'SITES OF STRUGGLE'

If you are writing an essay on Romantic poetry, you will probably still find that most of the books in your library are about the handful of major male poets (Wordsworth, Coleridge, Keats, etc.) who constitute the received literary canon of this period. Since the 1980s (as we saw in Chapter 4), there has been an important broadening of interest beyond these figures and on to women writers, prose and travel writers, and 'labouring class' male poets of the time; but there is still a long way to go before substantial individual collections of writers like these are in print at widely affordable prices. In the mean time, using online materials can provide the best opportunity to work on writers outside the magic canonical circle of mainstream, male, middle-class poets. With this aim in mind, you might decide to explore the resources of the

---

4   Cross-checking the *Two Gentlemen of Verona* example of 'too too' in the *Oxford Text Archive* fails to find this example. The reason is that the Oxford text includes a hyphen, printing the two words as one ('too-too'). This illustrates the limitation of searchable databases, which is that they will always and only give you exactly what you say you are looking for, and cannot interpret your wishes, or use their common sense. The dialogue you can have with them is like the dialogue in a law court, in which the plaintiff is only allowed to answer either 'yes' or 'no' to the barrister's questions.

5   An extremely useful source of information on Shakespeare and the internet is the chapter 'From Codex to Computer; or, Presence of Mind', pp. 111–36 in David Scott Kastan, *Shakespeare and the Book* (Cambridge University Press, 2001).

Electronic Text Center of the University of Virginia Library, <http://etext.lib.virginia.edu/>, which is one of the pioneer collections of 'e-texts' (founded in 1992) and now a major source of online full texts. The *ETC* has texts in various languages, so click on 'Collections' on the entry page, then on 'English' in the list of languages represented in the database entry page, and then on 'Online Holdings'. Scroll through the list till you find a likely-looking source of Romantic texts, in this case 'British Poetry 1780–1910: A Hypertext Archive of Scholarly Editions'. Within this, the relevant period texts are Mary Robinson's *Sappho and Chloe* (1796) and the *Poetical Sketches* (1795) of Ann Batten Cristall, who was associated with the circle of the major romantic poet William Blake. The entire text of this latter work can be accessed at <http://etext.lib.virginia.edu/toc/modeng/public/crisket.html>, and there is an accompanying introductory essay on the poet by Jerome McGann, the foremost Romanticist in the USA at <http://etext.lib.virginia.edu/britpo/intro-crisket.html>. The material includes facsimiles of the title pages, and modern notes in 'hypertext' form (click on a phrase in the text, and the related note appears on your screen), made as part of a class project by Jerome McGann's graduate course at Virginia in 1993. Your own essay might compare Cristall's treatment of selected topics with that of one of her better-known Romantic contemporaries, whether favourably or unfavourably, and it would have the potential of stepping outside received judgements and considering new material. You might or might not conclude that Cristall is a major neglected talent, but the point is, again, that the electronic form permits universal access to a text previously available only to specialists, so that you can make up your own mind independently.

The effect, really, is to enable work of postgraduate character to be done by undergraduates. Of course, there may be anxieties that major figures may suffer neglect when too much time is devoted to exploring the byways which the electronic media have suddenly opened up for us. It is possible that students taught the post-1980s 'New Romanticism' might end up knowing the byways of Romanticism without ever having walked the highways (never having read Wordsworth's *Prelude* or Keats's Odes, but familiar with Ann Laetitia Barbauld, Felicia Hemans, Ann Yearsley, and Ann Batten Cristall). This *is* a risk, but we must always seek to present our subject in ways which will engage students, and English Studies has always valued the student's first-hand engagement with an author above passive acceptance of the received judgement of posterity, or that of great critical 'authorities'. Such engagement is more likely to take place with authors on whom there is not a vast body of secondary material in existence. One could argue that McGann is one such authority, whose influence on which writers we study on degree courses is very strong. But the whole point of McGann's work has been to show that we cannot understand how Romanticism really felt as a living experience if we only know what later generations came to call Romanticism, which was for long limited to the 'Big Five' (Wordsworth, Coleridge, Keats, Shelley, and Byron) who emerged as the defining poetic superstars of the age: as lived, Romanticism was about seeing these poets' work as part of a continuum which included the run-of-the-mill poems in the books and journals of the day, many of which (like Cristall's work, in my view) showed much less evidence of ever having made a break with the diction and poetic practices of the eighteenth century. The e-texts, then, offer an important way of under-cutting the former rigidities of our conventional periodizations of literary history. They open up the byways so that, potentially, a much wider perspec-tive on the past can become available again. The ultimate effect *may* be to show that posterity was right to single out the Big Five (as is evident, this tends to be my own view), but English Studies would immediately become a sham if students were simply to accept their teachers' word for that. If you find Wordsworth's 'egotistical sublime' a bit trying (and many have done), then do explore other poetic voices of the time as well – the electronic media will help you to do so.

Working on the Victorian period in a similar 'canon-breaking' spirit might take us to the *Victorian Women Writers Project* <http://www.indiana.edu/~letrs/vwwp/>, which is a highly rated and attractive resource set up by Indiana University. The writings made available on this site include 'antholo-gies, novels, political pamphlets, religious tracts, children's books, and volumes of poetry and verse drama'. This description is from the invaluable *CTI Textual Studies: Guide to Digital Resources for the Humanities*, which first alerted me to the existence of this site.[6] I click on the 'List of Works Available' banner on the entry page, and can now either scroll through the list, looking for some-thing that seems potentially relevant to what I wish to write about, or else click on the appropriate letter of the alphabet if I am looking for a particular author. I click on 'L' to bring up 'Levy, Amy (1861–1889)', having heard about this writer at academic conferences, but without finding much of her work currently in print. Four items are available, so I go back to the entry page, and click on 'Proceed to the Victorian Women Writers' Collection'. I check 'HTML' for 'mode

---

6   By Frances Condron, Michael Fraser, and Stuart Sutherland, Humanities Computing Unit, University of Oxford, 2000. If your library doesn't have it, complain to the Librarian. See especially the chapter 'Literature in English and Other Languages', pp. 71–120. I have drawn upon this book several times in the present chapter. The CTI, the Computers in Teaching Initiative, was a project supported by the UK higher education funding bodies which ran from 1989 to 1999.

of collection' and then click on 'Proceed to Collection'. I click again on 'L' in the alphabet and 'Levy' in the listing, and this takes me to a set of four texts. I then click on 'A Ballad of Religion and Marriage' and I am through to this highly subversive text, which was crudely printed in 12 copies for private circulation around 1915, probably by a suffragette group, long after the young author's tragic death.

A BALLAD OF RELIGION AND MARRIAGE

Swept into limbo is the host
    Of heavenly angels, row on row;
The Father, Son, and Holy Ghost,
    Pale and defeated, rise and go.
The great Jehovah is laid low,
    Vanished his burning bush and rod—
Say, are we doomed to deeper woe?
    Shall marriage go the way of God?

Monogamous, still at our post,
    Reluctantly we undergo
Domestic round of boiled and roast,
    Yet deem the whole proceeding slow.
Daily the secret murmurs grow;
    We are no more content to plod
Along the beaten paths—and so
    Marriage must go the way of God.

Soon, before all men, each shall toast
    The seven strings unto his bow,
Like beacon fires along the coast,
    The flame of love shall glance and glow.
Nor let nor hindrance man shall know,
    From natal bath to funeral sod;
Perennial shall his pleasures flow
    When marriage goes the way of God.

Grant, in a million years at most,
    Folk shall be neither pairs nor odd—
Alas! we sha'n't be there to boast
    "Marriage has gone the way of God!"

Facsimiles of the printed text are given, and the effect is to give the web-user a powerful sense of immediacy of contact with a long-ago struggle against oppressive social forces. Strangely, this most up-to-date of media can give us a strong feeling of being in direct contact with the literary past.

'SITES OF RENEWAL'

The topic in this section is online study materials (other than full texts) on major canonical authors. What can online resources do for the most familiar canonical texts, the ones which are taught daily in schools and universities worldwide? Essentially, the adaptability and flexibility of the electronic medium means that it is able to provide fascinating materials for teaching and study purposes as well as for research. Often these sites have an extremely precise focus – not, perhaps, on a single author, or even a single work, but on *part* of a work, even being centred upon a specific scene in a play, or on the different textual and manuscript versions of a single poem. I will take two renowned sites as examples of this kind of thing: the first is one called 'Hamlet on the Ramparts' <http://shea.mit.edu/ramparts/>, which is (as described in *CTI Textual Studies*) 'a collection of texts, images, and films related to Hamlet's first encounter with the ghost (Act 1, scenes 4 and 5)'. This resource is (says its home page) 'a public website designed and maintained by the *MIT Shakespeare Project* in collaboration with the Folger Shakespeare Library, and other institutions. The aim is to provide free access to an evolving collection of texts, images, and film relevant to Hamlet's first encounter with the Ghost (Act 1, Scenes 4 and 5)'. The site, then, contains a range of materials, including the various versions of the text, early editions, prompt books, a century and half of paintings of the scene, and much about the 80 or more extant film versions of the play – one of the first films ever made was a film version of *Hamlet.*

There are also detailed lessons and tutorials: one of these, for instance, contains a fine suggestion about Hamlet's 'dram of evil' speech (i.iv.13–38), which occurs just before the ghost's entrance in Act I Scene 4. In the speech Hamlet (having heard the sound of drunken late-night partying floating up from the castle below) talks rather obsessively about defects of character, and especially those people whose character is ruined by 'the stamp of one defect' (i.iv.31). In such cases, whatever virtues the person has are tainted by that one vice, since (it ends) 'The dram of evil/ Doth all the noble substance often dout/ To his own scandal' (i.iv.36–8). The tutorial idea suggests that, before starting to read out the speech to a class, an eyedrop is used to release a single drop of red food dye into a glass of water, and as the speech unfolds (in all its slow, syntactic tortuosity) the red colouration will gradually suffuse the whole glass. The class is then asked to talk about the connection between the speech and the drop of dye in the glass. We don't have to actually *do* this, or see it done, to feel the force of this powerful image – this is effective even as a pedagogic theatre of the mind which finds a living image to illuminate the verbal image of the speech. Even if we still don't quite understand the precise meaning of every word in lines 36–8 about the 'dram of evil' (a 'dram', of course, is a small drop), we undoubtedly now understand the significance of what it says.

Another section of material on the site concerns the various films of *Hamlet*, especially in connection with the long tradition of the role of Hamlet being played by a woman actor. But in one film version Hamlet is played not just *by* a woman but *as* a woman, namely the 1920 film with the Danish star Asta Nielsen in the title role. Nielson was an international icon – Ann Thompson is quoted to the effect that 'by 1914, she was the most popular film star in Germany and was known all over the world. There were "Asta" cigarettes, pastries and hair-styles in Germany, and Asta Nielsen cinemas in San Francisco, Dusseldorf and Nagasaki. Her picture decorated trenches on both sides during World War I.'[7] This was a silent film, of course, and Nielsen plays Hamlet as a woman forced to pretend she is a man for the sake of the crown. The narrative frames in the film explain that it uses Edward P. Vining's thesis, in *The Mystery of Hamlet* (1881), that Hamlet was not only a 'womanly man' but 'in very deed a woman, desperately striving to fill a place for which she was by nature unfitted'. The material examines the implications of all this, using a series of stills from the film alongside quotations from film theorist Laura Mulvey on the male and female gaze, and there is also a series of clips from the film. The full extract from the film (nine minutes) can be run using 'RealPlayer' (which is downloadable if you don't already have it installed), and this is then broken down into a series of short clips with commentary. My brief comments here have touched upon aspects of only two of the items on the site, but they indicate, I hope, how such online material can revitalize the study of a text so familiar that studying it may threaten to lapse into pedagogic routine.

The second of these 'Sites of Renewal' I wish to consider is an Oxford University site called 'Virtual Seminars for Teaching Literature' <http://info.ox.ac.uk/jtap/>. The 'Virtual Seminars' resulted from a funded project to develop online materials for the teaching of First World War poetry. This now consists of three strands of material: first, the seminars themselves; secondly the Wilfred Owen Multimedia Digital Archive (WOMDA), which consists of facsimiles of the papers and manuscripts of British war poet Wilfred Owen, who was killed on 4 November 1918, exactly a week before the end of the war (his parents received the news of his death on Armistice Day). All this material is owned by the Oxford English Faculty Library. Also included in WOMDA are interviews with war veterans, photographs, letters, and video clips. Strand 3, 'Publications of the War', contains facsimiles of postcards,

7 In *Shakespeare the Movie*, ed. Lynda E. Boose and Richard Burt, Routledge, 1997, p. 216.

soldiers' newspapers, propaganda pamphlets, and issues of the journal *Hydra,* which was produced at Craiglockhart Military Hospital in 1917–18 while poets Wilfred Owen and Siegfried Sassoon were convalescing there. All the material in strand 3 is from the John Johnson Collection in the Bodleian Library, Oxford. I will discuss just the seminar material, the first of these three strands.

There are four seminars in this strand, the first being a general introduction to First World War poetry, using the selection of poems provided. The second seminar is a close study of a single poem, Isaac Rosenberg's 'Break of Day in the Trenches', first published in the famous Chicago journal *Poetry* in 1916. (Rosenberg was from the working-class Jewish community of the East End of London, and was killed during a night patrol in April 1918.) The seminar uses a range of provided materials, including a 'Hypermedia' version of the poem, in which clicking on various parts of the text takes you to annotation, information about textual variants, and so on. I will skip the third seminar for a moment. The fourth and final seminar is 'An Introduction to Text Analysis', using the 'TACTweb' online concordance tool to investigate word frequencies, co-occurrences of specified clusters of words, collocations patterns (for example, which words most commonly occur immediately before the word 'blood') and the vocabulary of specific registers (for example, words associated with music and musical instruments). This seminar is an excellent example of the way the online format immeasurably increases the possibilities of the concordance tool.[8]

To return now to the third seminar: this one is entitled 'Manuscript Studies', and its aim is 'to introduce editorial practices and manuscript studies'. The student is asked to prepare a text of Owen's poem 'Dulce et Decorum Est' for an edition of his work. This involves study of 'the primary sources (the manuscripts which contain the poem), choice of a base manuscript, collation of manuscript variants, and the production of your own edition'. The poem survives in four different manuscript versions (two at Oxford, two in the British Library), and facsimiles of any two can be put on the screen at the same time, and then scrolled down together, so that the variations can be noted. We see, for instance, that in the first manuscript the poem is dedicated 'To a certain

---

8   It is possible to download software which enables you to compile your own concordances. See the following site, maintained by Rob Watt, currently at the University of Dundee: <http://www.dundee.ac.uk/english/wics/wics.htm>. The software is a commercial product, but it can be tried out free for 30 days. Completely open-access concordances to Wordsworth, Coleridge, Keats, Shelley, and Hopkins are available at the same site. For an expert overview on concordances see: *Electronic Texts in the Humanities,* by Susan Hockey (Oxford University Press, 2000), ch. 4, 'Concordance and Text Retrieval Programs'.

poetess', in the second it has no dedication, in the third the dedication is 'To Jessie Pope etc' (Pope had published some rather facile patriotic verse, which Owen had seen), and in the fourth the dedication 'To Jessie Pope' is deleted and 'To a certain poetess' is substituted. The first line, 'Bent double, like old beggars under sacks', was originally 'Hunched double' in one version, and the same version has 'rag & bone men' instead of beggars. Line 8 of the poem caused the most trouble. The soldiers in the poem are so tired that they are 'deaf even to the hoots/ Of falling shells', which are described in various ways in the different drafts:

Of tired, outstripped five-nines that dropped behind.

or

Of gas shells dropping softly that dropped behind.

or

Of disappointed shells that dropped behind.

Of course, the effect differs greatly each time the line is changed: the precise description of the shells as 'five-nines' shows an officer's necessary technical knowledge of the calibre of shells, and his ability to recognize them and take appropriate action when possible: the second version, in which the 'five-nines' are just 'gas shells', is very much a 'plain language' rendering, with the repetition of 'dropping' perhaps suggesting the tiredness referred to. The final version is distinctly more fanciful – the shells are 'disappointed' because they overshoot their targets and fail to fulfill their death-dealing destiny. Which version is best? Which is the true voice of the poem? It is the editor's impossible task to decide, and the seminar takes us in the most vivid way into both the dilemmas of the editorial process and the creative struggle of the poet in the act of composition. Owen sent one of the versions of the poem to his mother with the intriguing remark that it was 'Not finished, but not private'. It remains suspended in this limbo for evermore. Here, then, is another example of the 'site of renewal', a set of online materials which show a high order of imagination and organizing skill, making a very substantial contribution to the revitalization of the study of what is included most frequently on our courses.

* * *

So far, we have talked about English as the study of literary texts, and about moving out beyond the text to consider matters of intertext, context, and history. We haven't given any specific consideration to the kind of English which involves studying language. There is a sleight-of-hand move which claims that, as literature *is* language, then we are in fact studying language all the time. In a certain limited sense, of course, this is obviously true, but the sense *is* limited, because the statement is only *literally* true. Indeed, a crude response to the crude assertion that literature is language is to say that literature is only language in the sense that paintings are paint. Studying paint will not necessarily tell you much about paintings. A less crude response is to assert that studying literature and studying language are different activities, but that both have a legitimate place in the study of English. The next chapter, therefore, is about English Studies as Language Studies.

SUMMARY OF SITES MENTIONED

The first date given indicates when the site went online in its present form (where known); the second date is the date of most recent access. If only one date is given, it is the date of most recent access.

1. Gateways

The Voice of the Shuttle. Ed. Alan Liu
Oct. 2001, U. California, Santa Barbara, 10 Apr. 2002
<http://vos.ucsb.edu/index.asp>

'Links Literary', Dundee University English Department, ed. Rob Watt
14 May 2001, U. Dundee, 10 Apr. 2002
<http://www.dundee.ac.uk/english/welcome.htm>

Humbul Humanities Hub
25 March 2002, U. Oxford. 10 Apr. 2002
<http://www.humbul.ac.uk>

2. Compendium databases

Oxford Text Archive
7 Feb. 2002, U. Oxford, 10 Apr. 2002
<http://ota.ahds.ac.uk/>

Electronic Literature Foundation: The Works of Jane Austen
10 Apr. 2002
<http://elf.chaoscafe.com/austen/mansfield/>

Internet Shakespeare Editions, ed. Michael Best
26 July 2001, U. Victoria, Canada, 10 Apr. 2002
<http://web.uvic.ca/shakespeare/index.html>

3. Consolidated databases

The Works of the Bard, ed. Matthew Farrow
U. Sydney, Australia, 10 Apr. 2002
<http://www.it.usyd.edu.au/~matty/Shakespeare/test.html>

4. 'Sites of struggle'

Undergraduate Introduction to Literary Theory, ed. Dino F. Felluga
31 May 2001, Purdue U. West Lafayette, 10 Apr. 2002
<http://omni.cc.purdue.edu/~felluga/theory2.html>

Introduction to Modern Literary Theory, ed. Kristi Siegel
6 Mar. 2001, Mount Mary College, Milwaukee, 10 Apr. 2002
<http://www.geocities.com/kristisiegel/theory.htm>

Electronic Text Center, ed. David Seaman
U. Virginia Library, 10 Apr. 2002
<http://etext.lib.virginia.edu/>

Victorian Women Writers Project, ed. Perry Willett
19 Jan. 2001, Indiana U., 10 Apr. 2002
<http://www.indiana.edu/~letrs/vwwp/>

5. 'Sites of Renewal'

Hamlet on the Ramparts, ed. Peter S. Donaldson
2000, MIT Shakespeare Project, 10 Apr. 2002
<http://shea.mit.edu/ramparts/>

Virtual Seminars for Teaching Literature, ed. Stuart Lee
Oct. 1998, U. Oxford Computing Services 10 Apr. 2002
<http://info.ox.ac.uk/jtap/>

10 English as Language

The word 'English' in 'English Studies' often means not just English literature, but English language as well, for many English departments, especially in the UK and Europe, are departments of 'English Language and Literature' (or equivalent). This means that their staff will comprise both literary theorists, literary critics, and literary historians, on the one hand, and, on the other, those who refer to themselves as 'linguists', not meaning that they are speakers of many languages (which I think is the usual lay meaning of this word), but indicating that their field of expertise is the study of language itself. Hence, the syllabus set for study in such departments covers both language and literature, and the language side of this joint syllabus is the topic of this chapter.

Let's begin by considering the following definition of linguistics (that is, Language Studies) from a helpful web site:

> In its broadest sense, Linguistics is the study of human language: how it is structured, how it is used to represent meaning, how it is used to communicate ideas, how it is formed, how it is decoded. Linguistics tries to look for commonality across all human languages, and shouldn't be confused with 'Language Teaching' which aims to teach a single language. It is confusing that an expert in languages is called a 'linguist', since it leaves no name for an expert in Linguistics – maybe he [*sic*] should be called a 'linguistician'![1]

The breadth of this definition makes it a useful starting point, but what are some of the main subdivisions of linguistics? The list below draws on the same source, and on the very useful *Concise Oxford Dictionary of Linguistics* (P. H. Matthews, 1997):

- *Stylistics*: the study of style in language, especially in literary texts
- *Sociolinguistics*: the study of language in its (usually contemporary) social context

---

1 <http://www.speechandhearing.net/entrance/intro.html>

- *Historical Linguistics*: the study of the origins and development of languages, and of historical change within individual languages
- *Syntax*: the study of the relationship between words and phrases within sentences
- *Semantics:* the study of meaning
- *Phonology*: the study of the pronunciation of words and sentences (what basic sounds are used by a language, what regular patterning occurs in words)
- *Phonetics*: the study of the production of speech by the human vocal mechanisms (how are sounds made, how do speakers of different accents differ?)
- *Psycholinguistics*: the study of the mental processes by which sentences are constructed and decoded by human beings

I will not, of course, attempt to represent that whole spectrum here. In fact, almost nobody would claim to have competence across that whole spectrum: to do so would be like claiming to be simply a scientist, without indicating what kind of scientist, and what areas of specialist expertise you possess. So I will concentrate on just the first four categories in the list.

STYLISTICS

Outside the changing rooms for the swimming pool on the campus where I work there is a large blackboard propped against the wall, on which is chalked the instruction: 'Please leave any footwear here'. 'Here' means 'in this room' (or so I have always presumed), but visitors sometimes seem in doubt, and occasionally (especially in the summer) you will find pairs of shoes clustered around the blackboard itself, indicating that the word 'here' has been taken to mean 'in the immediate vicinity of this blackboard'. The ambiguity stems from the fact that the word 'here' is what linguists call a 'shifter' (the term was coined by the influential Russian linguist Roman Jakobson, 1896–1982), meaning that its referent is contextually defined: if *I* say 'Come here' it means 'to where *I* am, and if *you* say it, then it means to where *you* are. By contrast, if the utterance were 'Come to London', it would mean the same thing no matter which of us said it (discounting, for a moment, the existence of London, Ontario). Shifters operate in routine and predictable ways in day-to-day speech, but in poetry their use can be very subtle and complex. Tracking language use in poetry using technical terms and concepts derived from linguistics (like 'shifters') is the kind of thing undertaken in the form of literary analysis known as stylistics. In this section I will try to give an impression of the 'flavour' of stylistics by illustrating how one specific set of terms and concepts might be employed, namely the cluster of devices known as 'shifters', 'deictic features', and 'orientational features'. I choose this cluster of items because analysing how they work is particularly illuminating in the discussion of poetry.

'Shifters' and deixis

As well as being a 'shifter', as just described, the word 'here' has what linguists call a 'deictic' function. 'Deixis' (pronounced 'day-ix-iss') comes from the Greek word *deiknuo*, which means to point or to show. Its root is contained in English words like 'in*dex*', as in 'index finger', meaning the finger which points, or the part of a book which 'in*di*cates' – another cognate word – the location of particular information. 'Deictic words', says Richard Radford, are 'orientational features', and they are 'particularly important in the criticism of poetry because the poem (unlike the reported speech acts of a novel or a play) is rarely attended by external evidence of its spatio-temporal or social context'.[2] In other words, in everyday life, the utterance 'He was here yesterday' is seldom ambiguous, because there is usually plenty of evidence of the 'spatio-temporal or social context' of the utterance. Rarely does someone phone with that message from an unknown part of the globe, making it necessary to ask '*Who* was, and what do you mean by 'here', and who are *you* anyway?' A poem, however, might well begin with precisely that phrase, 'He was here yesterday', and be without any 'spatio-temporal indicators', so that *all* those questions would become relevant, including the last, since the speaker in the poem might well be a proxy 'persona', rather than the author speaking 'autobiographically'. Deixis is a linguistic concept of peculiar conceptual breadth, on the one hand, and, on the other, of stark precision in application. Of their nature, 'orientational features' of various kinds are a feature of poetic openings; once a poem is 'orientated' the need for them progressively declines. Romantic and Victorian poetry, in particular, is often very keen to establish the 'spatio-temporal context' of the utterance, fixing what becomes the 'locatory pivot' of the entire poem.

2 Richard Radford, *A Linguistic History of English Poetry* (Routledge, 1993), pp. 40 and 207. See also Radford's *Roman Jakobson: Life, Language, Art* (Routledge, 1994), pp. 92–3, on shifters and poetry.

Taking a ghost for a walk

Take, for example, Matthew Arnold's 'Thyrsis', one of his best poems, written (as the epigraph says) to commemorate his Oxford friend and fellow poet Arthur Hugh Clough. It opens with the line 'How changed is here each spot man makes or fills!' But where is 'here'? The reader's problem is like that facing the reader of the notice by the swimming pool: does it mean here in general ('here on earth', say), or is it referring to a specific place (Oxford, for instance)? As the poem unfolds, it becomes clear that the poet is retracing a specific walk in the Cumnor Hills near Oxford which he and Clough had often taken together as students, so that the sense of the word 'here' has again shifted when re-used in the penultimate line of the first stanza, 'Here came I often, often, in old days'. In the first line of the second stanza it is used again, and again with a shifted sense: 'Runs it not here, the track by Childsworth Farm'. Since his student days, the terrain has become unfamiliar to him, though, as he says in stanza 3, line 4, 'Once pass'd I blindfold here, at any hour' (in other words, 'There was a time when this track was so familiar I could have walked it blindfolded, day or night').

   I won't track the word 'here' any further than this through Arnold's poem, but I think it is clear that the shifters have a *double* shift in poetry, and that this has a strongly enriching effect. Thus, the opening phrase 'How changed is here . . .' has a double meaning within the context of the poem, one being 'subjective', indicating how the world itself, to the middle-aged speaker, does indeed seem transformed – nothing now *feels* the same – and the other being objective, registering the fact of specific physical and social changes which have altered this terrain since Arnold was a student. By making this commemorative walk Arnold is laboriously seeking to relocate and reactivate the youthful ideals he shared with Clough (symbolized by 'the single-elm that looks on Ilsley Downs', which they used to walk to). It is the internal change, of course, that is the more troubling. The poem's act of mourning and willed restoration of purpose takes the form of retracing a walk in the Oxford hills which Arnold and Clough had frequently taken together as students, and ends with a defiant proclamation of inner continuity with their youthful idealism, as the voice of Clough says to the poet, *'Roam on! The light we sought is shining still . . . Our tree yet crowns the hill.'* This is a typical trajectory in Victorian poetry; the poet begins with a gloomy registering of change or decay, and then assertively proclaims a hope or a resolution in the face of that perception (this movement is seen in Tennyson's 'Ulysses', for instance, and in Hardy's 'Darkling Thrush').

Yet the deictic pointers have a further and crucial level of ambivalence when they are used in a poem. The word 'here' seems to locate the utterance on the ground itself, as if Arnold is 'speaking' these precise words, or, more accurately, sub-vocalizing these precise thoughts, actually on the spot. Of course, the poem is more likely to have been composed retrospectively in the poet's study (or in many different places), so that the deictic pointers ought strictly to say 'there' rather than 'here'. But the convention is otherwise, for poems 'talk through' and 'walk through' a past event, revitalizing it, revisiting the spot, rethinking the thoughts. The paradox embodied in poetry is that poems often re-create a 'past' moment of reflection which actually exists *only* in the re-creation; the poem is a verbal 'copy' of an event for which there is no original, since the verbalization is itself the event. Doubtless Arnold actually did revisit the ground and thought about Clough as he did so,[3] and that revisit is happening 'To-night', as the speaker seeks out the once familiar route again ('Runs it not here, the track by Childsworth Farm'). But the 'here' is part of a verbal *re*-enactment of something which never was enacted exactly as related. 'Here', then, is neither the globe, nor Oxford, nor a particular spot on the hills; it's a setting as cerebral as the un-place on the stage in which Beckett's *Waiting for Godot* is acted out. Yet, at the same time, the poem's force is also highly dependent on its loco-specificity (Oxford, the two Hinkseys, the Cumnor Hills, Childsworth Farm, and so on), just as the 'un-place' in which *The Waste Land* is set also gains its emblematic force from the 'loco-specificity' of Lower Thames Street, St Mary Woolnoth, and all the other parts of London mentioned in the poem. Likewise, the 'to-night' of the poem, 'this winter-eve', is no actual moment, now receding further and further into the past, but a moment of being, a moment of realization which has both multiplicity and specificity, and is at the same time both general and particular.

This discussion may not seem different in kind from conventional close reading, and indeed, I don't think it is entirely. The defining feature of literary stylistics is simply that it uses concepts and terminology from linguistics as part of its repertoire, but it doesn't seek to use *exclusively* linguistic material, and will necessarily work in tandem with more familiar approaches to reading. My example uses the notion of the 'shifter', but there are, of course, hundreds of linguistic terms which this kind of analysis could potentially employ: here

3   Clough died in November 1861; in January 1862 Arnold wrote to his widow of 'Oxford, where I shall go alone after Easter – and there, among the Cumnor Hills where we have so often rambled, I shall be able to think him over as I could wish.' The actual composition of the poem seems to have taken place during 1864–5: see the note to the poem, p. 206, in *Matthew Arnold*, ed. Miriam Allott (Oxford University Press, 1995).

is a random list from a useful essay which sets out to exemplify the stylistic analysis of a poem in a systematic way. Stylistic investigators, then, might focus upon such elements as: the use of *stative verbs* (those which denote a state, like 'to own', rather than an action, like 'to buy'); *collocational clashes* (when words occur in unexpected combinations, as, for example, in the term 'an elegant rant'); the use of *cataphoric words* (words which refer forward to something which follows, like 'these' in 'The most important considerations are these:'); the occurrence of *cohesive chains* (groups of words, perhaps from different parts of a text, which have the same associations, for example 'battle shouts' and 'death cries'); the poet's choice of *premodification* (as 'a red-hot poker') or *postmodification* (as in 'a poker which was red-hot'); the significance of the *head nouns* ('poker' is the head noun in both the previous examples, irrespective of whether the modification comes before or after); the occurrence of *lexico-semantic deviations* (all the deviations from normal usage a poet might employ – for example, the word 'rainbow' might be used as a verb – 'the sun rainbowed the window').[4]

The stylistician, then, examines the language of the poem using categories and terms of the above linguistic type. The aim is not to provide an exhaustive stylistic description, of course, but to use such data as part of a literary-critical argument. In my comments on Arnold's 'Thyrsis', the focus on 'shifters' serves to highlight the sense of 'precariousness' Arnold has, of his own world shifting and changing, and his familiar moral landmarks being dislodged. The 'shifters' provide what is in effect a linguistic reinforcement or embodiment of this pervasive feeling. It should be added, finally, that stylistic analysis is not confined to literature. Any text can be analysed in this way, and you might find yourself engaged in stylistic analysis of (say) newspapers, advertisements, sports commentaries, fashion brochures, and so on. I have chosen to stick to literary stylistics as the main example, to emphasize that literary criticism and stylistics can (and often do) very usefully complement each other. In the past the two approaches were often enemies, but there seems no reason to perpetuate a situation which resulted in lost opportunities for both sides of the divide.

---

4 All the terms listed occur in the essay 'To Analyse a Poem Stylistically: "To Paint a Water Lily" by Ted Hughes' (but the exemplification is mostly my own). This is ch. 1 in *Twentieth-Century Poetry: From Text to Context*, ed. Peter Verdonk (Routledge, 1993), a title in the excellent 'Interface' series, the aim of which is 'to build bridges between the traditionally divided disciplines of language and literary studies'.

SOCIOLINGUISTICS

Stylistics, as just argued, has close affinities with long-standing practices of close textual scrutiny in English Studies, and this is also true, although to a lesser extent, of sociolinguistics. A common element in many English courses used to be that attention would be given at some point to such matters as the language of newspapers, popular culture, and advertising, usually in a highly critical spirit which was keen to expose the use of cliché in newspapers, and the pandering to shallow, populist assumptions.[5] Among other things, sociolinguistics too scrutinizes the language of newspapers, advertisements, and of social and professional groups, but in a spirit which is generally more openly descriptive and investigative than prescriptive and condemnatory. We can define sociolinguistics, then, as the study of language and language use in its social context.

Reading the papers

The focus of sociolinguistics may be of various kinds: for instance, it might be *lexical,* that is, concerned mainly with lexis (what lay people usually call 'vocabulary'); we might note, for instance, the way certain words seem 'tied' to a specific context: for instance 'wed' (meaning 'to get married') occurs in newspaper headlines, but isn't used in day-to-day speech: nobody says 'He's going to wed next week', but in newspaper headlines the word is favoured for its shortness, so we might see the headline 'Rock star to wed', in which context it looks quite normal. A sociolinguistic study could also be *syntactical,* that is, concerned with what lay people usually call the grammar and structure of sentences. Thus a headline, again, might say 'New school to close', which contains no unusual lexis, but structurally is immediately recognizable as a newspaper headline. Why, exactly? Well, think of how one person might convey this news to another in actual conversation: the utterance might take the form 'The new school's going to close'. The usual telegraphic concision of the headline eliminates many of these words: '[The] new school ['s going] to close': if we now 'audit' what is omitted, we have (1) the definite article ('the'), and

---

5 This kind of work perhaps has its ultimate source in Q. D. Leavis's PhD thesis, and later book, *Fiction and the Reading Public,* and in student texts like Denys Thompson's edited collection *Discrimination and Popular Culture* (Penguin, 1964), which has essays on advertising, radio and TV, the press, film, magazines, pop music and design, mostly by prominent Leavisites.

(2) the auxiliary parts of the main verb ('is going'). Performing this kind of analysis on a corpus of newspaper headlines would enable investigators to produce a list of the linguistic features which constitute the recognizable 'register' (that is, style) of newspaper headlines (omission of definite articles and auxiliary parts of verbs, preference for short words, etc.). Even from these brief comments, it will be clear that sociolinguistic investigations lend themselves very well to practical, investigative work of an enjoyable kind. It will be clear, too, that the main emphasis in such work would be *de*scriptive rather than *pre*scriptive.

Language and gender

Apart from the language of the media, what other aspects of language in society are commonly investigated from a sociolinguistic perspective? Well, one topic is that of language and prejudice, for instance in relation to gender: areas investigated might begin with such apparently innocent matters as the 'rank ordering' within gendered pairings of words – pairs like 'men and women', 'husbands and wives', 'sons and daughters'. Do these terms seem to have a 'natural' running order, just like 'fish and chips', 'sausage and mash', 'roast beef and Yorkshire pudding', where the first word in each phrase is the main element of the meal – the protein – and the second is the secondary, accompanying element? Is the analogy correct, and if so, how do we explain it? Likewise, consider the prevalence in the English vocabulary of 'praise' compounds bearing masculine elements, like 'masterpiece', 'MasterCard', 'master bedroom', 'master's degree', and so on. Try to make a similar list with feminine elements. Consider which list is longer, and ask why.

Yet another level of sociolinguistic investigation within the ambience of gender might be an attempt to investigate differences in language use between men and women. This kind of work was characteristic of the 1980s, and at the time common findings were that:

(a) Men tend to use 'unqualified' statements ('It's too late to go now'), whereas women more often had 'question-tagged' statements which allowed the possibility of other views, as in 'It's too late to go now, isn't it?' Here, 'isn't it?' is a 'tag' in question form which is added to the statement 'It's too late to go now'.

(b) Male speech tends to have 'falling intonation' (that is, the tone drops at the end of the sentence – *Let's go now*), whereas female speech (especially that of younger women) often has the rising intonation characteristic of questions, even when questions are not being asked (*Let's go* now).[6]

(c) Male speech tends to have more slang and neologisms than female.

(d) In the case of male and female speakers of the same social class, the regional accents of the male speakers are more marked.

(e) Male speakers seldom ask questions (notoriously, male drivers totally lost in a strange city will drive round for hours rather than stopping to ask directions).

(f) Male speakers use fewer 'phatic' features (these are the brief verbal signals which indicate to someone speaking that you are taking in what they are saying – phrases like 'Yes', 'I see what you mean', and 'Really?').

(g) Only women speakers use 'disclaimers' (these are 'prefacing' elements like 'I don't know if you'll agree with this, but what I think is happening is . . .'

My impression is that these differences are generally less marked now than then, and that there has since been a move towards greater homogenization of speech patterns, reflecting much wider social trends. It will be clear, I think, that sociolinguistics is likely to stray from its aim of being purely descriptive when it begins to deal with topics like gender or prejudice. I don't think there is anything wrong with this. All the same, in such cases the potency of the investigation can be increased by suspending evaluative judgement *for as long as possible*.

Jargon

Another typical area of sociolinguistic investigation is that of jargon, especially the characteristic usages of particular social and professional groups. In considering the language of governmental and commercial spokespersons, for instance, we might notice a strong preference for 'aesthetic euphemisms', that is, for terms which 'dress up' the mundane: thus, in a report on the country-side we may hear of 'single-purpose agricultural structures' rather than 'barns', or of 'organoleptic analysis' rather than 'smelling things to see what they are'.

---

6 Since the 1980s, the phenomenon of rising end intonation has become very marked, especially among younger English speakers worldwide, and particularly in certain national language communities such as Australia. For instance, in listening to an account of an incident you will often detect a rising inflection (as for a question) on the italicized elements in a string like the following: 'So I went *home*, opened a can of *lager*, started punching in the *numbers*, and this is what I came up with.'

These verbal preferences may be a harmless way of giving an air of learned professionalism to otherwise trite observations. But the use of 'semantic euphemisms' (that is, euphemisms which seem to want to *disguise* meanings, dressing them down rather than up, so to speak) may be less so: many of these are connected with warfare, the most notorious perhaps being the use of the term 'collateral damage' as a way of avoiding mention of the killing of civilians. At the time of the war in Afghanistan, there was discussion of the possibility of allowing the use of 'physical interrogation' of terrorist suspects in that country (*Guardian*, November 2001). Being 'physically interrogated' doesn't sound very pleasant, but it sounds a lot better than being tortured. It is difficult to imagine discussing language use of this kind in a neutral and purely descriptive way. But, again, suspending judgement for as long as possible does give us a greater chance of understanding what its users want this language to do for them. Those who use this kind of euphemistic language know, of course, that *we* know what the words actually refer to (they know, in other words, that the euphemistic veil is transparent). But the effect of using controlled language is to give the impression that we are in control. The jargonistic trick can still work on us even though we have seen through it.

Brave new words

Another fascinating area for sociolinguistic investigation is lexical innovation, that is, the entry of new words into the language. These, of course, directly reflect social trends and technological change, and, again, they lend themselves very well to investigative activities. A key practice is simply to keep a log of 'first sightings', that is, writing down in a designated notebook precise details of the first time new words, or catchphrases, or technical terms were encountered. Sometimes these moments will stick in the mind – I can recall vividly the moments in the early 1970s when I first heard the terms 'bio-degradable' and 'hassle' – but usually a conscious effort is required to record the details. I kept such a record for teaching purposes in the early 1990s, and the following are some of the entries:[7]

---

7 The record is subjective, of course, but keeping it trains us to register the presence of new words before they become a taken-for-granted element in our verbal environment. Also, the value is as much in the list as a whole, and the snapshot it gives of a specific year or part of a year, rather than in the details of individual words.

WORD	MEANING	SOURCE
teleplomacy	Diplomacy conducted by telephone link-ups	*Observer*, 13 Sept. 1990
trilogue	Negotiations involving three parties	*Guardian*, 1 Dec. 1990
hold-jockey	A disc-jockey who chats and plays records for those 'on hold' waiting to get through to the offices of large organizations	BBC Radio Four, 27 Sept. 1991
ETOPS	A term in the aviation industry, meaning 'Extended Twin-engined Operations, i.e. the trend towards building long-range commercial aircraft with two engines rather than four	TV travel programme, Dec. 1991
eco-holidays	Holiday tours especially for those with a social and environmental conscience	BBC Radio Four 'Breakaway' travel programme, 17 Jan. 1991
spin-doctors	Political consultants who advise politicians about news presentation	Mar. 1992
float-operated valve	Reputedly now the preferred term in the building trade for the plumbing device previously known as a 'ball-cock'	BBC DIY programme, 1991
vision statement	A refinement of the already current 'mission statement', a kind of official proclamation of corporate aims and ambitions	UK college prospectus, Mar. 1994
bear hug	An aggressive take-over bid on terms too attractive to shareholders to be refused by management	BBC Radio Four, Mar. 1994

Even a sampling as brief as this gives an immediate sense of the period, and the record is valuable even when the full occurrence details are not to hand. A useful language-based task would be to classify the various ways in which such new words are formed: many, for instance, are so-called *back-formations*, that is, words or phrases which are based on the model of already existing words or phrases – for example, 'hold-jockey' is a back-formation from 'disc-jockey'. Others are *metaphorical extensions* of existing words – the phrase 'bear hug' already existed, but the new usage extends its range and specificity. Some are blends of two existing words ('telephone' and 'diplomacy' together give 'teleplomacy'), and some are based on acronym*s* (like ETOPS, and like all those designations for target audiences, supposedly used in advertising agencies, like 'DINKIES' ('Double Income No Kids', i.e. middle-class professional couples without children). Again the key questions seem to concern what it is we want language to do for us, and how language use doesn't just *influence* our thinking, but *becomes* our thinking.

* * *

Sociolinguistics, then, is a popular area of language study which provides many opportunities for practical work. It investigates language synchronically, that is, across the whole spectrum of usage today, rather than diachronically, which means 'through time', or historically. It is interested, especially, in language variation – variations, for instance, between different national varieties of English, between 'standard' and 'regional' forms, between the language of different generations, and between that of men and women. It is interested, too, in the jargon associated with various professional groups, in the language registers typical of various trades and professions, and in recreational slang. It is, for many, the most attractive and the most contextually rooted form of language study.

HISTORICAL LINGUISTICS

If sociolinguistics is mainly synchronic (i.e. about language now), then historical linguistics is mainly diachronic (about language then), and concerns the history and development of language. The eighteenth- and nineteenth-century linguists studied interrelationships between languages, aiming especially to work out the origins and sources of the languages of Europe and India. The study began with the imperial expansion which brought Westerners into contact with the languages of India, the Middle East, and the Far East, leading to the perception of similarities and parallels between them. The founding figure was the Orientalist William Jones (1746–94) whose presidential address to the Bengal Asiatic Society in 1786 included the seminal statement about the ancient languages Latin, Greek, and Sanskrit that 'no philologer could examine them all three without believing them to have sprung from some common source, which, perhaps, no longer exists'. This, says David Crystal, is 'generally quoted as the first clear statement asserting the existence of Indo-European'.[8] Indo-European is the ancient common ancestor language of most of the modern languages of Europe and India – it is the extinct 'missing link' between them. Realizing the common origins of most of the languages of India and Europe was a major breakthrough in this kind of study, and there was general acceptance of the hypothesis that there exists an Indo-European language family, one of the 30 or so major language families worldwide.

The detailed picture reconstructed by the linguists of the nineteenth century is the result of painstaking linguistic detective work involving close scrutiny of the forms of many words across many different languages. The story they tell is that around 3000 BC the civilization now called Indo-European developed in Eastern Europe, with its own language, which was the common ancestor of most present-day European and Indian languages. Around 2500 BC this civilization broke up (perhaps because of climate changes) and these peoples migrated towards many different regions, including present-day Greece, Germany, Russia, and India. In each place of settlement the language spoken continued to evolve, and of course evolved differently, so what had been a single language began to split into several languages. In particular, six main branches developed, these being the Celtic, Germanic, Italic, Balto-Slavic, Hellenic, and Indo-Iranian. From these major Indo-European branches of the ancient world have developed the language groups of today: the *Celtic* group includes Gaelic, Welsh, and Breton: the *Germanic* group includes the languages of north-west Europe (English, German, Dutch) and the Scandinavian languages (Swedish, Danish, Norwegian, Icelandic): the *Italic* (or *Romance*) group includes French, Spanish, Italian, Portuguese and Romanian: the *Balto-Slavic* group includes Russian, Polish, and Czech: modern Greek is the descendent of the ancient *Hellenic* branch: the *Indo-Iranian* branch has Hindi, Urdu, Bengali, and Gujarati, and many other Indian languages; this branch, finally, also has modern Farsi (Persian), an Indo-European language which happens to be written in Arabic script. This kind of information seems to open up a whole new vista of knowledge, across vast

8 David Crystal, *The Cambridge Encyclopedia of Language* (Cambridge University Press, 1987), p. 296.

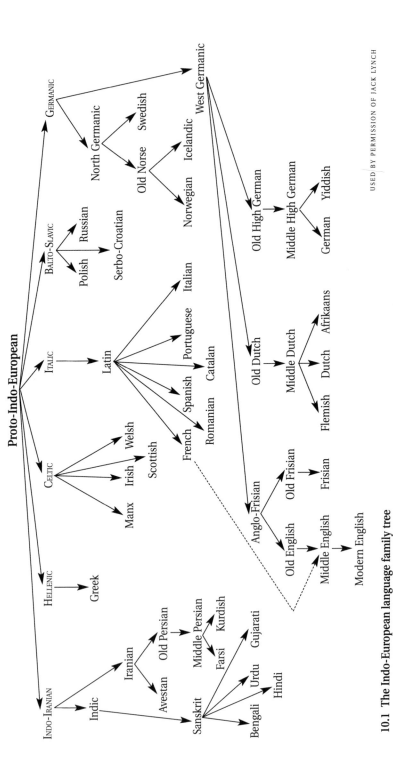

10.1 The Indo-European language family tree

(In the interests of readability, I have left out dozens of languages, grossly simplified some language families, and left out the historical phases of some languages.)

epochs of time, across continents and ice ages, which is awesomely impressive, as if a whole area of human experience and interconnections has suddenly been revealed. This is how Keats felt, perhaps, 'On first looking into Chapman's Homer'.[9]

Clandestine relationships

There is also something especially intriguing about the nature of the evidence which supports the picture of language relationships just given, and this links back to the basic attractions of English as a discipline as sketched out at the start of this book. This is to do with the fact that some of the evidence is concerned not with the *overt* similarities between words in these different languages but with *covert* connections between them. 'Overt' connections are the kind which are evident in the present form of words; for instance, it is evident at once that it cannot be coincidental that the word for 'mother' in English must be related to the German *Mutter,* or the Dutch *moeder,* or the Swedish *moder.* But consider the words in the following list:

ENGLISH	FRENCH	ITALIAN	GERMAN	LATIN
father	*père*	*padre*	*Vater*	*pater*
fish	*poisson*	*pesce*	*Fisch*	*pisce*
foot	*pied*	*piede*	*Fuß*	*pes/pedis*
hill	*colline*	*collina*	*Hugel*	*collis*
hundred	*cent*	*cento*	*hundert*	*centum*
heart	*cœur*	*cuore*	*Herz*	*cor/cordis*

Here, there is, for instance, little overt similarity between the word 'father' and its French equivalent, *père,* or between the English 'fish' and the French *poisson* – these words do not look as if they could be 'cognate' (words are said to be cognate when they derive from the same source word). However, we do notice that in both these cases an English word beginning with 'f' has a French

---

9   This account of language families follows the traditional 'nationalist' bias of the early formulations: in other words, it privileges the development of national languages, rather than regional dialects, or language forms which cross national boundaries. In reality, the distinction between a dialect and a language is a political one – a well-known Yiddish saying, atttributed to Max Weinreich, expresses this neatly, maintaining that a language is a dialect with an army and a navy (see a note in *Language in Society* 26:3 (1997) – my source for this information is Adrienne Bruyn of the Linguistics Department of Manchester University).

equivalent which begins with 'p', and, if we noticed (as did nineteenth-century philologists compiling lists of word equivalents across various languages) that this happens quite often (there is another example in the list), then we would have to conclude that it can't be an accident. Likewise, we notice another pattern of this kind, of words which begin with 'h' in English and German ('heart' and *Herz*) beginning with 'c' in French, Italian, and Latin (*cœur, cuore, cor*). On this basis alone we might conclude that, while all five languages ultimately come from the same source, English and German are more closely related to each other than they are to the rest, forming one group of close relatives; the same is true of French, Italian, and Latin, which form another distinct group of close relatives within the languages mentioned. But the relationship between, say, English and French is more distant, perhaps resembling that of second or third rather than first cousins.

The complex patterns of sound equivalences in Indo-European languages (like those indicated above), which disguised the close relationships between these words, are explained by 'Grimm's Law', which was worked out by the philologist Jakob Grimm (1785–1863) in his Germanic grammar of 1822 (Grimm, with his brother, was also famed as a compiler of fairy tales). The 'law' explains a pattern of nine different interlocking sets of consonant shifts, which also covers other equivalences, for instance, between Germanic 'd' and Romance 't': hence, the apparently unrelated words 'hundred' and *cent* declare the fact that they are really the same word when we know Grimm's Law and can see that the roots '*hund*' and '*cent*' correspond quite closely to each other, once we take into account the correspondences between the initial 'h' and 'c', and the concluding 'd' or 't'. This kind of work reveals the close connection between two words which now belong to different languages and have very little surviving *morphological* similarity (that is, their current external forms show few affinities).

Meanings on the move

If the major characteristic of philology is its interest in investigating language 'diachronically', then another important area of philological interest is the study of *semantic change*. 'Semantic' means 'concerned with meaning', and the focus here is not the words themselves as spoken sounds or written marks, but on the changes in what words signify. The fact that words change their meanings is evident when we read any document from the past: even in a nineteenth-century novel, many words and phrases have meanings different from those they bear today. For instance, the sudden mention of Mr Collins's love-making in Chapter 23 of Jane Austen's *Pride and Prejudice* is at first rather startling to a modern reader:

> Mr. Collins returned most punctually on Monday fortnight, but his reception at Longbourn was not quite so gracious as it had been on his first introduction. He was too happy, however, to need much attention; and luckily for the others, the business of love-making relieved them from a great deal of his company.

In the nineteenth century 'love-making' meant expressing romantic admiration verbally, that is, talking flirtatiously one to one, making remarks like 'You have very fine eyes', and so on, which Mr Collins was doing with his betrothed. If we go further back in time, our realization will be intensified that although the *words* are nearly the same as now their *meanings* are often different. Thus, when King James II first viewed the new St Paul's Cathedral in London, he expressed his profound admiration of the building by saying that it was 'amusing, awful, and artificial'. Today, this would be a pretty devastating verdict on any work of art, but all these words have undergone 'semantic' change since the time of James II: 'Amusing' then meant 'pleasing', 'awful' meant 'awe-inspiring', and 'artificial' meant 'skilfully wrought'.[10]

Like so much else in language history, semantic change isn't random, but follows predictable patterns. We may think of words as being 'anchored' to their meanings – the word 'aeroplane' isn't suddenly going to drift off all over the place and come to mean 'flowerpot'. But a ship at anchor doesn't remain rigidly still – a certain amount of 'play' is observable around the point of anchorage. Semantic shift or 'play', then, can be envisaged as having two main axes: along one axis, words can take on a meaning which is either more *restricted* or else more *extended* than it used to be. Along the other axis, words can gather overtones which are either more negative (or *pejorative*) than

---

10 This example is from Simeon Potter's book *Our Language* (Penguin, 1950), which is packed with information about the history of English, and is the source of my own initial interest in the topic. It is now, sadly, out of print, but was once a bestseller, and is still quite easy to find second-hand. Potter's follow-up book, *Language in the Modern World* (Penguin, 1960), was an impressive distillation of many key aspects of language study, including an engagement with contemporary linguistics. He makes a distinct step, from 'humanist' to 'scientific' forms of language study, between these two books, but without lapsing into aridity or dryness. Potter was the first in an illustrious line of British linguists able to write effectively about language for a large audience. His successors have included Randolph Quirk (*Language in Use*, 1962, now out of print), Jean Aitchison (*Language Change: Progress or Decay?*, 3rd edn (Cambridge University Press, 2001), and David Crystal, *The English Language*, new edn (Penguin, 1990).

before, or else more positive (or *meliorative*) than before. We can arrange these two axes to form what I call 'the semantic cross', as below:

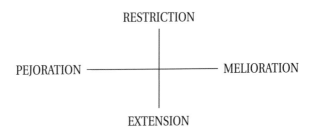

RESTRICTION

PEJORATION —————————————— MELIORATION

EXTENSION

The centre of the cross marks the meaning of the word at a given moment in the past (this being roughly the time of Shakespeare in the case of the examples given below). If the arms of the cross are taken as compass directions, we can say that northerly semantic drift, towards *restriction*, is more common than southerly, and that westerly drift, towards *pejoration*, is more common than easterly. The following words are examples of each kind of semantic change:

RESTRICTION
meat: this word used to mean any kind of food (see the expression 'It was meat and drink to her'); now it means just one kind.
starve: used to mean to die in any way (e.g. 'to starve for love'); now it means just one kind of death.
deer: used to mean any kind of animal (see the German word *Tiergarten,* which means a zoo (literally 'animal garden'), and King Lear's remark in Shakespeare's play about 'mice and rats and other small deer'); now it means just one kind of animal, not animals in general.
wed: used to be any kind of contract (e.g. you could be 'wed' to deliver goods by a certain day); now it means just the marriage contract.

EXTENSION
hazard: used to mean a specific game of chance played with dice; now it means any kind of risk or danger.
virtue: used to mean just strength, potency (from Latin *vir,* a man); now it means any admirable quality in anybody.

PEJORATION
counterfeit: used to mean any likeness, not one intended to deceive. Hamlet says to his mother, showing her the pictures of his uncle and his father, 'Look

on this likeness, and on this, the counterfeit presentment of two brothers'.
silly: used to mean 'happy' or 'fortunate'. When Troilus has successfully wooed Cressida (in Chaucer's *Troilus and Criseyde*) he is called 'silly Troilus'.
lust: used to mean just 'vigour' or 'enjoyment' – a headteacher might encourage lusty hymn-singing from the school choir.
crafty: used to just mean 'skilful', 'well made', the sense which survives in expressions like 'country crafts'.

MELIORATION

success: used to mean any outcome, not just a happy one – you could have 'good success' or 'bad success'; the word literally just means 'what follows', as in 'successor'.
enthusiasm: used to mean fanaticism, especially religious fanaticism: a seventeenth-century bishop famously remarked: 'If religion is ever to perish it will be because of enthusiasm.'

Semantic change is a fascinating topic, which offers many opportunities for discussion and debate. Why, for instance, should northerly and westerly drift predominate over their opposites? What is it (in human nature?) which brings about that change in the meaning of a word like 'success'? Whatever it is, a similar change seems to affect related words, like 'result': when football managers say 'We came here to get a result' they don't just mean that they are hoping to be included in the results round-up on the Saturday evening sports programmes – to 'get a result' means to win, just like success.

Borrowed words

Another important aspect of language change which is of great interest to historical linguists is the phenomenon of the so-called 'loanwords', which are words 'borrowed' by one language from another (with no intention of ever returning them, in spite of the name). An interesting form of this kind of lexical study is to consider the early growth of English, as it absorbed words from adjacent languages to build its own characteristically 'layered' vocabulary, in which there is often a choice of words, each with a slightly different 'flavour', to designate a single thing. (See, for example, the trio *blessing* from Anglo-Saxon, *benison* from French, and *benediction* from Latin.) If we think of the English vocabulary as being like a cake made up of several layers, then the bottom (or earliest) layer consists mainly of the 'West Germanic', or 'Anglo-Saxon', words brought in by the Germanic invaders of the fifth and sixth centuries who displaced the indigenous Celtic peoples of Britain. These words are often monosyllabic, concrete, and basic – words like *man, wife, house, meat,* and so on; some characteristic sounds are 'ch' (as in 'church') and 'sh' (as in 'shirt').

The second layer is the North Germanic, these being words of Scandinavian origin brought in by the Viking invaders from the eighth century onwards. These are also short, basic words, often recognizable by the initial 'sk' sound (the word *sky,* for instance, which displaced the West Germanic *welkin,* though in *Hamlet* Claudius's drunken revels 'make the welkin roar'): other common 'sk' words are 'skin' and 'skull'. Other characteristic sounds which indicate words of Scandinavian origin are the hard 'g' (as in 'go', as contrasted with the soft 'g' in 'gin'), and the 'k' sound, as in 'kirk' (the Scandinavian version of 'church') and 'kin'. That hard 'g' sound is in words like 'leg' and 'egg'; the latter word began to replace the West Germanic equivalent word, *eyren* (meaning 'eggs'), but the process was gradual, and the printer William Caxton, writing as late as 1490, has a story of merchants in his own day sailing from the Thames to Holland and going ashore, when becalmed off the south-east coast, where they knocked at a house door to ask for food (the passage is given here in the original spelling – 'goode wyf' means 'housewife'):

> [He] axed for mete; and specially he axed after eggys. And the goode wyf answered, that she coude speke no frensh. And the marchaunt was angry, for he also coude speke no frenshe, but wolde have hadde egges, and she understode hym not. And thenne at laste a nother sayd that he wolde have eyren. Then the gode wyf sayd that she understod hym wel.[11]

The confusion was due to the fact that there were two forms of the word 'egg' then fighting it out for supremacy in the English vocabulary: the country woman uses the older Anglo-Saxon word *ey,* which is *eyren* in the plural, this being one of the Anglo-Saxon 'weak' plurals, made by adding 'en', rather than 's', to the singular form (the surviving examples of the weak plural form are the words 'oxen', 'brethren', and 'children'). The London merchants, by contrast, use the newer form 'egg', derived from Scandinavian, with that characteristic hard 'g' sound. Sometimes two competing words made a kind of truce, as it were, each taking a slightly different sense. Thus, the Anglo-Saxon word 'shirt' with the 'sh' sound characteristic of West Germanic, had its North Germanic

11 The anecdote occurs in Caxton's preface to a translation of a French version of the *Aeneid.* It is quoted in many histories of English, e.g. in Lincoln Barnett's *History of the English Language* (Sphere, 1970), pp. 104–5.

equivalent 'skirt', with that 'sk' again. Instead of one replacing the other (the 'egg'/*ey* scenario), both underwent a semantic shift in a 'northerly' direction, towards a more restricted sense: a 'shirt' became a garment for the upper part of the body, and a 'skirt' one for the lower part, with both words later acquiring additional gender-specific connotations. A similar demarcation pact was made between the words 'church' and 'kirk'.

The third major lexical layer of the vocabulary cake is Norman French, these being words from French which were brought into the language by the Norman invaders of the eleventh century; many of these words concern aspects of culture – religion, government, the law, and cooking. It is well known, for instance, that the French words for common farm animals were incorporated into English to designate that animal when it had been cooked as food: English 'pigs' when cooked become French *porc* (later 'pork'): 'cows' become French *bœuf* (later 'beef'): English 'deer' become French *venison*, and English 'sheep' become French *mouton* (later 'mutton').

The fourth major layer of the vocabulary is represented by the incorporation into English of many words derived from Greek and Latin, around the time of the Renaissance. These are typically longer, polysyllabic words, with a 'learned' or abstract feel; again there are characteristic spellings. Longer words with 'eu' probably come from Greek, representing the Greek root which means 'good' or 'well': another indication of Greek origins in longer words is the letter combination 'ph', representing 'phi', the Greek letter 'f': so a word like 'euphemism' is from Greek *eu-pheimi*, literally meaning to 'good-speak'; 'philosophy' is from Greek *philo-sophos*, a lover of wisdom; and so on. The Latin words include many with the characteristic 'um' ending of Latin nouns – like 'equilibrium', 'pendulum', 'auditorium', 'maximum'. Sometimes Latin prefixes were used to generate words (like 'in' meaning 'not' – as in 'inconsiderate', 'inconvenience'), and suffixes like 'able' (from Latin *habilis*, meaning easily held or handled) were added to words of whatever origin (as in 'understandable', 'manageable', and 'laughable'). The fifth layer, finally, contains words from the many languages from which English has 'borrowed' words, especially during the period of British imperial expansion: often these words are recognizable by their obviously un-English spellings – 'yacht', from Dutch, 'guru' and 'pundit', from Hindi, 'kiosk' and 'yoghurt' from Turkish, and so on. Of course, the layers don't stop at five, but this basic five-layer model of lexical acquisition is a useful way of conceiving the basic loanword process.

* * *

There are, of course, many other topics which are studied within the approach known generally as historical linguistics, such as the study of place-names and surnames, and the consideration of the development of languages in terms of their syntax and structures as well as their vocabulary. But, in my experience, matters of vocabulary and meaning are usually perceived by non-specialists as being much more immediately interesting than aspects of structure and form. By contrast, structure (in its various senses) is of particular importance to the professional linguist; so our final focus is on syntax, which is the very heart of linguistics.

SYNTAX

All three areas so far considered in this chapter (stylistics, sociolinguistics, and historical linguistics) are branches of linguistics, which calls itself the *science* of language – that is, it is a systematic form of enquiry *which is scientific in tone and character*. It is concerned with the meticulous observation and categorization of linguistic phenomena, and with the testing of specific hypotheses about language; and it clearly requires some aptitude for abstracting and classifying, and for working with encoded data. The three topics considered so far lie on the edge of this domain because they can be studied with all due rigour within a 'Humanities' ambience. The study of syntax, on the other hand, lies at the heart of the *science* of linguistics – it is highly technical, depends upon the rigorous application of logical principles, and involves the manipulation of formulae written in (as it will first seem) arcane algebraic notation. What follows is just a brief taster.

Syntactical manoeuvres

One way of describing the key difference between the three types of language study looked at so far and this final one is to say that, whereas stylistics, sociolinguistics, and historical linguistics are often crucially concerned with *words*, the study of syntax is about *sentences*, that is, about how words group together into meaningful structures – it is concerned with grammar, in the generally accepted sense of that term. Put it another way: eighteenth- and nineteenth-century linguistics were above all *lexical*, while twentieth- and twenty-first-century linguistics are above all *syntactical*. This distinction between those who are interested in words and those who are interested in sentences also broadly reflects the distinction between 'amateurs' and 'professionals' in language study. There are plenty of lay people with an obsessive interest in words (where they come from, how they change, what their 'true' meaning is, how they should be pronounced), but very few, in my experience, have any serious interest in grammar and syntax – and by 'serious interest' here I exclude the pedantic writers of letters to the press who object to usages like 'between you and I'.[12] What began the shift of emphasis in linguistics from lexis to syntax was the work of the so-called 'father of modern linguistics', the Swiss linguist Ferdinand de Saussure, who died in 1911. Saussure was interested not in individual words but in words as elements in mutually defining structural constellations: consider, for instance, the following list of words and phrases denoting an event which has negative consequences in relation to some enterprise:

flea-bite, blip, setback, severe blow, disaster, catastrophe

Each phrase in the sequence is defined by those on either side of it: a 'setback' is more than just a 'blip', but not as bad as 'a severe blow', for instance, and likewise for the other terms in the sequence. Reasoning something like this led Saussure to his famous proclamation: 'In a language there are only differences, with no fixed terms.' Thus, linguistics moved on from the 'fixed terms', the individual words, and began to think in terms of broader linguistic structures. Later in the century, the phenomenal prestige and success of the work on syntax of the American linguist Noam Chomsky (b. 1928) led to the widespread assumption that linguistics had the key to understanding the human mind itself. Chomsky's first book, *Syntactic Structures* (1957), altered the field for ever. Chomsky introduced the notion of *deep* and *surface* grammar. To get a glimpse of what this distinction might mean, consider these two sentences, which have the same 'surface' grammar, but different 'deep' syntactical structures:

(1) *The chicken is ready to eat.*

(2) *The chairman is ready to eat.*

'To eat' in the first sentence is an 'active' verb, in terms of its surface grammar, but its 'deep' grammar is passive – it means 'to be eaten'. Chomsky's notion of 'transformational grammar' explains the series of 'moves' by which the

12 For the record, David Crystal's view about this usage (*The English Language*, p. 27) is that both 'between you and I' and 'between you and me' are OK – they are just different in tone, the former being slightly more formal than the latter. In the early 1980s Crystal was asked by the BBC to monitor complaints about language use on radio and TV. He made a list of the 'top 20' complaints over a one-year period, and this item was the most frequent object of complaint.

different 'deep' structures of these two sentences are transposed into the same surface structure. The reader of the two sentences doesn't just slavishly read the surface, but has an awareness that the two occurrences of the phrase 'to eat' are not really the same at all – one is transposable to the underlying form 'to be eaten', and the other isn't. We aren't machine readers, as we encounter these two sentences, but imaginative (even creative) readers, literally *making* sense of what we read, and this is how we learn to deal with language as we acquire it as children.

Chomsky, indeed, placed enormous emphasis on the creative aspects of language use – very sensibly, since all but the very simplest utterances and exchanges are unique inventions which have never occurred before and will never occur again. The very sentence I am writing now, though completely ordinary, is also unique, and will never be produced again (unless someone quotes it). For Chomsky, we could never learn to be constantly inventive in this way if language acquisition were merely imitative, merely a matter of copying what we hear. Whereas the behaviourist B. F. Skinner had believed that we learn language simply by copying what we hear spoken around us, Chomsky used telling examples to argue that what is really happening is that complicated sets of syntactical rules are being internalized by the young child, as is evidenced by the characteristic production, at certain stages of the language-learning process, of 'error forms' which the child will never have heard used by anybody. For instance, a child might make an utterance like 'Don't giggle me'[13] or 'She wented home'. Using these 'never heard' forms shows an understanding (respectively) of 'transitivity' (as in forms like 'Don't push me'), and of the English language rule that we make past tenses by adding 'ed' to the basic verb form. The child, of course, could not formulate the 'rule', in this or any other form, and seems to have inside (says Chomsky) a 'Language Acquisition Device' (LAD) which enables it to perform these complex mental operations. Chomsky's ambition was to produce a 'generative grammar', a kind of compendium of rules which, in application, would generate 'all and only' the syntactical structures of English.

Of course, Chomsky's work was later modified and criticized, but his influence (on cognitive psychology, on educational thinking, and on many other spheres) has been immense, and largely responsible for the late twentieth-century prestige of linguistics. Many linguists who subsequently became important figures themselves cite him as their inspiration. Chomsky opened up what was almost a new American intellectual frontier – linguistics became 'the American science' – and his new-found land of linguistics was

13 Steven Pinker's example, in *The Language Instinct* (Penguin, 1995), p. 21.

syntactical at its core. More recently, something like the same worldwide success (in joining linguistics to ultimate questions about human cognition) has been achieved by Steven Pinker (Chomsky's younger colleague at MIT, the Massachusetts Institute of Technology), with his bestseller *The Language Instinct,* and this too has contributed to the ongoing success and prestige of linguistics.

'S = NP1 + V + NP2', and all that

The aim of this kind of 'high', Chomskyan syntactical study might be described as showing the *real* relationships of the components of sentences, rather than their *apparent* relationships. A slightly more complex example than the one about chickens and chairmen is the pair of sentences 'John is easy to please' and 'John is eager to please'. Conventional 'parsing' of the two sentences will give the same structure for both: John (subject) is (verb) eager/easy to please (verb complement): this is reasonable, as they have the same 'surface' grammar: but their 'deep' grammar differs: 'John is easy to please' is equivalent to 'It is easy to please John', but the sentence 'John is eager to please' cannot be transformed in the same way into 'It is eager to please John'. Generative grammar, therefore, seeks a form of analysis which takes into account these underlying deep-structural differences. The method involves IC analysis, that is, the display of the Immediate Constituents of the sentence, using tree diagrams which show how a simple sentence (S), such as 'The girl chased the dog', is broken down into its constituent parts: a noun phrase (NP), 'the girl', and a verb phrase (VP), which consists of the verb (V), 'chased', and another noun phrase (NP), 'the dog'. The two noun phrases in the sentence can be further broken down into a 'determiner' (DET), 'the', and a noun (N), 'girl' and 'dog'. So the complete phrase marker (P-marker), or tree diagram, for the sentence will look like the diagram below.

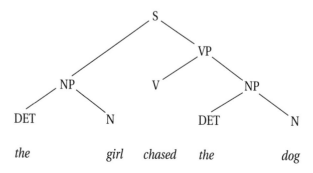

The string S = NP + V + NP then becomes a generative rule, able to generate all English sentences of this type ('The professor astounded her audience', and so on). The generative rules will be able to explain the 'transformations' by which two sentences with the same meanings but different surface grammar (such as 'The girl chased the dog' and 'The dog was chased by the girl') are related by their deep structure, which permits the first sentence (NP1 + V + NP2) to be transformed into the second by the formula:

$$NP1 + V + NP2 = NP2 + Aux + Ven + by + NP1.$$

This means that the second noun phrase (NP2, 'the dog' is moved to the front of the sentence, then an auxiliary (Aux) is added ('was'), then a past participle (V*en*), 'chased', and finally the first noun phrase (NP1, 'the girl'). This formula enables any passive sentence to be generated from any active sentence structured like 'The girl chased the dog'.[14]

My purpose in discussing these examples is mainly to demonstrate the 'flavour' of this kind of syntactical analysis. This kind of discussion is the heart of linguistics, and clearly, if you undertake it, you will need to be confident of your ability to hack out a trail through whole forests of tree diagrams, and unravel spaghetti-like heaps of formulaic strings. You will need the ability to read with intense concentration, and, when you realize that you have missed a point from earlier on, you will need the self-discipline to go back and work at it again. Without this, your understanding of these topics will remain forever wobbly and unreliable. But there will be rewards: an engaging recent textbook by Geoffrey Poole (another MIT product), begins with this bold pronouncement:

> This may sound like an odd thing to say about a book entitled *Syntactic Theory*, but the fact that this book is about syntactic theory is, in certain respects, incidental. I've written a book about syntax, and not quantum hydrodynamics, simply because I happen to know a little more about the former than the latter. . . . What this book is really about is theory-building: how to examine data, formulate and test a hypothesis, and evaluate the results.[15]

14 This example, and much of the detail, is from Crystal's *The Cambridge Encyclopedia of Language*, pp. 96–7.
15 Geoffrey Poole, *Syntactic Theory* (Palgrave, 2002), p. xiv.

This typifies the pervasive scientific and intellectual ambition of linguistics, and especially that of its syntactical core: the aim is not just to understand how *one* language works, but how language as such works, and thereby to give access to an understanding of how all human conceptualizing works. Linguistics in this sense has very little interest in cultural difference – it is always looking beyond that, reaching in the most ambitious way for universals. Doing syntax, then, will be hard work. But it is also a way of learning how to think.

It should be added that Chomsky's ideas about generative and transformational grammar are by no means universally accepted within the discipline. Indeed, he is a figure rather like Freud, whose most fundamental propositions are still widely disputed, whose methods are held by some to be in no way genuinely scientific, in spite of their scientific veneer, but whose influence on our thinking remains immense. The critique of Chomsky ranges from Ian Robinson's *The New Grammarian's Funeral* (1975), an early attack from outside the discipline of linguistics, to Geoffrey Sampson's *Empirical Linguistics* (2002), an attack from within the discipline – to be precise, from the branch known as computational linguistics, which collects computer corpora (electronic databases of language samples), thereby basing its views about language on the kind of empirical (rather than theoretical) data which Chomsky's work lacks.

We haven't so far, though, tried to hint at a more proximate goal for this kind of syntactical analysis than that ultimate goal of understanding the structures of the human mind. More immediate goals can become apparent if we work with actually occurring example sentences, rather than with those formulated expressly for syntactical analysis. Something like this happens in the textbook *Varieties of English,* when Dennis Freeborn and his co-authors analyse newspaper reports of disturbances at the funeral of an IRA hunger striker at the height of the Northern Irish 'Troubles'. One of the reports contains the sentence: 'Plastic bullets were replied to with stones.' The structure of this sentence is oddly complicated – how and why did it get that way? The answer is complex, but bear with me for a moment, and (as always) if you lose the thread in the course of the following exposition go back to the start of it and work through again more slowly.

The surface structure of the sentence ('Plastic bullets were replied to with stones') is a complex double transformation of two 'deep-structure' sentences with the pattern: NP1 + V + NP2. The two sentences would be:

1. *Soldiers* (NP1) *fired* (V) *plastic bullets* (NP2)

2. *Rioters* (NP1) *threw* (V) *stones* (NP2)

Passive transformations of both of these would give the pattern: NP2 + Aux + Ven + by + NP1. That is:

1. NP2 (*Plastic bullets*) + Aux (*were*) + Ven (*fired*) + by + NP1 (*soldiers*)

2. NP2 (*stones*) + Aux (*were*) + Ven (*thrown*) + by + NP1 (*rioters*)

This form would be non-committal about the precise sequence of the events, although we would probably tend to read 'and' as meaning 'and then' if we sympathized with the rioters (the soldiers fired first, and the rioters responded to the shots by throwing stones). But if our sympathies lay with the soldiers we would read 'and' as 'because' (the rioters started throwing stones and the soldiers responded by firing shots). But, whether active or passive, the sentence would require the 'agents' of both actions (the shooting and the throwing) to be designated by a noun. The noun 'soldiers' is presumably a neutral designation acceptable to both sides, but what about 'rioters'? Isn't that a word which implies hooliganism or criminality? If we wanted to avoid that word, what other one could be put in its place? If we are on the side of the 'rioters', then it's quite a problem, isn't it? 'Rioters' is not a neutral term like 'soldiers'. The peculiarly contorted 'blended passive' wording of the sentence as printed ('Bullets were replied to with stones') avoids both this problem and the problem of the ambiguous 'and' (since using the term 'replied to' makes it clear that the firing came first). So now we begin to see how that syntactically odd sentence got to be the way it is. Freeborn discusses the sentence as part of a comparative analysis of two newspaper accounts of this same event, one in a 'loyalist' paper and one in a pro-IRA paper. Which paper do you think this sentence appeared in?[16] The example illustrates, I hope, that syntactical analysis, especially of devices like the passive, can have direct relevance to many questions concerning power, prejudice, and the manipulation of opinion. Syntactical analysis at its best teaches us to think, yes, but not just about language.

* * *

Apart from the discussion of language study in this chapter, everything we have said about English so far has taken for granted the view that English involves the study of imaginative writing which already exists, rather than the creation of new stories, or poems, or plays. In recent years, however, there has

16 The example is in exercise 9, ch. 8 of *Varieties of English: An Introduction to the Study of Language*, by Dennis Freeborn, with David Langford and Peter French (Macmillan Education, 1986). My treatment of the example differs from theirs.

been a trend towards the inclusion of some element of creative writing on English courses, and the trend has not yet reached its peak. This development seems a very logical one; it brings English courses more into line with those in (say) music, which involve classes in the composition and performance of music, as well as its history and appreciation. Furthermore, the creative aspects of English courses can contribute to the revitalization of the critical aspects too, for often the best way to understand what the writer of a masterpiece is doing is to attempt to do something oneself in the same field or genre. Creative writing, then, a new and expanding presence within the field of English, is the topic of the next chapter.

TEACHING ELEPHANTS: CREATIVE WRITING IN AMERICA

The organization of writing degrees in the United States is highly distinctive, not least because of the vast scale of the enterprise. A recent count (by the AWP, Associated Writing Programmes, the organization for the teaching of creative writing in higher education in the USA and Canada) gives a total of 1,119 degree courses in creative writing being offered by the approximately 1,500 colleges and universities in the United States. To its detractors, this huge enterprise is the bizarre joint product of the counterculture of the 1960s and the business enterprise culture of the 1980s.[1] But creative writing programmes are much older than is popularly supposed, stemming from the English Composition course established at Harvard in 1873,[2] where a course in Advanced Composition was also available from 1884, with the emphasis on 'practice, æsthetics, personal observation, and creativity rather than theory, history, tradition, and literary conservation' (Fenza). Students on this course, taught by Barrett Wendell, had to hand in a piece of writing *every day*, but it still recruited 150 students in its second year. This may be a testimony to the negative qualities of the philological courses which were the alternatives, for early Composition was, among other things, an attempt to approach literature in the more student-friendly manner (as we would say) of the 'generalists' discussed in Chapter 7. These early Harvard courses were taught from the 1880s through to the 1920s. In 1930 Norman Foerster, another noted generalist, became the director of the School of Letters at the University of Iowa, and started 'classes in creative writing and a new emphasis on literature as an art',

1 This is the argument of a piece called 'Creative Writing in the Academy', by David Radavich, published by the Modern Language Association (the MLA) in *Profession 1999*, and cited in 'Creative Writing and its Discontents', by D. W. Fenza (the chair of AWP), an article first published in the AWP's journal *The Writer's Chronicle* (Mar./Apr. 2000). I am drawing on Fenza's piece throughout this sub-section. It is also available on the AWP website at <http://awpwriter.org/magazine/writers/fenza1.htm>
2 See Gerald Graff, *Professing Literature: An Institutional History* (University of Chicago Press, 1987), p. 46.

so that this graduate school 'was the first to contain the basic components of today's creative writing programmes: a course of study leading to a graduate degree; seminars for writers on the issues of craft and form; the study of literature as an art; and a creative work for a thesis' (Fenza). The related Iowa Writers' Workshop was founded in 1942, specializing in 'the education and nurturing of literary artists' and leading to the Master of the Fine Arts (MFA) degree. Similar programmes followed, at Johns Hopkins University in 1946, at Stanford and Denver in 1947, and at Cornell in 1948. The creative writing movement, then, had close connections with a range of liberalizing tendencies in the history of the discipline, including the broadening of literary studies beyond the language-based philological approaches of the nineteenth century, and the desire to study modern literature in general and American literature in particular. It involved, for instance, several of the New Critics of the 1940s who were writers as well as critics (such as John Crowe Ransom at Vanderbilt and Yvor Winters at Stanford) and it was also aware of the progressive educational philosophy of educators like John Dewey, who pioneered such ideas as 'learning by doing' rather than 'learning by rote'. Much of the remaining antagonism against creative writing seems to replay old battles between 'theory' and 'practice' within the discipline, between those who accumulate 'knowledge about' literature (dates, sources, variant readings, and so on), and those who 'merely' do it, whether that means writing it, enjoying it, or finding ways of communicating the grounds of their enjoyment to others. When Harvard appointed the novelist Vladimir Nabokov to a professorship, the linguist Roman Jakobson famously remarked, 'What's next? Shall we appoint elephants to teach zoology?' Hence the title (which I have adapted for this subsection) of the best-known book about the development of creative writing at American universities, *The Elephants Teach: Creative Writing since 1880*, by D. G. Myers (1995).

The range of undergraduate writing programmes currently available in the United States includes those which enable students on an English degree to major in creative writing, as well as those which are exclusively a BA in Creative Writing. Typically, both these require the study of the literature of the past and the present, and some study of the English language itself, as well as practical tuition in the writing of fiction, poetry, drama scripts, and 'creative non-fiction' prose. All are a world away from the outdated caricature of courses that simply encourage self-expression, or teach a cynical and uncritical manipulation of 'market' preferences. Those who teach such courses are invariably active and published writers, their work often supplemented by readings and workshops taken by major writers who are more loosely affiliated to the programme. The permanent Faculty members often have an MFA degree, which is becoming the main professional qualification for the teaching of creative writing at college and university level, equivalent to the PhD, which has long had the same status for English Faculty members outside the creative writing programmes. These MFA degrees tend to be intensively taught, two-year, highly selective programmes, taking a small number of students each year – often around a dozen – and involving tuition in both the pedagogy and the practice of creative writing. MA degrees in creative writing, usually with a larger enrolment, and without the pedagogic element, are also widely available.

CREATIVE WRITING IN UK HIGHER EDUCATION

The teaching of writing, both as 'composition' and as 'creative writing', has long been part of the curriculum in the United States, but this has until fairly recently not been the case in what publishers call 'RoW' (the Rest of the World). In the UK, indeed, the separation between English departments on the one hand and living poets and writers on the other often seemed to be enshrined in the constitution. Creative writing, therefore, did not formally become part of the higher education system until 1970, when an MA in Creative Writing was founded at the then recently established University of East Anglia, by the novelists Angus Wilson and Malcolm Bradbury. This famous enterprise remained a workshop-based course in the writing of fiction for a quarter of a century, with well-known contributing tutors like Angela Carter and Rose Tremain, and an increasing list of highly successful graduates, including Ian McEwan, Clive Sinclair, and Kazuo Ishiguro. As it was founded by novelists, the East Anglia course retained its exclusive concern with fiction until 1995, when the poet Andrew Motion became the director and a poetry strand was added, followed by one on script-writing.

It isn't surprising that university courses in creative writing in the UK should have started at what was then a new university, nor that courses of a similar type did not become common until much later. Other early entrants to the field were the MA in creative writing at the then Sheffield Polytechnic (now Sheffield Hallam University), the Creative Writing MA started in 1981 at Manchester Polytechnic (now Manchester Metropolitan University), and another at Lancaster University, started in 1983. One of the marked features of the field is that provision at postgraduate level (which is to say, mainly MA) preceded the existence of BA programmes, which began to emerge only in the 1990s. Initially, these BA programmes were set up outside the traditional university sector – in the post-1992 universities, and at university colleges. A survey of BA courses with components in creative writing, made by Dymphna Callery in 1995, listed 17 undergraduate degrees, of which only one (BA English Literature with Creative Writing at East Anglia) was at a pre-1992 university.[3] Why should this have been so? In one sense, the answer is obvious – tradition is often the enemy of innovation, so the institutions most conscious of their status as guardians of traditional academic values have been slowest off the mark.

Another important element in building pedagogic confidence was the fact that the former polytechnics had long had the practice of subjecting new courses to external validation and scrutiny (originally under the auspices of the former CNAA, the Council for National Academic Awards). This meant that they were accustomed to making aims, objectives, assessment criteria, and syllabuses very explicit, and this helped them (indeed, required them) to think out methods and rationale very carefully in a manner which could be defended to outsiders. Consequently, the pervasive anxieties which surround this field (for instance, anxieties about whether creative writing can be assessed and graded at all) could be openly faced and worked through, and the rigours and public spectacle of the CNAA 'validation event' was reassuring to sceptical colleagues. By contrast, in the days before academic audit became part of daily life in all sectors of British higher education, these anxieties were never really worked through at traditional universities, and so they retained their primitive hold and tended to deter innovation.

Yet another reason for the growth of creative writing provision outside traditional universities was that they had always been somewhat remote from the creative arts, whereas the large polytechnics of the 1980s were usually amalgamations of several institutions within a region, often including a college of art and a college of (higher) education which had probably started life as a monotechnic teacher training college. Institutions of the latter kind usually had strong performance traditions in departments of Art, Movement and Dance, and Music, and even in their English departments, which had long been involved in the teaching of creative writing techniques for use in primary and secondary schools. Such institutions routinely included practitioners of various arts as members of their staff (my own colleagues at one such institution included composers, artists, potters, dancers, fabric designers, poets, and writers of children's books), and this produced an institutional ambience and mindset quite different from that of a traditional university. This is the soil in which the teaching of creative writing took root in the UK.

---

3   'Writing Courses in Higher Education', in *Writers' and Artists' Yearbook* (A. & C. Black, 1995), pp. 492–7.

At the time of writing, the momentum of the discipline in the UK remains powerful. At 12 institutions creative writing can be pursued right up to PhD level. At 40 it can be taken at MA level, and at 120 it can be taken as an entire degree, or as a named part of a degree, or as an optional strand within a degree.[4] The effects of this massive expansion are as yet difficult to determine, but one beneficial result may be to contribute something towards the survival of contemporary poetry. To be blunt, that survival depends upon the survival of contemporary poets, and this cannot be ensured merely on the proceeds of selling poetry books. (In each generation in Britain, W. H. Auden once said, there are just two people who can live on the sales of poetry alone.) Even well-known figures may sell under 1,000 copies of a title, so most poets survive by means of the reading circuit, which provides them with reading engagements at literary festivals, literary societies, schools, and other educational institutions. The fees from these may add up to a fairly low-grade working salary, but at the personal cost of leading a nomadic existence which (the poets say) is barely compatible with the maintenance of family life and relationships, let alone with securing the kind of stability and work-space a writer needs. One effect of the creative writing boom, then, is to provide some poets with a degree of security, with regular contact with a seriously interested audience, and with a work routine that allows sustained utilization of and engagement with their craft.

CREATIVE WRITING AND ENGLISH DEPARTMENTS

The spread of creative writing right through the university system in recent years can be traced to a variety of causes. Firstly, when provision existed at MA level only, it was difficult to integrate tutors fully into departments, or to provide them with sufficient work to constitute a full-time appointment. Offering a few additional or supplementary creative writing modules at BA level was one way of doing so, and these often became over-subscribed, strongly suggesting that there must be an untapped demand for a formal creative writing strand at BA level too. Secondly, the 1990s began to see some erosion of the traditional student base of English by newer degree subjects like Media Studies and Theatre, Film, and Television Studies. The appeal of these subjects was partly the creative opportunities they offered, for example for film editing, film making, script writing, and so on, and it therefore seemed that

---

4   These figures are from Dr Graeme Harper, who runs the Development Centre for the Creative and Performing Arts at University of Wales, Bangor.

offering this kind of opportunity as part of undergraduate study in English departments would be a sensible step.

Another likely beneficial effect of the creative writing courses on the English departments which host them is more difficult to specify, but it concerns the potentially liberating effects of the presence of practising writers among them. In practical terms, there seems to be a growth, right across English degrees, in more flexible attitudes towards assessment (that touchy and volatile area), so whereas in the past the academic essay was the sole form of 'assessed outcome' in most English departments, we are now seeing more flexible variations or alternatives, particularly in the form of 'critical/creative' kinds of assessment (the term, I think, is from Rob Pope, author of *The English Studies Book*). Examples of this would be (say) assessing the qualities of Henry James as a short-story writer by taking one of his tales and supplying an alternative ending, and then discussing the relative aims and merits of the two versions. Likewise, a tutor might decide that the best way to appreciate the qualities of Wordsworth's iambic blank verse, as used in his verse auto-biography *The Prelude*, is to narrate an incident from one's own childhood in this form. Or we might decide that the best way to appreciate Hemingway's ultra-sparse narrative style is to rewrite one of his stories, framing it in a conventional omniscient authorial overview, instead of Hemingway's own 'vacuum-packed' presentational method. Practices like these clearly derive from the pedagogic techniques of the creative writing class.

What, finally, are some of the key characteristics of the creative writing course at undergraduate level? There is, I think, a fairly high degree of consensus concerning both the intellectual content and the format of such courses. Firstly, the dominant pedagogic format is the workshop, in which members of the group in turn read out or present a piece of work for discussion. The reading may take five or ten minutes, and as the course develops the tutor will stress the importance of making comments helpful, specific, thoughtful, and supportive. Some tutors like to have a couple of minutes' silence after a piece is read, or read out, during which group members jot down some thoughts and responses, so that the atmosphere in the room is suitably reflective, and the comments offered are not just off the cuff. Sometimes the writing will have taken place outside the session and will have been circulated to members for reading beforehand. Sometimes the tutor will ask students, individually or in pairs, to start a piece on the spot in response to an idea or a piece of writing presented in the session by the tutor. In these cases, the piece thus started may be worked upon during the following week, and then presented in a more developed state at the next session.

A second common feature is that material produced in the workshops will be collected in some way into a student's course portfolio, which will be presented for assessment when the module is complete. Typically, the aim of the portfolio will be to stimulate reflective practice, so that the material presented will be not just the completed product (a poem, a story, a dramatic sketch) but also evidence of the process it went through, in the form of a series of drafts, with explanatory comments on the various stages through which the work passed. The comments will explain the reasons for, and the intended effects of, some of the changes made, and this kind of work (the intention is) will begin to produce the 'reflective practitioner', one who consciously reflects on the craft of writing. The creative writing course very much embodies the view that writers aren't just naturals who either know or don't know how to do it; rather, the assumption is that we can learn skills, hone our methods, clarify our intentions. We can benefit from trying to explain to others what we are trying to do, and we can learn how to keep working at an idea until we have refined and improved its execution. Becoming a writer, these courses assume, is a *cumulative* process.

A *final* characteristic of creative writing courses is the assumption that creative writers need to be creative readers too. Hence, they commonly involve the simultaneous study of literature alongside students not in the creative writing stream, and they require, in particular, the reading of literary criticism and literary theory. Hence the influences (between the English Department and the Creative Writing course) are mutual, and these degree-stream courses in creative writing are thus different from the classes in writing which can be taken outside degree programmes in extramural departments. Such courses do not usually entwine the practice of writing with the systematic study of literature, and especially, they do not usually involve any exposure to literary theory. Creative Writing degree courses, by contrast, mostly believe that the study of (for instance) poststructuralism, structuralism and narratology is of great benefit to the short-story writer; the belief embodied in the courses is that the kind of formula used by the literary theoretician attempting to pin down some aspect of the relationship between language and the world closely parallels the struggle the poet undergoes in that 'intolerable wrestle with words and meanings' which is the composition of poetry. These courses, then, present writing in an integrated manner, as part of an established set of intellectual practices. Struggling to say what they mean, the creative writer and the literary critic or theorist face the same challenges, and this is why creative writing courses have come so quickly to seem at home in English departments, in spite of their long banishment thence.

* * *

Of course, creative writing will never be the only kind of writing which takes place on English courses. As we have seen, even on a dedicated creative writing course, some of the required writing will be predominantly critical in character, asking students to analyse their own creative work in terms of current literary theory, for instance, or requiring them to compare their own methods with the techniques and approaches of established writers. But on English courses generally the critical, theoretical, or analytical essay accounts for nearly all the assessed writing which students have to do. No matter how deep or brilliant your insights, if you don't learn how to write a good essay you may well find the overall experience of taking an English degree something of an anticlimax. But, in any case, 'writing back' is a vital part of the 'dialogue' with writers past and present which I have emphasized a good deal in the book. It is of great importance that you should have your say effectively, so the last chapter in the book is about writing essays.

12 The Essay: Crossing the Four Frontiers

DESCRIPTION

It is possible to identify four basic levels of literary discussion, which can be called, in ascending order of complexity, description, commentary, discussion, and analysis. They can be illustrated by extracts from a hypothetical essay on Charlotte Brontë's novel *Jane Eyre*, all taken from the point in the essay where the matter under consideration is the relationship depicted early in the novel between the heroine and the Reed family. Firstly, then, in the kind of literary-critical writing which I am calling description, a sentence of the following kind might occur:

> Jane is mistreated by the Reed family, and, although she is solely dependent on them to secure her livelihood, she speaks out against her harsh treatment. [*The essay then moves on to a different point.*]

Self-evidently, this is just a statement of what happens in the book. It simply describes events in the narrative. It merely indicates that the writer has read the novel and knows its plot, but there is no indication of whether anything has been understood about the significance of the events depicted. Such writing retells the story, or a section of it, usually sticking to the order of the events as they occur in the book; when encountered in extended form, it is characteristic of the weakest kind of student essay.

COMMENTARY

An essay on the same novel which is predominantly *commentary*, by contrast, might begin in the same way, but would then take matters a little further:

> Jane is mistreated by the Reed family, and, although she is solely dependent on them to secure her livelihood, she speaks out against her harsh treatment. This shows that she is becoming something which society disapproves of – a woman with a voice and opinions of her own. [*The essay then moves on to a different point.*]

Here, the factual description of what happens at this stage in the book is supplemented by comments on the *significance* of those events (as in the final sentence). Such comments are often fairly limited in scope, especially in student essays, and, typically, an essay which is written mainly at this level would go on to cite or describe several other incidents from the book, each time attributing more or less the same significance to them. Hence, the overall structure of such an essay is often that of a list or catalogue of cited incidents, none of them examined closely, and without much 'thematization', beyond the reiteration of a single point of significance.

DISCUSSION

Perhaps the limitations of *commentary* can best be seen by comparing it with the next level, which I am designating *discussion*:

> When she protests against her treatment by the Reeds, Jane, of course, engages in a laudable act of rebellion and self-assertion. But the emphasis of the passage is not really upon this, but upon the heroine's realization of her own powers, which are tested in this episode for the first time. ('What strength had I to dart retaliation at my antagonist?' she begins by asking herself.) When she makes her verbal assault ('I gathered my energies and launched them in this blunt sentence') she is herself shocked at the force of her own words, as Mrs Reed is silenced and rebuffed ('Mrs Reed looked frightened ... she was lifting up her hands ... and even twisting her face as if she would cry').

Here the essay moves from commentary, which is essentially a *series* of more or less isolated points on some aspect of a book, to discussion, which is made up of a *sequence* of points linked together and having a single focus. In the example just quoted, what is said concerns just one aspect of the scene, which is the heroine's acquiring for the first time a sense of the force of her own personality. This is an underlying facet of this literary text which the essay picks out and highlights. It gives us, in other words, that vital ingredient – thematization. If the essay writer had merely praised Jane for her self-assertiveness, or blamed her for her failure to restrain her outburst, then the writing would probably have remained at the level of commentary, for it would merely be part of a catalogue in which actions are approved or disapproved of with reference to a fixed moral or social point of view. So the defining quality which promotes the passage from commentary to discussion is that it resists simple closure of that kind; it picks up on a less than obvious facet of the text and then takes time to tease out its implications in greater detail. Commentary passes rapidly over the textual terrain at high level, flying a predictable course and quickly moving on elsewhere. Discussion, in contrast, involves doubling back over the territory in question and moving in for a much closer look.

ANALYSIS

So what, finally, does the fourth level, *analysis,* look like? It takes up elements from the discussion level and incorporates them into something more wide-ranging:

> When she protests against her treatment by the Reeds, Jane, of course, engages in a laudable act of rebellion and self-assertion. But the emphasis of the passage is not really upon this, but upon the heroine's realization of her own powers, which are tested in this episode for the first time. ('What strength had I to dart retaliation at my antagonist?' she begins by asking herself.) When she makes her verbal assault ('I gathered my energies and launched them in this blunt sentence') she is herself shocked at the force of her own words, as Mrs Reed is silenced and rebuffed ('Mrs Reed looked frightened . . . she was lifting up her hands . . . and even twisting her face as if she would cry'). The outburst here prefigures the moment near the end of the novel when she again has the undoubted satisfaction of releasing the full force of her tongue and telling others exactly what she thinks of them: this happens at the moment when she rejects St John Rivers, telling him 'I scorn your idea of love . . . I scorn the counterfeit sentiment you offer; yes, St John, and I scorn you when you offer it.' In this later exchange, the matters at issue are the same as in the scene with Mrs Reed; on both occasions she refuses to take part in a masquerade of love – 'I am not deceitful', she tells Mrs Reed, 'if I were I should say I loved you' – and on both occasions she resents the assumption by the other party that she can repress her feelings in an inhuman way – 'You think I have no feelings, and that I can do without one bit of love or kindness', she says to Mrs Reed. In that sense, taking up St John Rivers's offer of marriage in adult life would involve re-imprisoning herself in the red room of Mrs Reed's childhood neglect.

This, then, is *analytical* writing. The main difference between this and discussion is that in analysis the sustained scrutiny of one aspect of a text, which is characteristic of the discussion level, is combined with the making of links and connections with other parts of the text. So, in the example, there is both detailed discussion of the early scene in the book and a series of suggestions which link that scene with other crucial episodes which occur later on. The example is using the incident under immediate discussion (Jane's early mistreatment by the Reeds) as a springboard to a series of connections with other parts of the novel. The essay is not simply moving chronologically through the events depicted in the book (the most common mark of writing at the description and commentary levels). Rather, it is establishing its own order, based on an underlying integrative thematization, that is, a thematization which integrates key details of the scene under discussion with other sections or aspects of the novel.

A further list of some of the other important characteristics of analysis would include the following: firstly, the last extract isn't just making simple assertions; points are being qualified, amplified, restated, and this is indicated by the nature of the connecting words and phrases: 'of course', 'but', 'not really', 'she is, almost', 'partly', 'all the same'. These words indicate that a debate, or a 'dialogue with the self', is going on. Secondly, the passage has slowed the pace of the discussion: the writer has paused, and then homed in on a specific episode. That episode is being looked at closely, yet in broad connecting terms too, so that its implications for the rest of the novel are being teased out. Thirdly, the passage is working in close-up with the text, picking out specific phrases – not quoting huge chunks but working mainly at what might be called 'phrase level', so that the sections quoted from the novel seldom amount to more than a single sentence, often the sign of real engagement in a literary essay. Of course, there are many different kinds of analytical writing. Some kinds, for instance, use sophisticated critical or theoretical vocabulary; but that is not a necessity, and it is not the case in the kind of analytical writing exemplified here.

When I try to describe (to myself and to students and teachers of literature) the rudiments of the traditional Anglo-American approach to literary texts I arrive at taxonomies like the one just set out. My motive is that I am constantly seeking some kind of synthesis and balance between old and new, between text-based and theory-based approaches. In practice, of course, a good literary essay will tend to move in a strategic way between these four levels – some element of description is essential in literary-critical writing, if only to speed up the process and facilitate the movement from one focus to the next. Likewise, it is possible to posit, beyond the four levels so far described, further levels in which connections are made with extra-textual issues of a literary-historical kind (level 5), of a social-political kind (level 6), and of a philosophical-linguistic kind (level 7). French theoretical writing about literature has a strong preference for abandoning levels 1–4 almost completely and staying at these 'higher' levels of discourse, especially 6 and 7. In my own writing, and with my students, I am usually trying to encourage the crossing of the divide between the first four and the rest, so that the writing covers levels 3–6 especially (I am conscious that my taste and talents at level 7 are fairly limited). As a writer, I find this kind of discursive taxonomy of essay writing very helpful, and I hope that others may do so too.

Postscript

In 1998, the American Council on Education and the University of California conducted a survey on the habits and aspirations of 275,811 new college students entering 469 institutions. The survey found, among other things, that 80.4% of these students had occasionally played a video game in the past year, while only 18.7% had frequently taken out a book or journal from a school library. Among their reasons for going to college, the ability to make more money ranked highest among 74.6% of these new college students.[1]

Playing video games is undoubtedly a more popular leisure activity than reading literature. It's easier, and it may well give most people a more immediate sense of pleasurable relaxation. Video gaming is fine, but it isn't everything. Reading literature, rather than just spending the evening in front of the TV, requires conscious effort, even for professors, but it can give a longer-term sense of satisfaction, which may well in the end add up to a greater measure of human contentment. In the same way, getting off the sofa and going for a run or a swim isn't always the most attractive option, but mostly (surely?) we find it more pleasurable in the end. Pleasure isn't everything, either, but if we don't read we become trapped in our own individual minds, never allowing somebody else's thoughts to alter our mental climate in subtle ways by thinking themselves inside us (that slightly spooky, yet somehow thrilling way of thinking about what reading is). Without reading, we can end up living in a mental weather system which is always the same, so that rain and sunshine become the same thing, and a sameness which isn't really total living begins to take hold of us. Of course, we can be moved and challenged by films and TV, and other electronic images too, but the City of Words has a unique intimacy and power, and that is where we live when we study English, and then take it into the rest of our lives.

As Ezra Pound said, education is what remains when we have forgotten everything we set out to learn. Perhaps when we revisit our own City of Words in later life, we will find much of it vanished, with only isolated sections of

---

1   D. W. Fenza, 'Creative Writing and its Discontents', *Writer's Chronicle* (Mar./Apr. 2000).

apparently unimportant suburbs remaining, or puzzling bits of broken monuments, which presumably once stood in an impressive urban centre of some kind, but are now stranded in territory which has reverted to desert. This, I realize as I write it, is the scenario of Shelley's short poem 'Ozymandias', so again, it's the 'already said' of literature (as we called it at the start of the book) which reverberates deep down in the mind. But it's also the ending of the film *Planet of the Apes,* in which a puzzling fragment is recognized as a piece of the Statue of Liberty, half-buried in land which has now become desert. Film image and literary image, then, can express the same thing, can work together, each with its own vividness, each with the characteristic tang of its own textuality. After all, all true cities are several cities, and in studying English we are not looking for an embattled citadel which is opposed to everything else in our own time and place. But this book has mainly been devoted to literary textuality, and it has covered the six kinds listed in Chapter 4 – textuality, intertextuality, contextuality, multitextuality, peritextuality, and metatextuality. It would be very rash to try to predict what kind of textuality will occupy the discipline next.

Since the era of high theory in the 1980s, we have seen various 'turns', including the 'turn' to history, which we have considered here, the turn to ethics,[2] and the turn to aesthetics.[3] Of course, all these 'turns' are really *re*turns, and in particular they are returns of what was repressed by the two revolutions in twentieth-century English Studies (the Cambridge-led textual revolution of the 1920s, and the Paris-led theory revolution of the 1970s). But that by no means diminishes their interest or potential. Beyond this, there is a growing contemporary interest in eco-criticism,[4] and in 'spectrality', which is currently something of a buzz-word in English departments.[5]

Increasingly, too, there is the general feeling that, whatever sub-group we belong to, we should have a literary 'suburb of our own' in the City of Words, rather than just being part of a wider literary culture. This reflects the taken-for-granted view that every voice is a partisan voice, and that there can be no transcendent cultural stratosphere where great books stand beyond issues of politics, race, and gender, equally available to all. If this is so, it must follow that we all need 'our own' authors, whether we are single women, gay men,

2   See Robert Eaglestone's *Ethical Criticism* (Edinburgh University Press, 1997).
3   See Isobel Armstrong, *The Radical Aesthetic* (Blackwell, 2000).
4   See *The Ecocriticism Reader*, ed. Cheryll Glotfelty and Harold Fromm (University of Georgia Press, 1996) and *The Green Studies Reader: From Romanticism to Ecocriticism*, ed. Laurence Coupe (Routledge, 2000).
5   See Julian Wolfreys, *Victorian Hauntings: Spectrality, Haunting, the Gothic, and the Uncanny in Literature* (Palgrave Macmillan, 2001) and Nicholas Royle, *The Uncanny: An Introduction* (Manchester University Press, 2002).

black youths, or just middle-class and middle-aged. The fact that so many of these categories overlap, and that none of us are *just* black, or gay, or female, does not seem to be a matter we want to deal with. In any case, the wider common literary culture will surely go on being undermined, albeit slowly. Perhaps one day only fragments of the City of Words will remain. Not many years ago, literary theory itself mainly seemed to be aimed at destroying that city; but literary theory's hold on the mind often seems to be oddly transient, and the same has proved true of its hold on the discipline itself. It can hit literary texts, and entire academic departments, with the force of a meteorite from outer space (like Coriolanus, in Shakespeare's play, who 'struck [the city of] Corioli like a planet'), but the resulting crater is soon recolonized by the usual fauna and flora, the familiar buildings reappear, and after a few years it can even be difficult to remember precisely where it was. Things today in English Studies seem much quieter. Too quiet, perhaps. Doubtless, at this very moment, that strange and frightening beast the Next Big Thing is slouching towards the City of Words, to be born.

What Next? Annotated Bibliography

Chapter 1 Introduction: The Appeal of English

The following books all give an overview of literature or literary studies. Bradford and Pope are big textbooks covering both criticism and theory and designed for systematic use as part of an English course. Eaglestone's is a short book which aims to bridge some of the gaps between 'A' level and degree-level English. Gribble's is an older book which defends more traditional methods in the face of the onslaught of theory. Widdowson's is a succinct and thought-provoking reflection on a vast topic.

Bradford, Richard, ed. *Introducing Literary Studies*, London: Harvester Wheatsheaf, 1996

Eaglestone, Robert, *Doing English*, London: Routledge, 2nd edn, 2002

Gribble, James, *Literary Education: A Revaluation*, Cambridge: Cambridge University Press, 1983

Pope, Rob, *The English Studies Book*, London: Routledge, 2nd edn, 2002

Widdowson, Peter, *Literature*, London: Routledge, 1999

Chapter 2 Reading the Lines

Close reading remains potentially a radical and transforming pedagogical practice, but many of those who have explicitly defended it in recent years have tended to become identified (sometimes unfairly) with mainly conservative allegiances. The books by Abrams, Alter, Ricks, and Steiner are works of this kind with great character and originality. Hopkins is a textbook working usefully to a systematic brief.

Abrams, M. H., *Doing Things with Texts*, New York: Norton, 1989

Alter, Robert, *The Pleasures of Reading in an Ideological Age*, repr. New York: Norton, 1997

Hopkins, Chris, *Thinking About Texts*, London: Palgrave Macmillan, 2001

Ricks, Christopher, *Essays in Appreciation*, Oxford: Oxford University Press, 1998
Steiner, George, *Real Presences*, London: Faber and Faber, 1989

Chapter 3 Reading Between the Lines

All these books are about prose fiction. Forster's was first published in 1927, and is relaxed but systematic. Hawthorn's is an excellent study book, detailed, practical, and comprehensive, and drawing upon the more 'high-tech', 'narratological' approach of Bal and Genette (both of which are written with pithy concision). Lodge's is a compendium of his very short pieces (originally published in a Sunday newspaper) on different aspects of fiction (beginnings, endings, the use of symbolism, and so on).

Bal, Mieke, *Narratology: Introduction to the Theory of Narrative*, 2nd edn, Toronto: University of Toronto Press, 1998
Forster, E. M., *Aspects of the Novel*, Harmondsworth: Penguin, 1962
Genette, Gerard, *Narrative Discourse*, Ithaca: Cornell University Press, 1993
Hawthorn, Jeremy, *Studying the Novel*, 4th edn, London: Arnold, 2001
Lodge, David, *The Art of Fiction*, Harmondsworth: Penguin, 1992

Chapter 4 Reading Beyond the Lines

Allen gives an orderly account of the many different versions of intertextuality within literary studies, whereas Chandler, in his Chapter 6, 'Textual Interactions', covers the same terrain from a perspective which takes in non-literary media as well. Clayton and Rothstein unravel notions of literary intertextuality from the related idea of literary influence. Newton takes a broader all-round view of matters of literary interpretation. Rylance and Simons offer a series of contextualized readings of major literary texts, illustrating the officially approved way of doing English in the UK.

Allen, Graham, *Intertextuality*, London: Routledge, 2000
Chandler, Daniel, *Semiotics: The Basics*, London: Routledge, 2001
Clayton, Jay and Rothstein, Eric, eds, *Influence and Intertextuality in Literary History*, Wisconsin: University of Wisconsin Press, 1991
Newton, K. M. *Interpreting the Text: A Critical Introduction to the Theory and Practice of Literary Interpretation*, London: Harvester Wheatsheaf, 1990

Rylance, Rick, and Simons, Judy, *Literature in Context,* London: Palgrave Macmillan, 2001

Chapter 5 English and History

This chapter deals with history and contextuality, and, while there are plenty of books and series which place individual writers in context, there are very few which raise the question of contextuality as a general issue. Brannigan gives an overview of the strengths and weaknesses of New Historicism. Chandler exemplifies the full-scale new historicist approach applied to Romanticism. Cunningham's lively and provocative book argues against the view of the literary text as self-contained and self-reflexive, seeking to reinstate the importance of reference and context, while Gallagher and Greenblatt show historicist approaches in practice. Veeser offers a very useful collection of material, not restricted to a single historical period.

Brannigan, John, *New Historicism and Cultural Materialism,* London: Palgrave Macmillan, 1998
Chandler, James, *England in 1819: The Politics of Literary Culture and the Case of Romantic Historicism,* Chicago: University of Chicago Press, 1999
Cunningham, Valentine, *In the Reading Gaol: Postmodernity, Texts, and History,* Oxford: Blackwell, 1994
Gallagher, Catherine, and Greenblatt, Stephen, *Practising the New Historicism,* Chicago: University of Chicago Press, 2000
Veeser, Aram, H., *The New Historicism Reader,* London: Routledge, 1994

Chapter 6 Literary Criticism and Literary Theory

All these books are introductions to literary theory for students. Eagleton's was the pioneer, the first book to try to make literary theory make sense for undergraduates, and the first to present its development as a single integrated narrative. The others are all 'second-generation' texts which build on that approach, but have much more material on practical applications of literary theory.

Barry, Peter, *Beginning Theory: An Introduction to Literary and Cultural Theory,* 2nd edn, Manchester: Manchester University Press, 2002
Bennett, Andrew, and Royle, Nicholas, *An Introduction to Literature, Criticism, and Theory,* 2nd edn, London: Prentice Hall, 1999

Eagleton, Terry, *Literary Theory: An Introduction*, 2nd edn, Oxford: Blackwell, 1996

Lynn, Steve, *Texts and Contexts: Writing about Literature with Critical Theory*, 3rd edn, New York: Longman, 2000

Tyson, Lois, *Critical Theory Today: A User-Friendly Guide*, New York: Garland Publishing, 1999

Chapter 7 English Now and Then

All these are about the history of English Studies. Court and Graff have a Nor American perspective, and Potter and Palmer centre on England. Crawf argues for the centrality of the Scottish model in what became English Stud worldwide. These, then, are all different versions of the 'many histories English discussed in the chapter.

Court, Franklin, E., *Institutionalizing English Literature*, Stanford: Star University Press, 1992

Crawford, Robert, ed., *The Scottish Invention of English Literature*, Cambridge: Cambridge University Press, 1998 (esp. chs 10 and 12)

Graff, Gerald, *Professing Literature: An Institutional History*, Chicago: University of Chicago Press, 1987

Palmer, D. J., *The Rise of English Studies*, Oxford: Oxford University Press, 1965

Potter, Stephen, *The Muse in Chains*, London: Jonathan Cape, 1937

Chapter 8 The Text as Text

All these are about literary editing. Pettit is the best one to start with as it introduces the issues for non-specialists, with essays on the texts of major novels. Kastan and McKenzie are brief books by excellent writers, using telling examples to focus the issues involved. Murphy's collection links literary editing and literary theory in provocative ways, and McGann and Greetham is a major work which had a profound effect on literary theory, literary editing, and literary criticism.

Kastan, David Scott, *Shakespeare and the Book*, Cambridge: Cambridge University Press, 2001

McGann, Jerome, and Greetham, David C., *A Critique of Modern Textual Criticism*, Virginia: University of Virginia Press, 1993

McKenzie, D. F., *Bibliography and the Sociology of Texts*, Cambridge: Cambridge University Press, 1999

Murphy, Andrew, ed., *The Renaissance Text: Theory, Editing, Textuality*, Manchester: Manchester University Press, 2000

Pettit, Alexander, *Textual Studies and the Common Reader*, Georgia: University of Georgia Press, 2000

Chapter 9 Online English

The Centre for Computing in the Humanities gives a useful overview of what is available online. On the home-page, under 'Contents', click on 'Resources'. Clark is a free, online public information resource giving basic data on literature in English worldwide. Condron is an excellent up-to-date guide to what is available online, both open-access and subscriber material. Section 2 of Goring is a very useful guide to electronic media in literary studies, and Hockey is a thoughtful and concise overview of the field.

Centre for Computing in the Humanities, Kings College London <http://www.kcl.ac.uk/humanities/cch/>

Clark, Robert, Elliott, Emory, Todd, Janet, *The Literary Encyclopedia and Literary Dictionary*, <http://www.litencyc.com/fridx.html>

Condron, Frances, Fraser, Michael, and Sutherland, Stuart, *CTI Textual Studies: Guide to Digital Resources for the Humanities*, Oxford: CTI Centre for Textual Studies, 2000

Goring, Paul, Hawthorn, Jeremy, and Mitchell, Domhnall, *Studying Literature: The Essential Companion*, London: Arnold, 2001

Hockey, Susan, *Electronic Texts in the Humanities*, Oxford: Oxford University Press, 2000

Chapter 10 English as Language

This chapter touches on four areas within a vast field of study: Bradford is a general introduction to the first of them, stylistics, and Toolan covers the area of *narrative* stylistics, balancing the fact that my own comments under this heading are mainly on poetry. Holmes is one of the best student introductions to sociolinguistics, and Burchfield is an able and engaging writer on matters of historical linguistics. Pinker's attractive and well-known book is an excellent starting point on linguistics generally.

Bradford, Richard, *Stylistics,* New Critical Idiom series, London: Routledge, 1997

Burchfield, Robert, *The English Language,* Oxford: Oxford University Press, 2002

Holmes, Janet, *An Introduction to Sociolinguistics,* London: Longman, 2001

Pinker, Steven, *The Language Instinct: The New Science of Language and Mind,* London: Penguin, 1995

Toolan, Michael, *Narrative: A Critical Linguistic Introduction,* 2nd edn, London: Routledge, 2001

Chapter 11 English and Creative Writing

This is currently a rapidly expanding field, with many excellent books competing for sales and influence. Bell has contributions from around 40 writers and covers a wide range of topics – viewpoint, setting, characters, endings, and so on – and the book is associated with the creative writing course at east Anglia. Brande is an older and very popular book now reissued (it's actually about fiction writing, in spite of its broad title). Newman's is a lively and practical book from the creative writing course-team at Liverpool John Moores University. Singleton is also a practical workbook, closely associated with a degree course, and Marshall is a book which has very quickly established wide popularity.

Bell, Julia, Magrs, Paul, Motion, Andrew, *The Creative Writing Coursebook,* London: Pan, 2001

Brande, Dorothea, *Becoming a Writer,* new edn, London: Pan, 1996

Marshall, Evan, *Novel Writing,* London: A and C Black, 2000

Newman, Jenny, Cusick, Edmund, La Tourette, Aileen, *The Writer's Workbook,* London: Arnold, 2000

Singleton, John, and Luckhurst, Mary, *The Creative Writing Handbook,* 2nd edn, Basingstoke: Palgrave Macmillan, 2000

Chapter 12 The Essay: Crossing the Four Frontiers

Marggraf-Turley is an extremely popular and user-friendly practical guide to essay writing, written by an English lecturer rather than a general educationalist. Gaskell too is an English lecturer, and the book has both general guidance on correct usage, and a series of quoted examples from critics with commentaries. Evans's is a lively and sensible book by a former newspaper editor writing for journalists about clear style, and valuable for English students too. Elbow's book is compulsive reading – I have found it an enormous help as a writer over many years. Hennessy's is a 'cure for essayphobia', its users say.

Elbow, Peter, *Writing with Power*, 2nd edn, New York: Oxford University Press, 1998

Evans, Harold, *Essential English*, new edn, London: Pimlico, 2000

Gaskell, Philip, *Standard Written English*, Edinburgh: Edinburgh University Press, 1998

Hennessy, Brendan, *Writing an Essay*, 4th edn, London: How To Books, 1997

Marggraf-Turley, Richard, *Writing Essays: A Guide for Students in English and the Humanities*, London: Routledge, 2000

Index

Note: page numbers in **bold** refer to illustrations.